# PRIVATE INVESTIGATION 101

## A guide for becoming a private investigator.

What is a private investigator?
Would I make a good investigator?
How much experience and training do I need?
Am I required to have a license?
How do I get started?
How much money can I expect to make?

By Norma Mott Tillman, PI

Cover Design by Bill Collier

Typography by Vicki Stephens, Nashville, Tenn.

Printed in the United States of America

ISBN 0-9634424-1-4

# Dedication

*This book is dedicated to my family and friends.*

*A special thanks to Don Huth for editing*

# TABLE OF CONTENTS

# INTRODUCTION

This handbook is intended to provide an overview and insight into the real world of private investigation. This handbook is not intended to qualify anyone to become a licensed private investigator or private detective. This handbook is in no way a complete guide to all types of investigations. This handbook is a basic overview of the profession based on over twenty years of investigative experiences and is intended only to be used as a guide.

I am often asked "How can I become a private investigator?" No doubt many people have a natural curiosity and would make good investigators, but the job requires more than just a natural curiosity. Having a natural curiosity is a good thing…it means you want to know more. If you are patient, tenacious, self-motivated, resourceful, and determined you will probably find whatever it is that you want to know more about.

Whenever someone tells me they want to become a private investigator I try to be encouraging and say "If I can do it, so can you," "nothing ventured, nothing gained," or "you will never know if you don't try." But for many people taking the first step is the hardest part. Making up your mind to do this is going to take a lot of determination and a good plan of action. You will need to have a source of income to rely on until you can become established and self-supportive. In some cases a spouse can provide that other source of income. In some cases another job or a retirement fund can provide the income. No one should give up their job with benefits and jump into the world of private investigation until they have a proven track record and are able to produce a good income. Like other professions you must first pay your dues.

A brain surgeon did not start out as a specialist…. it took many years of training and experience to achieve that status. An actor did not start out winning an Academy Award…. it took many years of training and experience to achieve that award. Every profession requires training and experience.

There is a lot of difference in an untrained or inexperienced private investigator, and an experienced investigator with a proven track record of winning cases for their clients. In order to gain experience a new private investigator may be willing to work for little or nothing. Some may work as interns and not get paid. Some may get minimum payment. Just as with any other profession, you don't start out at the top…. you have to climb the ladder of success…one-step at a time. It may take time, but it is not unattainable. Knowing where you want to go and how you are going to get there is like taking a trip using a good road map.

So with this said, if you think you would make a good private investigator, you probably will. It starts with believing in yourself, because if you don't believe you would make a good private investigator, no one else will believe it either. If you think you can do something, you can. You have to be determined. No one can do this for you.

When you accept the challenge and find your niche, you will eventually feel the exhilaration of victory. For me I found my niche was locating and reuniting families and friends. It is very rewarding and fulfilling.

I do not recommend doing what I did when I started. That is, I never set out with a plan or goal…. things just happened to me. As a volunteer at the police department the "bug" bit me to learn more about law enforcement. Attending the police academy and studying criminal law was quite a learning experience and quite challenging. I enjoyed working in law enforcement and especially enjoyed the challenge of finding a missing criminal, preferable one no one else could find. Over the years I honed my skill and became better and better at finding criminals. It was many years later, after I "burned out" in law-enforcement, that attorneys called and asked me to find people who were not criminals, such as a witness or an heir. These people left a trail…. and the trail was easy for me to follow. Finding missing persons who had not done anything wrong, and who were not deliberately hiding was so much fun. I could not believe I could get paid to do this. Of course in order for me to work for attorneys and get paid I had to have a private investigator license. So for me, becoming a private investigator was not something I set out to do…. it just happened.

One person referred another and the phone started ringing. Soon I was very busy and realized that the clients were all word of mouth, referrals, and repeat clients. I did not advertise but figured out the reason my business was growing was because of the way I treated my clients. I always had a good contract and a good understanding of what I could or could not do so the client would not be disappointed, have unrealistic expectations, or expect me to do something that I did not agree to do. I wanted to give the client what they needed to win their case and never took a client's money unless I gave them what I agreed to do. I worked on a variety of cases including background investigations, insurance claims and fraud, domestic cases, missing persons, and criminal defense. Eventually I specialized in finding missing persons (family and friends) and offered a guaranteed search. Certain information is required to qualify for a guaranteed search, but no one else was doing this.

My first web site on the internet began in 1994 with a database and messages for missing persons. The missing persons on my web site were not criminals or people who owed money. They were not wanted because they had done anything wrong. They were not deliberately hiding. They just did not know anyone was looking for them. The database and web site eventually grew to messages for over 300,000 missing persons and received over 10,000 hits per day from 12 countries around the world.

Have you ever said to yourself, "Private investigation sounds very inter-esting and exciting but what exactly does a private investigator do? Exactly how do I get started? Would I make a good investigator? How much money can I expect to make? How much experience and training do I need? Am I required to have a license? Hopefully this book will help guide you to get started. Or if you have already started maybe you can pick up some new tips that will be beneficial.

There is a big difference between being a private investigator and law enforcement. A private investigator is not a police officer and a police officer is not a private investigator. A private investigator has no arrest powers other than what any ordinary citizen may have, and is not allowed to carry a weapon without a permit. A private investigator may be hired to investigate either a criminal case or a civil case. However, a police officer can only investigate criminal cases and are not hired to investigate civil cases unless they have a private investigator license.

Law enforcement officers are trained to work criminal law cases. They are not trained for civil law cases. Having experience of working on criminal cases does not qualify a law enforcement officer to work a civil case. A law enforce-ment officer is trained in report writing, may have surveillance experience, have knowledge of background information, have use of criminal databases, and have court room experience testifying in cases. All of these experiences are useful but these experiences alone may not qualify a law enforcement officer to own and operate a private investigation agency. Law enforcement officers may be dependent on others, such as a dispatcher or partner to assist them; they may not be experienced working alone. Law enforcement officers have their equipment furnished. Private investigators may have to purchase their own equipment unless they work for an agency that will provide it. Law enforce-ment officers may have no experience in sales or soliciting business, charging for their services, marketing their services, negotiating a contract, paying for their equipment, billing clients, and keeping up with expenses.

Private investigation is a demanding profession that is more mental than physical work. It is not as glamorous as portrayed in movies and on television. A case may take weeks, months, or even years to solve. It has been said that an investigator is only as good as his or her sources. The object of working a case is to produce results for your client. In order to charge more for your services you must have a proven track record. In this age of high technology a private investigator must keep on top of their game. Knowledge is power.

This book is a guide for becoming a private investigator. This book is intended for the novice who wants to become a private investigator as well as for former law enforcement, former military intelligence, security personnel, paralegals, legal professionals, or other individuals. Learn how to obtain a license, how to set up a private investigation agency, how to market your services, how to find information, types of investigative cases, contracts and report writing, and much more. There is no guarantee that reading this book is going to qualify anyone for a private investigator license.

# *About the Author*

## NORMA TILLMAN

Norma Tillman is not the typical stereotyped private investigator. Her background includes working with law-enforcement eleven years, two years of insurance fraud investigations, and fifteen years of private investigations. She has a proven track record for winning cases for attorneys and clients. With over twenty years of experience she has worked on almost every type of investigation including background investigations, divorce and child custody, insurance fraud, criminal defense, copyright infringement, and environmental cases, but her specialty is locating and reuniting long lost families and friends for television shows.

As a professional speaker she is never at a loss for an interesting story based on her true experiences including: posing as a street person to track a mentally disturbed woman who was hiding from her family; working undercover in a topless bar to attempt to save a man from suicide; finding out that an adopted daughter is having an affair with her biological father; or rolling under a mobster's Jaguar in a crowded parking lot to install a tracking device.

Over 2500 professional investigators across the country have attended her training seminars.

Whether she is a guest on a television or radio show, speaking or conducting a seminar, her behind the scenes look at the real world of private investigation is informative, entertaining, inspirational, and motivating.

She is the author of "Private Investigation 101," "How To Find Almost Anyone, Anywhere," "The Man With the Turquoise Eyes and other True Stories of a Private Eye's Search for Missing Persons," and "The Adoption Searcher's Handbook."

Norma has appeared on many national and local television shows including Oprah, Barbara Walters (The View), CNN, NBC, and about a hundred talk shows.

Her current web sites are: www.nationwidelocate.com, www.get-intouch.com, www.getintouch.tv, and www.tvreunions.com.

# CHAPTER I

## WHAT IS A PRIVATE INVESTIGATOR?

**"A private detective or investigator is a person who accepts employment to conduct an investigation for the purpose of obtaining information that may be used for civil or criminal investigative cases."**

Another simple definition of a private investigator is a problem solver for hire, a person who is employed to obtain information for a client. A problem solver is also a truth seeker. Some laws may state that if you are paid to obtain information for another person, you are required to have a private investigator license. Before you begin you will need to check your state's laws.

Among other things, a private investigator needs to be intuitive, creative, innovative, decisive, tenacious, determined, patient, resourceful, and have a good sense of direction with great instincts and intuitions. Remember that your opinion, instincts, and intuitions are not factual and that a private investigator must remain impartial.

You will need good instincts and intuitions to decide whether or not to work a case for a client. Con artists, criminals, prisoners and others may try to hire you for illegal purposes. You will learn when to say "no" to a client. Is working a case that involves breaking the law worth losing your license and receiving a fine or possibly being charged with a crime? Today's private investigator is an information specialist, a fact finder, and a truth seeker. It is possible for a private investigator to surpass the capabilities of government investigators. If you cannot provide beneficial results to your client, you will not become successful. The bottom line for success is about results.

Private investigators often work irregular hours because of the need to conduct surveillance or contact people who are not available during normal working hours. Early morning, evening, weekend, and holiday work is common. It may not be the ideal job for those with family demands. The job can be demanding and can consume your life if you are not careful to keep your life in balance. Recognize and realize what is most important to you and don't lose site of your values and principals. If it is important for you to be home with your family at night and on weekends, don't take a case that will take you away from them. A self-employed private investigator will constantly be making choices.

Some investigators spend time in the field, away from their offices, researching records, conducting interviews, or doing surveillance, but some work in their office most of the day conducting computer searches and making phone calls. Those with their own agencies employ other investigators and may work primarily in an office with normal business hours.

When working on a case away from the office, the environment might range from a plush office to a seedy bar. Store and hotel detectives work in the businesses that they protect and may have set hours.

The job can be stressful and dangerous. Some situations call for the investigator to be armed, such as certain bodyguard assignments for corporate or celebrity clients. The appropriate authority must license detectives and investigators who carry handguns. In most cases a weapon is not necessary because the purpose of their work is gathering information and not law enforcement or criminal apprehension. A private investigator has no police powers. Prior to beginning an investigation, a good contract and a good understanding with a client of what this investigation will or will not involve should prevent a distraught or unhappy client.

According to the U.S. Department of Labor's Bureau of Labor Statistics in 2002, private detectives and investigators held about 48,000 jobs. About a third of those were self-employed, including many who held a secondary job. Almost a fifth of the jobs were found in investigation and security services, including private detective agencies, while another fifth were in department or other general merchandise stores. The rest worked mostly in state and local government, legal firms, employment services, insurance carriers, and credit intermediation and related activities, including banks and other financial institutions.

There are no formal educational requirements for most private detective and investigator jobs, although many private detectives have college degrees. Private detectives and investigators typically have previous experience in other occupations. Some work initially for insurance or collections companies or in the private security industry. Many investigators enter the field after serving in law enforcement, the military, government auditing and investigative positions, or Federal intelligence jobs.

Former law enforcement officers, military investigators, and government agents often become private detectives or investigators as a second career because they are frequently able to retire after 20 years of service. Others enter from such diverse fields as finance, accounting, commercial credit, investigative reporting, insurance, and law. These individuals often can apply their prior work experience in a related investigative specialty. A few enter the occupation directly after graduation from college, generally with associate or bachelor's degrees in criminal justice or police science.

The majority of states and the District of Colombia require private detectives and investigators to be licensed. Licensing requirements vary widely, but convicted felons cannot receive a license in most States and a growing number of States are enacting mandatory training programs for private detectives and investigators. Some states have few requirements, and 6 states—Alabama, Alaska, Colorado, Idaho, Mississippi, and South Dakota—have no statewide licensing requirements while others have stringent regulations. For example, the Bureau of Security and Investigative Services of the California Department of Consumer Affairs requires private investigators to be 18 years of age or older; have a combination of education in police science, criminal law, or justice, and experience equaling 3 years (6,000 hours) of investigative experience; pass an evaluation by the Federal Department of Justice and a criminal history background check; and receive a qualifying score on a 2-hour written examination covering laws and regulations. There are additional requirements for a firearms permit.

For private detective and investigator jobs, most employers look for individuals with integrity, ingenuity, persistence, and assertiveness. A candidate must not be afraid of confrontation, should communicate well, and should be able to think on his or her feet. Good interviewing and interrogation skills also are important and usually are acquired in earlier careers in law enforcement or other fields. Because the courts often are the ultimate judges of a properly conducted investigation, the investigator must be able to present the facts in a manner a jury will believe.

Training in subjects such as criminal justice is helpful to aspiring private detectives and investigators. Most corporate investigators must have a bachelor's degree, preferably in a business-related field. Some corporate investigators have master's degrees in business administration or law, while others are certified public accountants. Corporate investigators hired by large companies may receive formal training from their employers on business practices, management structure, and various finance-related topics. The screening process for potential employees typically includes a background check of criminal history.

Some investigators receive certification from a professional organization to demonstrate competency in a field. For example, the National Association of Legal Investigators (NALI) assigns the Certified Legal Investigator designation to licensed investigators who devote a majority of their practice to negligence or criminal defense investigations. To receive the designation, applicants must satisfy experience, educational, and continuing training requirements, and must pass written and oral exams administered by the NALI.

Typical private detective agencies are small, with almost no room for advancement. Usually there are no defined ranks or steps, so advancement takes the form of increases in salary and assignment status. Many detectives and investigators work for experienced detective agencies at the beginning of their careers and, after a few years, start their own firms. Corporate and legal investigators may rise to supervisor or manager of the security or investigations department.

Keen competition is expected because private detective and investigator careers attract many qualified people, including relatively young retirees from law enforcement and military careers. Opportunities will be best for entry-level jobs with detective agencies or as store detectives on a part-time basis. Those seeking store detective jobs have the best prospects with large chains and discount stores.

Employment of private detectives and investigators is expected to grow faster than average for all occupations through 2012. In addition to growth, replacement of those who retire or leave the occupation for other reasons should create many job openings. Increased demand for private detectives and investigators will result from divorce, fear of crime, increased litigation, and the need to protect confidential information and property of all kinds. More private investigators also will be needed to assist attorneys working on criminal defense and civil litigation. Growing financial activity worldwide will increase the demand for investigators to control internal and external financial losses, and to monitor competitors and prevent industrial spying.

Private investigators may use many sources and means to determine the facts in a variety of matters. To carry out investigations, they may use computer searches, surveillance, or interviews. To verify facts, such as an individual's place of employment or income, they may make phone calls, interview neighbors or friends, search public records, or visit a subject's workplace. In other cases, especially those involving missing persons and background checks, investigators often rely on computer database information, public records, and interview people to gather as much information as possible about an individual. Private investigators assist attorneys, businesses, and individuals with a variety of legal, financial, insurance, and personal problems.

A variety of services are offered by private investigators, including executive, corporate, and celebrity protection; pre-employment verification; and individual background profiles. They also provide assistance in civil liability and personal injury cases, insurance claims and fraud, child custody, divorce, premarital screening, and criminal defense cases. Proving or disproving marital infidelity is one of the most requested types of investigation.

Most private investigators perform surveillances, often for long periods of time, in a car or van. They may spend hours, days, or weeks observing a home or workplace of a subject. The surveillance will probably require the use of still and video cameras, binoculars, radios, and a cell phone, until the desired evidence is obtained. They also may perform computer database searches, or work with someone (a vendor) who does. Computers allow detectives and investigators to quickly obtain massive amounts of information on individuals' prior arrests, convictions, and civil legal judgments; telephone numbers; motor vehicle registrations; associates and relatives; prior residences; and other information.

In cases for employers involving fraudulent workers' compensation claims, for example, investigators may carry out long-term covert observation of subjects. If an investigator observes a subject performing an activity that contradicts injuries stated in a workers' compensation claim, the investigator would take video or still photographs to document the activity and report it to the client.

Experienced private detectives often specialize in whatever type of investigation they enjoy and do best. Some investigators may focus on white collar crimes or intellectual property theft. Some may investigate and document acts of piracy or copyright infringement, help clients stop illegal activity, and provide intelligence for prosecution and civil action. Other investigators specialize in developing financial profiles and asset searches. Their reports reflect information gathered through interviews, investigation, surveillance, and research, including review of public documents.

Legal investigators specialize in cases involving the courts and are normally employed by attorneys. They frequently assist in preparing criminal defenses, locating witnesses, serving legal documents, interviewing police and prospective witnesses, and gathering and reviewing evidence. Legal investigators also may collect information on the parties to the litigation, take photographs, testify in court, and assemble evidence and reports for trials. Whether for a criminal defense attorney or for a prosecutor, the role of the legal investigator is to provide the "bullets for the attorney's gun" in order for an attorney to win a case.

Corporations, banks, and other businesses employ security investigators to conduct internal and external investigations. In internal investigations, they may investigate drug use in the workplace, ensure that expense accounts are not abused, or determine if employees are stealing merchandise or information. External investigations typically prevent criminal schemes originating outside the corporation, such as theft of company assets through fraudulent billing of products by suppliers.

Financial investigators may be hired to develop confidential financial profiles of individuals or companies who are prospective parties to large financial transactions, settlements, liens, or judgments. They search for assets in order to recover damages awarded by a court in fraud or theft cases. Although not required, financial investigators often are Certified Public Accountants (CPAs) and work closely with investment bankers and accountants.

Detectives who work for retail stores or hotels are responsible for loss control and asset protection. Store detectives, also known as loss prevention or security, safeguard the assets of retail stores by apprehending anyone attempting to steal merchandise or destroy store property. They prevent theft by shoplifters, vendor representatives, delivery personnel, and even store employees. Store detectives also conduct periodic inspections of stock areas, dressing rooms, and restrooms, and sometimes assist in opening and closing the store. They may prepare loss prevention and security reports for management and testify in court against persons they apprehend. Hotel detectives protect guests of the establishment from theft of their belongings and preserve order in hotel restaurants and bars. They also may keep undesirable individuals off the premises.

**Q. Do I need a private investigator license?**

Most states have laws and regulations that govern the licensing and business of private investigations. To obtain information on state requirements for private investigators contact by phone, mail, fax, or email the state board of regulator's office and request a packet of information on how to become a licensed private investigator.

This packet of information may contain the state laws for private investigators. It may also contain recommended materials that may help a person to become a qualified licensed investigator. Each state may have separate requirements.

Some states may have reciprocal agreements. This means that if you are licensed in one state and have a case in another state that, depending on the law, you may have the right to work in the reciprocal state without being licensed in that state. The states with reciprocal agreements recognize each other's licensing. It is best to always check the laws before working a case in another state other than the one in which you are licensed. If you work in a state that does not recognize your license, you could jeopardize the case for your client.

A list of state agencies may be found in Chapter IX.

### Q. Do I need a law-enforcement background to become a private investigator?

A private investigator differs from a police officer, a bounty hunter, a collection agency, a bondsman, a security guard, and other similar professions. Each of these professions has a distinct function, and none of them are the same.

A police officer is trained to enforce criminal laws. Police officers are not trained to work on civil cases. A private investigator may work on either a criminal or civil case but has no powers of arrests. A private investigator has no special privileges that allow him/her to break a law, make an arrest, work an accident, or carry a gun (without a permit). Having a law enforcement background may help with criminal defense cases, and may help with report writing, court testifying, and lots of other things, but it is not necessary to become a private investigator. Most former law enforcement officers are not accustomed to being their own boss and have no experience running a business. The government agency has provided their equipment and paid their salaries with benefits. They did not have to generate clients, keep up with billing, purchase their own equipment, or price their services.

Becoming a private investigator with your own company requires knowledge of how to operate a business. It is a good idea to have a business plan. Most beginner private investigators experience "feast or famine." With a proven track record and a good reputation, word of mouth spreads and that is one of the best ways to make your business grow. For a beginner it is a good to have another source of income and not "put all your eggs in one basket."

Because most private investigators do not work set hours it is very difficult for a dedicated private investigator to work full time and balance a good family life. It is not a good profession for a family man or woman with small children. Oftentimes private eyes with small children will have to make a choice to neglect their family in order to work a case. Let me tell you, family needs to come first. It is not worth the sacrifice if you choose to work a case and neglect your family. You will need to learn to prioritize and make good choices.

Sometimes a client will ask a private investigator to do something that may be unlawful. A good private investigator will tactfully tell the client that they will try to obtain the information in a lawful way. It is not worth losing your license or going to jail to obtain information illegally. A good investigator will find a legal way to get whatever they need. If an investigator has to lie, cheat, or steal to obtain information for a client, then they are not a good investigator.

A pretext is a lie. It is not the truth. Unfortunately many private investigators think this is how to obtain information. It is not necessary. Information can be obtained by telling the truth. A good investigator knows not to volunteer too much information…just enough to get what they need. This is a learned technique. The art of asking the right questions is necessary for being a good investigator. Learn to re-phrase the question several ways. Practice various ways to ask for the same thing. Always have plans "b, c, d, and e" in case plan "a" does not work.

The mind of an investigator has to think ahead and be prepared to react to the unexpected at all times. You will need to "think smarter, not work harder."

In working on a case, the mind of an investigator will learn to automatically eliminate anything that is not a fact. Always have pen and tablet ready to keep a working log of what happens. Always put a date, time, and place when taking notes. As facts are gathered list them in chronological order. Working a case is like working a puzzle. You will get a little piece of the puzzle at a time until you complete the whole puzzle. You must be able to separate facts from opinions. You must also learn to listen to your instincts and intuitions for they are usually correct. If something does not sound right, look right, or feel right…it is not right. Your instincts and intuitions will tell you when something doesn't sound right, look right, or feel right. You need to tune in to these instincts and recognize and develop them. When you feel like something is not right examine what has made you feel that way. Learn to analyze facts. Keep going over and over whatever information you have. Recognize what is missing and what you need to discover. If you reach a brick wall, probably you have overlooked something. There are usually clues that leave trails. You will learn to recognize these clues and follow the trails.

Private investigators employ techniques such as public record and computer database searches for background checks, pre-employment screening and locating missing persons. Private investigators interview people to gain information, gather evidence, and verify facts. Private investigators may provide assistance in civil liability and personal injury cases, insurance claims and fraud, child custody cases, premarital screening, martial infidelity, missing persons, white-collar crimes, criminal defense cases, and a multitude of other types of investigations. Some private investigative firms offer executive and celebrity protection, alarm services, and some serve court papers. Security services and alarm services may require separate licensing.

Private investigation is a field that is vast and diverse, from fraud to missing persons, to criminal defense, there's a need for virtually all types of investigators and for a vast array of skills. Probably the most important investigative skill is the desire to get at the truth. Most investigators possess an almost bloodhound like tenacity (hence, the symbol of the bloodhound dog with the magnifying glass, used so often by private investigation firms). If you enjoy a scavenger hunt, digging for clues, following every thread of evidence, and solving puzzles you will likely make a good investigator. One major trait common among investigators is the desired to help people and fulfill the client's needs. Most investigators have a natural curiosity that makes them want to find the truth.

**Q. How much income can I expect to earn?**

Getting started is not easy and most PIs have to "pay their dues" by working for a low salary or nothing just to establish a track record. An intern may work for a beginner's salary is negotiable, depending on qualifications and experience. In the year 2006 with experience and a good track record a self-employed private investigator can expect to earn from $50. to $150. per hour, plus expenses. The phone is your cash register and if the phone doesn't ring, you don't get paid. Those who charge less than $50.00 per hour usually live in lower income areas or may have less experience. Those who charge more than $50.00 an hour may have a good specialty and/or is located in an affluent part of the country. Most who bill $100.00 or more an hour may have advanced degrees or a strong links to some specialty market. Once a PI is established and has a proven track record he or she can expect repeat and referral business. Word of mouth is the best advertisement and in order to get word of mouth advertising you have to treat your customers with respect and give them what they asked for or what you agreed to do for them. It has been said that what goes around comes around. If you treat clients right, they will tell someone else about you. If you don't treat your clients right they will also tell that and no one will want to hire you. Good customer service is the secret to a successful business.

According to government statistics median annual earnings of salaried private detectives and investigators were $29,300 in 2002. The middle 50 percent earned between $21,980 and $41,710. The lowest 10 percent earned less than $17,290, and the highest 10 percent earned more than $57,370. In 2002, median annual earnings were $29,030 in investigation and security services, and $22,250 in department stores.

Earnings of private detectives and investigators vary greatly depending on their employer, specialty, and the geographic area in which they work. According to a study by Abbott, Langer & Associates, security/loss prevention directors and vice presidents had a median income of $77,500 per year in 2002; investigators, $39,800; and store detectives, $25,000. In addition to typical benefits, most corporate investigators received profit-sharing plans.

Some private investigators enjoy well-paying and worthwhile careers. Experienced private investigators may make over $100,000.00 a year while deriving satisfaction from helping people and working cases.

**Q. Are there many opportunities for work as a PI?**

In addition to working as a self-employed private investigator or for a private investigation agency there are other work opportunities with related duties including process serving; bill collecting; insurance claims investigators; corporate investigators; financial investigators; store detectives; security.

Are you an adventurer? Are you interested in a well-paid challenging profession that rewards both initiative and skill? Would you like to be able to locate missing persons, catch cheating spouses, run background checks, conduct surveillance employing the latest high tech equipment? Have you dreamed of owning your own private investigation agency?

**Q. Are there equal opportunities for both women and men investigators?**

Yes, there are opportunities for people who can do the job regardless of whether they are male or female. The key prerequisite for a career as a private investigator is your desire and determination to succeed.

Women are naturally inquisitive (nosey). By nature we're more detail oriented (real nosey). A woman tends to think differently from a man. Women tend to look at a case from a different angle than a man.

If you've ever considered a career as a professional investigator and you are financially ready to break into this exciting industry there is no reason why you cannot do this. New specialties and areas of expertise are being created frequently, necessitated by an unquenchable demand for information.

The investigative and security industries are big and getting bigger. Each year new high-tech clients vie for the services of experienced private investigators that understand the diverse technologies and have acquired the latest skills required to meet those exacting demands.

Private investigators employ techniques such as public record searches for background checks and pre-employment screening. Private investigators interview people to gain information, gather evidence, and verify facts about individuals, events, or companies. Private investigators may provide assistance in civil liability and personal injury cases, insurance claims and fraud, child custody cases, premarital screening, and martial infidelity. Some private investigative firms offer executive and celebrity protection, and some serve court papers.

If you have a desire to do this, or if you are already licensed, taking the first step may be the hardest. Start by believing you can do this. Then believe that you can do it better than anyone else. Believe in yourself before expecting anyone else to believe in you. Next you will need a proven track record. You will need to have some satisfied clients. Sometimes working a case pro-bono (unpaid) or by barter (swapping) can be rewarding in that you can capitalize on this experience by getting your client to give you a written testimonial that you can use for various purposes such as on a web site, brochure, or press release. Try to get testimonials from your satisfied clients. This helps prove you have a track record. If your client is satisfied they will tell someone else and hopefully refer other clients to you.

## Q. What are the advantages and disadvantages of being a PI?

1. Work hours often are irregular, and the work can be dangerous.
2. About a third of all licensed investigators are self-employed.
3. Applicants typically have related experience in areas such as law enforcement, insurance, the military, or government investigative or intelligence jobs.
4. Keen competition is expected because of the large number of qualified people who are attracted to this occupation; opportunities will

be best for entry-level jobs with detective agencies or as store detectives on a part-time basis.

*Tip: To get started you might work a free case, get permission to publicize it, solve it, and publicize it. Once you receive publicity wait for your phone to ring.*

*Learn to barter. If someone cannot pay for your services ask him or her if they can swap or trade something. That's how I got my first computer. I bartered with someone who built computers...I found his father and he gave me a computer, printer, and all the software I needed. Bartering can be a good thing!*

## CHAPTER II

## HOW TO BECOME A LICENSED PRIVATE INVESTIGATOR

Almost every state has laws pertaining to the license of private investigators and private investigation companies. Some states require a written test. Some states have reciprocal agreements. Some states require experience working with a licensed company. Not all states are the same so it is recommended that before you begin obtain a copy of the state laws for private investigators. A list of state offices and state associations are provided in this chapter. Many laws are available online.

Most public libraries will have a reference section with law books in which you can look up these laws. A reference librarian is usually available for assistance. It would be a good idea to make a copy of the laws and study them to be sure you completely understand them.

**Q. How do I get started?**

Becoming a private investigator begins with understanding the state laws and requesting requirements from the state board of regulators office. Each state has a board of regulators that govern the licensing of private investigators, as well as every other profession. Chapter IX has a list of laws and where to find these laws.

If your state requires you to first work with a licensed company to obtain experience you may have a hard time getting your foot in the door. A licensed company has to be a mentor and become responsible for you. They have to train you and share information, secrets, and sources with you. Unless they have a non-compete agreement, a trainee can be trained then go and compete with the mentor. To take an untrained and inexperienced investigator a licensed company may feel the trainee should pay for their training. A trainee may expect to be paid for something they are unqualified for. So being trained by a licensed company may be an internship. That means it is a trade off – no pay for the education and no pay for the experience. The benefit of this is that the licensed company gets a free employee and the trainee learns the trade secrets free of charge. Listen to your instincts and intuitions and work only with a reputable investigator with a proven track record. Many good investigators will not spend their time training a new person. Oftentimes an investigator will seize the opportunity to take advantage of a free employee. Some experienced investigators may even try to charge for their time to train you. So beware of whom you are talking to and working with. Don't be afraid to check them out.

Although not required, all new businesses should first develop a plan. Your chance at success will become better if you follow a plan. There are five basic types of businesses:

1. Sole proprietorship – The owner is totally responsible for operating the business and everything involved in running the business.
2. Partnership – More than one person shares the responsibility for operating the business.
3. C corporation – Corporate papers must be filed with the secretary of state's office. It some states it is possible to download a form online and submit with the filing fee. This type of corporation is used as a shield from lawsuits. Taxes must be paid on any profits plus taxes must be paid on any dividends from stock. Taxes are paid twice.
4. S corporation – This type of corporation may shield an owner from personal liability, but any profits or losses from the corporation are reported on owner's personal tax return. Taxes are only paid once.
5. LLC – Limited Liability Company – This type of company has the liability advantages of a corporation, but may not be taxed at the state or federal level. Check state laws to be sure.

Always have a good contract no matter what you are doing. If you go to work for another company, have a good contract. If you start your own company and have clients, have a good contract.

A good contract is a sign of a good business deal. If you have a good understanding up front and put it into a contract, then you should not have a misunderstanding later on. This is so important so please don't take it lightly. Anyone who is legitimate should not mind signing a contract.

# CHAPTER III

## HOW TO START AND BUILD A PRIVATE INVESTIGATOR BUSINESS

One of the hardest parts of becoming a private eye is taking the first step and getting started. Getting your foot in the door is not going to be easy. Like most businesses the more you know, the better job you will do. If you have no experience, it is wise to work with an experienced and successful investigator (if you are lucky you might find one who will become your mentor). Learn what you can from the more experienced person, and then develop your own style. The person you work with might not do things the way you think they should be done. You can learn some good and bad lessons from other investigators and then decide what you prefer. You don't have to do what someone else does. It is usually a learning experience to observe others.

Depending on your background and experience, if you work with another investigator it might take a two-year internship before you are ready to jump in on your own. You could possibly open a branch for the existing service, or start your own company. If you work with another investigator it might be required that you sign a non-compete agreement that will limit what you can do with your own company. You may not be able to contact former clients, or practice within a certain area. On the other hand after you start your own business you might refer clients to each other and help each other as sub-contractors.

After you are licensed, one of the first things you will need is a nice business card. You should get in the habit of keeping cards in your pocket or billfold at all times and don't hesitate to hand them to every person you meet. You now become a prospector and a networked. Hand them to people who work at the courthouse, attorney's offices, or other public buildings, church, neighbors, friends and relatives. Don't be afraid to strike up conversations with people everywhere you go and mention that you are a private eye in case they ever need anything or know someone who might need a PI. A cheap business card is a reflection on you and how your potential clients will see you. Invest in one that looks professional even if it costs more.

Each and every person you come in contact with is a potential client or referral to another person. In a sense you are now a sales person, in the business of selling your services. If you don't make a sale, you don't get paid. The phone will become your cash register. If the phone is not ringing, the cash register is not making any money.

Also image is important. Your appearance is going to become a factor in getting business. A neat, well-groomed, conservative appearance is going to reflect a sign of success. An unkempt appearance and sloppy attire will reflect a sign of failure. Dress appropriately for whatever you are doing. Naturally if you are working undercover or on surveillance you will dress to blend in to the environment where you are working. But if you are testifying in court, look your professional best. If you are trying to solicit business, look your best. If you want to succeed, look your best.

A convenient and good place to order affordable and sometimes free professional business cards, stationery, brochures, and other products on the web is Vista Prints, www.vistaprints.com.

### Q. What is the secret of good customer service?

First, you must believe you are the best private eye in the world, and then you will convince others. If you don't believe you are good, neither will anyone else. It all begins with how you see yourself, your attitude, and determination. When you meet your prospective client if you are not clean and well dressed and do not look successful more than likely you will not get the job. You must look successful to become successful. You must look a client in the eye and know exactly what you are talking about. You have to have self-confidence and self-esteem. If you don't, the client will sense it. No one will want to hire some-one with no experience or track record, so you must prove yourself. You must treat each client and each case with respect and integrity. Do not take a case that you cannot solve. Do not take a client's money and not give them what you told them you could do for them. Treat each client the way you would want to be treated. If you treat people right you will get referrals and repeat business. That's the real secret to making a business grow.

### Q. Why should I have a business plan?

A business plan is like a road map. Although it is not required, to get from where you are to where you are going you will probably need a map to show you the best way to get there. It is true with a start up business. Throughout the process of creating a plan keep in mind your objective of the plan. There are two types of business plans, an annual plan that is used to manage a business, and a business plan, which is used to attract capital. If you plan to borrow money to start or run your business, banks or other lenders may require a copy of each year's annual plan. The start up business plan is used as a basis for operating the business.

**Q. What information should the business plan contain?**

Make the plan one page if possible…. keep it short and simple.

1) Describe your services.
2) State why your service has promise.
3) Do you already have a track record for generating clients and sales?
4) Identify your client market.
5) Do you have any statistics to show how many people may need your services?
6) State who will be working with this business and what their special qualifications and experiences are.
7) What is your financial objective? How much income do you hope to produce? If you are going to borrow money, how do you plan to use the money and how do you plan to pay it back?
8) Describe where your business will be located and how much the overhead and expenses are expected to be.
9) Explain how your services will differ from the competition.

**Q. What information should a marketing plan contain?**

1) How large is the client market?
2) How many competitors are there?
3) How will you market your services?
4) Evaluate your client market. What services are most requested? What will the average client spend? How many clients can you expect per month?

**Q. How do I analyze the competition?**

1) Identify who your competitors are, who is generating the most business, and determine what makes them successful.
2) What are the competitive advantages and weaknesses of your business?

**Q. How do I generate clients and market my services?**

1) Advertising in the yellow pages can be expensive and may produce a lot of inquiries about your services, but if you don't get the sale it is worthless. Many people who use the yellow pages are just comparing

rates and looking for a good deal. Unfortunately this type of advertising probably will not produce the kind of business you hope for. Try calling the numbers listed; most will not work because they have not had enough business to justify the expense.

It is important to have a real person answer the phone and not an answering machine. An answering service might be what you need if you cannot answer the calls yourself, or have someone do it for you. If you answer the call you have a better chance of making the sale. Think of your phone as your cash register. If the phone is not ringing, you are not generating sales; therefore you are not producing income and will probably not survive solely on the income from private investigation.

Make an appointment to meet with each person who calls. Learn to negotiate a good deal.

2) Business card or brochure? You will definitely need business cards. Never go anywhere without having a business card at your fingertips and hand them out to everyone you meet. You could also have a printed brochure and distribute them by mail, or hand delivery to attorneys or other potential clients.

3) Potential clients are everywhere. You can be a guest or guest speaker at a civic function such as a Rotary club. You can join the local Chamber of Commerce. Members of these organizations are primarily made up of the business leaders of the community. Potential clients are your neighbors, people you go to church with, friends of friends or family members. Anyone and everyone is a potential client. Learn to prospect and network.

4) Join and become active in professional associations. Attend professional conferences. This is a tremendous source of networking, information, and referrals.

5) To become successful you need to dress and look professional. You will also need a proven track record.

Many private investigators have good investigative skills, often they have law-enforcement backgrounds, but few have experience in marketing, management, sales, or finance. They have been taught to be great investigators, but don't have a clue how to get clients, operate a business, make a sale, manage a budget, or make a profit. The information contained herein is intended to help supplement the other things that were taught at the police academy. Unfortunately the police academy did not prepare you to work anywhere else except law-enforcement. What are you planning to do after retirement? Life goes on, you know? And it can get better. You have a choice of making it better or not. The choice is yours and there is no reason in the world why you cannot become a great private investigator. You can make your own decisions now, and you don't have to ask anyone for permission to work on something. You can choose to work on whatever appeals to you.

**Q. What kind of advertising and marketing will produce new clients?**

Almost every state has a legal association that publishes a bar journal, magazine, or newsletter. These are publications that are read by attorneys. Many of these publications accept outside advertising. Your ad will have to stand out from the rest. A photo-ad is good. A caption that has a "hook" might read: "Do you need my help?" Asking a question in an ad draws attention. Placing the ad on the right side of a publication will result in more people seeing it.

Professional newsletters are also a good place to make an announcement or a special offer or special service.

You can also submit a press release to any publication. Free publicity is hard to beat. For publicity you can also submit an article for publication. Publicity will help to give you credibility and legitimacy.

Mailing can be expensive, but mailing lists can be purchased and often you can purchase ready to mail labels. You may consider direct mailing announcements of a new service, a new location, or something that will inform recipients of your the services you offer. How about a special rate with a deadline?

A brochure can become an essential part of promoting your business. It needs to answer some key questions for someone who is considering using your services:

1) Who is this investigator?
2) Why should I hire this investigator?
3) How much will this cost?
4) Where is this investigator's office located?

The brochure should answer these questions by describing your services and the benefits you offer your clients. You need to show you have a proven track record. Don't be afraid to include a few references or testimonials from satisfied clients who have used your services. Sell your strengths rather than offer a multitude of services.

If you are computer literate you might like to invest in some brochure software. You can create brochures, labels, stationery, and your own business cards if you have the right software and the knowledge of how to use it. I have created brochures using Pagemaker as well as with special brochure software. You can probably produce them using whatever Word program is in your computer. You can cut and paste and type whatever you want it to say. It is really not that hard. You can produce a "master" copy and take it to your local Kinko's or office products store and have as many copies as you want printed. You can leave a place to put a label and mail them, or you can hand them out at various places. You can print them in color or black and white. You can add photos, or logos, or whatever you want. You can print them on heavy stock paper, slick paper, or colored paper. Everything is your choice, so you get to decide.

## Q. Do I need a web site?

If you really want to look professional and have a place for people to read about you and your services, by all means have a web site. It won't hurt. But of course if no one knows you have a web site, and no one ever visits your web site, it is useless. If you have a web site you have to drive traffic to it. You have to promote and advertise your web site on your business cards, stationery, reports, and brochures.

First you will need to register a domain name for your web site. You can easily register a domain name at www.myhosting.com or www.netsol.com. Many other companies also offer domain registration. To find them go to your favorite search engine and enter "domain name registration." My favorite search engine is GOOGLE. Another favorite is www.ask.com. I can usually find most anything using these two services.

For those who are really computer literate and want to create your own site, you will need the software for designing. I have used FrontPage for many years. Many professionals use DreamWeaver. Check with your local computer software supplier for other products.

Just as your phone needs a phone service to make it work, a web site will need a host server (ISP) to make it work.

**Q. How do I get my first cases?** *"If it is to be, it is up to me."*

It will be up to you to generate clients. Probably no one is going to do this for you. You must think of yourself as a sales person and getting a case as "making a sale." Without "sales" you won't have a business. It is vital that you learn to make sales. A good sales person must believe he or she offers the best service in town. You must believe in yourself, or no one else will.

First identify what markets and types of investigation you want to target. Do you want divorce or child custody cases? Do you want insurance fraud cases? Do you want to work on surveillances? Do you want to sit at a computer and do all your work from home? Do you want to work for lawyers, insurance companies, banks, businesses, or individuals?

In towns where there is a courthouse you will probably find a nearby building filled with attorneys. Attorneys like to have their offices near a courthouse for convenience. Try to talk to an attorney in every office. Make them an offer they cannot refuse. Ask them to give you a case that has not been solved and if you cannot solve it they won't owe you anything. Prove that you can get results.

It has been my experiences that seldom do lawyers pay me directly. Most prefer their clients' pay. It does not matter to me who pays, as long as I get paid. I do not begin working a case without a contract and a retainer. Attorneys don't work cases without a contract and retainer either. Most professionals have their clients, patients, or customers sign some type of agreement with how they are to be paid. Private investigators are professionals too, and should proceed accordingly.

Don't be shocked at how many friends and family members will try to use you to get "free information." If you want to work for free, at least learn to tell them you can do them a favor but they will need to pay for whatever your expenses are. Don't let them take advantage of you. Be ready to barter for something of equal value.

Almost anyone can also start out serving process for attorneys. That can be time consuming and not always under the best of circumstances, but for each subpoena served, that is a potential $50–$75. Not too bad if you can serve several in one day. If you can find an attorney who needs subpoenas served immediately, they may be willing to pay extra. (The client actually has to pay.)

Everything you do is negotiable. You can add extra for mileage, gas, or other expenses.

When meeting with a client be sure to take notes on everything. Be sure to put a date and time on all notes. Start a file and keep everything in the file. When it is time to produce a report you will have everything organized in chronological order.

## Q. How do I price my services?

What is the going rate of the average private investigator in the area where you are working? Are you going to have a niche or offer services that are better than your competitors? This is how you determine what to charge. If a client can hire another investigator for less than you charge, why should they hire you?

For many years I charged $100 per hour, plus expenses for my services. I tell my clients that they can hire any other investigator for $50 an hour, however that investigator may work twice as many hours. I will produce results in less time than most. I have even gone so far as to guarantee my services. If I don't get the desired results, the client does not have to pay.

Also, when I show them something to prove I have a track record, which usually makes me credible. I have a "press kit" with articles about me, testimonials from clients, and books that I have written. I can show I have a proven track record. I don't need a case I cannot solve. I want to prove how good a job I can do.

You must learn to evaluate a case by:
    1) Type of investigation.
    2) What is the client's goal?
    3) How much time is estimated to work the case?
    4) How much will it cost to work this case?
    5) Will I have expenses?
    6) Do I need to work this case on a flat rate or an hourly rate?

Often clients will call and want to meet in your office, an attorney's office, or a restaurant. So when you meet with a client in person, look your best. You have already spoken with the client by phone and you have had time to think about the case. Come to the meeting prepared with a contract ready for them to sign. You can fill in the blanks as you talk and agree on the terms of the contract.

Every investigation is different and every client is different. The more experienced you become the easier it will be to work a case. You will automatically do things without having to give it much thought.

You can also offer to do an investigation in stages. Phase one might include gathering background information. Phase two might include moving or stationery surveillance. Phase three might include taking photos of a subject involved in some activity that may be beneficial to the case. There is no set rule of what you must or must not do. This is part of the beauty of working for yourself, you get to choose and decide on just about everything.

Learn to be innovative and creative. Be different from your competition. Listen closely to your clients and analyze what they want and expect from you. Explain to them what you can or cannot do and how what you are going to do will benefit their case. You will have to sell your services. A doctor must analyze the problem, diagnose the problem, and prescribe a solution. A private investigator does the same thing.

## Q. What equipment will I need?

Depending on what type of investigations you are going to work will determine how much equipment you will need to get the job done. Of course a cell phone, a camera, a camcorder, and a computer are some of the first things you will probably need.

To obtain information from a professional database you will first need a computer and a printer. If you already have a computer you probably already have access to the internet thru an ISP (Internet Service Provider).

In order to have access to the professional databases you will need to first be licensed. After you are licensed you will complete an application for access to the database. There are many professional databases for private investigators. More information on databases is in Chapter VII.

If you plan to work on surveillances you will need a camera and a camcorder. Look for a camera that takes good pictures at night or under low light conditions. Look for a good camcorder that will zoom from a distance. Date and time features are also good to show when the photos were taken.

Some states may allow tracking devices for surveillance work. Always check state laws before using this type of equipment.

## Q. Where can I purchase electronic equipment?

Electronic equipment, software, or "spy toys" may be purchased online, thru a catalog, by phone, etc.

If you attend some of the larger association conventions you will find many vendors selling equipment.

Online you can find software, "spy toys," and other equipment at:

http://www.undercoverpress.com/private.html
http://www.spygear4u.com/index.asp?PARTNER=mkissiah
http://www.gadgetuniverse.com/category.asp?CAT=CATSS&MENU=
SPY&CTITLE=Spy+and+Security
http://www.dynaspy.com/
http://www.spy-dome.com/spyrec.html
http://www.spy-tronix.com/record.html
http://www.spyville.com/
http://www.tscm.co.za/
http://www.computer-monitoring.com/
http://www.computer-spy.com/
http://www.internet-monitoring-software.com/
http://www.exploreanywhere.com/
http://www.usaspyshop.com/
http://www.spy-gadgets.com/
http://www.softactivity.com/
http://www.spygalaxy.com/
http://needtoknowsurveillance.com/
http://www.spysupplystore.com/
http://www.mjelectronics.com/
http://www.startechoutlet.com/
http://www.joenterprises.com/
http://www.spy-cams.com/
http://www.spytrac.com/
http://classifieds.pioutlet.com/
http://www.amtel-security.com/
http://www.surveillance-spy-equipment.com/
http://www.pishop.net/
http://www.gotspy.com/
http://www.security-camera.com/
http://www.longintech.com/
http://www.cornerstonesecurityservices.com/
http://x-recon.com/
http://www.spy-tools-directory.com/
http://www.flantopia.com/

http://www.miniwirelesscamera.com/
http://www.spysupplyinc.com/
http://www.microvideox.com/
http://www.spytechs.com/
http://www.covertonesecurity.com/
http://www.cctvshack.com/
http://www.purelysecurity.com/
http://www.deltadeals.com/
http://www.spy-equipment-buying-guide.com/
http://www.myspytech.com/
http://www.theprotectionpros.com/
http://www.2mcctv.com/
http://www.cctvblowout.com
http://www.ritevideo.com/
http://www.magic-cctv.com/
http://www.thetrackerforyou.com/
http://www.diydefense.com/index.asp
http://trackingtheworld.com/
http://www.advancedhomeandbusiness.com/
http://www.cbsurveillance.com/
http://www.spyopsusa.com/

**Q. Should I join an association?**

It is not required, but a good way to learn more about the business and network.

**Q. Am I required to obtain continuing education courses?**

Check the state law in Chapter IX.

**Q. How many types of investigations are there?**

This is a partial list:
- Accident investigation
- Asset search
- Background check, background investigations
- Child custody investigation
- Copyright infringement

- Crime scene investigation
- Criminal defense investigation
- Criminal records
- Court records search and retrieval
- Civil Investigations
- Divorce investigations
- Death Investigation
- DMV / Motor Vehicle records search and retrieval
- Environmental investigations
- Federal records search
- Fraud investigations
- Hidden camera surveillance
- Homicide investigations
- Insurance claims investigation
    1. Arson
    2. Death claims
    3. Disability claims
    4. Medical malpractice
    5. Workers compensation
- Insurance fraud
- Internal theft investigations / loss prevention
- Locate missing persons
- Medical malpractice
- Personal injury investigation
- Public document retrieval
- Pre-Employee Screening / Background Check
- Process Server
- Process Service
- Records Retrieval
    - Asset records
    - Bankruptcy records
    - Corporate records
    - Criminal records
    - Divorce records
    - Death records
    - Marriage records
    - Medical records
    - Phone records
    - Police reports

- – Real estate records
- – Title search
- – UCC filings
- – Utility records
- Sex offenders
- Subpoena Service
- State records search
- Surveillance
- Tenant Screening
- UCC Filings
- Vehicle Tracking Systems
- Vessel / Aircraft investigations
- Video Surveillance
- White collar crimes
- Wiretap detection
- Witness locate

## Q. What are public records?

Public records are records that are available for public inspection or purchase. These records may be found at a court house, a public library, a local archives library, a state archives library, state offices, federal government offices, and many other places. Researching public records can be like a treasure hunt. When you find the information you need it is like finding the "golden egg." Some types of public records are:

Census records
Social Security Master Death Index
Marriage records
Divorce records
Lawsuits
Liens
Bankruptcy
Judgments
Probate records
Criminal records
Utility records (may not be available in all jurisdictions)
UCC filings
Unclaimed property

**Q. What type of records are not public information?**

These records may not be available as public information and may require a subpoena or written authorization to obtain:
- Phone records
- Medical records
- Financial records
    - Banks
    - Credit cards
    - Investments
- Driving records (check the DPPA law)
- Vehicle registration (check law)

## CHAPTER IV

# REPORTS, CONTRACTS, AND CHECKLISTS

### Report Writing
### Investigative Reports

In order to write a good report it is vital to keep good notes or a daily log in chronological order as the investigation progresses. Factual information must be compiled, analyzed, and arranged in appropriate categories. It must be easily readable and easy to understand.

There are four basic types of investigative reports, each with a distinct purpose:

1) **Preliminary Report.** The preliminary report may be prepared within the first few days of a new investigation and should explain
   a) the history of the case
   b) what the initial investigation involved

2) **Progress Report.** This report is a chronological record of what the investigator has done or learned and is an ongoing report until the case is finished.

3) **Final Report.** This report explains the outcome of the investigation.

4) **Supplemental Report.** This report is a record of something that occurs after the final report such as new evidence or the court disposition.

### The Preliminary Report

This report needs to be written when a case is opened and explains the purpose of the investigation; the information provided by the client, the initial actions that were taken, what additional information was obtained, and what else needs to be done. The preliminary report needs to include everything known or involved in a case. Don't rely on your memory to provide this information later on.

Before a private investigator is hired for a criminal defense case, law enforcement has already investigated the case, and the case is ready to be prosecuted. The crime scene is cold and more than likely any evidence has already been discovered and confiscated. Witnesses have already been interviewed and their memory of what happened may not be clear. Regardless of what has already occurred it is up to the private investigator to recreate the scene, interview witnesses, look for new evidence, look for mistakes or oversights in the law-enforcement investigation, and provide additional facts for the defense attorney.

## Opening Statement

The opening statement should contain the date, time, and location of meeting with a client. It should contain a list of all persons involved in the case to be investigated such as the client, the client's attorney, information provided by the client or attorney, witnesses to be interviewed, and actions that need to be taken. Provide as much information on each person or each action to be taken as possible. Example:

On February 21, 2006, at 10:00 A.M. this investigator was contacted by phone by criminal defense attorney Glen Franks of 109 Second Ave., Nashville, TN 37202, (615-555-1212), who explained that he represented a client named Patrick Marshall, 1200 Winding Way, Nashville, TN 37206, who was being charged by the Davidson County District Attorney with the murder of his girlfriend, Amy Harper. Mr. Franks asked me to meet with him at his office at 3:00 P.M. on this date so that he could provide me with additional information regarding the case.

At 3:00 P.M. on February 21, 2006, I met with Mr. Glen Franks at his office. Mr. Franks and I signed a contract for my investigative services in which I agreed to obtain certain information pertaining to this case. Mr. Franks explained to me that his client Mr. Marshall, was innocent and that he needed me to prove that he could not have murdered Ms. Harper which occurred at approximately 8 P.M. on February 8, 2006. In order to represent his client, Mr. Franks needed copies of the police investigation, crime scene photos, copies of the warrant for Mr. Marshall's arrest, and other information pertaining to the investigation.

All reports should contain relevant facts of who (Client, Attorney, Prosecutor, Witnesses, etc.), what (type of investigation), when (dates and times involved), where (location), why (why the investigation is necessary), and how (how incident occurred).

## Body

The preliminary report should also contain a chronological list of events that occur as the investigation progresses. For example: a list of records and reports that are obtained, witnesses that are interviewed, visits to crime scenes or other locations, and photographs that document pertinent facts.

On February 22, 2006, at 11:00 A.M. records of the police investigation of the case involving Mr. Marshall were obtained from the Metro Police Department. Copies of these records are attached to this report.

On February 22, 2006, at 1:30 P.M. I drove to the crime scene at the Park Avenue Apartments at 100 Park Avenue, Apt. B-5, Nashville, TN 37221. Photos were taken of the exterior of the building and parking lot. Photos are attached to this report.

On February 22, 2006, at 2:00 P.M. I interviewed Ms. Mona Gossett, the apartment manager of the Park Avenue Apartments, 100 Park Avenue, Nashville, TN 37221 (615-555-1212). Ms. Gossett stated that she had met Mr. Marshall and had observed him coming and going from Ms. Harper's apartment on numerous occasions. Ms. Gossett further stated that she had no knowledge of any problems between Ms. Harper and Mr. Marshall. A report of the interview with Ms. Gossett is attached. A copy of the security camera tape for the date and time of the murder was requested.

**Ending**

This report should contain a list of additional information to be obtained, actions that need to be taken, or persons that need to be interviewed.

A meeting is scheduled at the Park Avenue Apartments on February 23, 2006, to interview Ms. Harper's neighbors, Ms. Jean Williams, Ms. Debra Sawyers, and Ms. Evelyn Odum.

A meeting is scheduled for February 24, 2006, with relatives of Ms. Harper at their residences: Ms. Debbie Sweeney, Ms. Elizabeth Woods.

A meeting is scheduled for February 25, 2006, with friends of Ms. Harper: Ms. Barbara Meroney, Ms. Melissa Meroney, and Ms. Nancy Nabors.

A meeting is scheduled for February 26, 2006, with Ms. Harper's co-workers, Ms. Jo Ann Goodman and Ms. Mary Oakley, at the corporate offices of Crownover Entertainment.

Copies of Mr. Marshall's credit card statements, cell phone records, and bank statements need to be obtained. Also a copy of a security tape for the date and time of the murder will be obtained from Mr. Marshall's employer.

## The Progress Report

A progress report contains updates of events and additional information pertaining to the investigation and is used primarily to record the results of the investigation or what else needs to be done by the investigator.

## The Final Report

At the end of the investigation the final report explains the factual events of the entire investigation and the end results or conclusion. The final report should contain evidence, facts, statements, substantiation, and proof.

Interviews with relatives, neighbors, friends, and co-workers of the victim, Ms. Harper, revealed that there were no known problems between Ms. Harper and Mr. Marshall.

Surveillance tapes from Mr. Marshall's employer revealed Mr. Marshall entered the building at 7:00 P.M. on February 8, 2006, and left the building at 10:30 P.M. on that date.

Surveillance tapes from the Park Avenue Apartment entrance gate revealed that between 7:00 P.M. and 10:00 P.M. on February 8, 2006, ten vehicles entered the complex. License tags of each of these vehicles were visible and legible. One of the license tags belonged to a former boyfriend of Ms. Harper's. Further investigation of the former boyfriend revealed that he had physically abused Ms. Harper and that she had a restraining order against him. Based on this new evidence the charges were dropped on Mr. Marshall.

The final report should be a summary of facts and explain the purpose of the investigation, the who, what, where, when, why, and how of the investigation, and list all facts in chronological order.

The final report should end with the investigator's conclusion based on the facts. The report should include all attachments such as statements, photos, documents and records, and anything else that was involved in the investigation.

## Supplemental Report

After the final report and the investigation has ended a supplemental follow-up report will include the court disposition, or any new evidence that might appear that could effect the outcome of the investigation.

## Report Writing Mechanics

Reports should include three main parts: Introduction, Body, and Ending. Separate paragraphs for each action, person, place, or time. The report should be written in past tense and first person. The report needs to be like a conversation. All reports should include the five Ws and one H: who, what, where, when, why, and how.

**Introduction**: This personal injury investigation was conducted between June 10, 2006 and August 10, 2006, and involves obtaining and documenting public records, photographs of the scene of the accident, and statements from witnesses.

**Body**: The body of a report should identify all persons involved and describe the evidence. Report only facts that are supported by evidence. Opinions don't count.

Be aware of the words describing persons or events. Be careful not to appear biased or judgmental.

On May 27, 2006, Ms. Barbara Mott left Albertson's Food Mart at 1500 Murfreesboro Rd., Nashville, TN 37013. A white Ford Mustang with Tennessee license ABC123 drove toward Ms. Mott and the male white driver reached out and struck Ms. Mott with a baseball bat, grabbed Ms. Mott's shoulder purse, and dragged her into the parking lot. As a result of this incident, Ms. Mott sustained a concussion. An ambulance transported Ms. Mott to Vanderbilt Hospital.

Interviews with the store employees and other witnesses provided a description of the driver of the vehicle.

A copy of the store's surveillance tape was requested for proof of the incident and identification of the perpetrator.

In writing a report help the reader by reporting facts without going into unnecessary detail. Your words are needed to make the reader understand what happened. After a report is written it will need to be edited until it is clear and concise. Look for spelling and grammar errors, omissions, punctuation, wordiness, repetitions, etc. Keep reading and rewriting until you don't find anything else to change.

**Statements:** Written statements are necessary–
- To document facts and observations of an individual.
- To record and report details that may be forgotten later.

- To verify that an incident occurred.
- To have proof for court.
- To identify the persons involved.
- To describe evidence.

Statements need to be written exactly as reported and should contain facts, not opinions. Statements should be signed, dated, and if possible witnessed. When taking notes think of working a puzzle and everything you discover is a missing piece of the puzzle. The puzzle pieces can be small details such as names, addresses, and phone numbers or important details such as photographs, records, physical evidence, statements from witnesses When all the pieces of the puzzle are complete you will have a picture of what happened. The case will be no better than the notes from which the report is prepared.

Statements need to identify all persons involved or related to the case. For each witness or person involved it is best to obtain their full name, date of birth, address, social security number, place of employment, spouse, and phone numbers. The purpose of obtaining personal information is so that that person may be located later in case they move.

Depending on the importance of the person to the case additional information such as relatives, friends, and neighbors will be helpful.

If a case involves evidence such as physical, forensic, eye-witness, photographic, or documentary, it must be identified and described:
- Blood was found at the scene
- A photo of the blood
- A photo of the victim's injury
- A copy of the medical report from the hospital
- Statements from witnesses.
- The store's surveillance tape.

A more detailed description of the evidence might read like this:

Blood (see photo of blood) was found in the front parking lot of the scene (identify location of incident). A baseball bat with bloodstains was found near the scene. Bloodstains that matched the blood type (see lab report) of victim (identify victim).

The findings of Dr. Bienvenu (see attending physician's report) are consistent with eyewitness accounts (see witness statements) of blows inflicted on victim (identify victim).

It is important to record the time and date that each item of evidence was obtained, how it was obtained, who obtained it, where it was obtained, and what was obtained. Also include the names of each physician, forensic examiner, or any other person who had knowledge of the incident.

A report of an investigation must include factual information. Opinions, theories, and suppositions are not facts.
- Blood was found at the scene.
- Bloodstains were found on a baseball bat.
- Blood matched the victim.
- Witnesses reported seeing the suspect reach out of the car and grab the victim's purse.
- The victim sustained a head injury.
- The store's surveillance tape.

Facts are supported by evidence. Each fact is like a puzzle piece that will eventually connect and form a complete picture of what happened at the scene of the incident.

**Past Tense**
Most of what you write has already occurred so you will use past tense to describe what happened, for example:
"The safe contained…"
"Mr. Minton stated…"

**First Person**
When talking about yourself use first person, for example:
"I went to the scene.."
"I interviewed Mr. Minton's employees…."

Do not refer to yourself as "this investigator," "the undersigned," or "the writer of this report." Do not use legalese, such as "the corpus delicti" or the jargon of professional investigators such as "perpetrator" or the M.O. or "modus operendi."

When your report is complete does it answer who, what, when, where, why, and how?

At approximately 12:30 A.M. on November 10, 2005, Mr. John Stewart, an employee of The Soup and Sandwich Shop, at 5000 Hill Road, Franklin, Tennessee, 37064, stole cash in the amount of $5,000.00 from the store's safe located in the main office at the end of the previous night's shift. Several eye witnesses reported observing Mr. Stewart put the money into the office safe at approximately 12:00 A.M. After 12:05 A.M. Mr. Stewart was the only employee to enter the main office.

**Who:** Mr. John Stewart, an employee of The Soup and Sandwich Shop.

**What:** Cash in the amount of $5,000.00 was stolen from the office safe.

**When:** At approximately 12:30 A.M., November 10, 2005.

**Where:** 5000 Hill Road, Franklin, Tennessee, 37064

**Why:** Mr. Stewart was deeply in debt.

**How:** Several employee witnesses stated that at the time of the incident (12:30 A.M.), Mr. Stewart was the only employee who entered the office where the safe was located.

### Worker's Compensation Statements

There is a purpose to obtaining information in writing:
1. To document facts and observations of an individual.
2. To document details of an individual, so that details will not be forgotten later when it goes to trial, and to avoid having a person change his/her mind as to the details.
3. To evaluate the credibility of the person from whom you are taking the statement.
4. To document evidence for trial purposes.
5. To document and verify details in support of photographs, such as verification of employment after the claimant is photographed going to work somewhere else, while collecting worker's compensation.
6. To verify or disqualify a signed document.
7. To verify that an incident actually occurred the way an individual described it.

Statements are written factual, as the person tells it. Like all reports, it should not contain your opinion or be altered in any way.

If it appears that a statement may be detrimental to a case, talk to the insurance adjuster before proceeding.

Each page of the statement should be signed, dated, and witnessed.

## Be Direct and Objective

In writing a report remember your opinion does not count, stick only to facts. Do not be judgmental or write with a hint of bias for or against anyone or anything. Avoid tagging names to people such as "wino," "pot head," "liar," "con artist," etc. Avoid comments that might be suppositions like "It would appear that..." or "In my judgement..." or "According to all indications...."

It is best to use direct words to describe an incident. Instead of using "blow away" use "shoot"; instead of using "beat up" use "assaulted"; and instead of "drunk" use "intoxicated" or "under the influence." Describe an incident. Instead of saying Mr. Jackson was uncooperative, describe what happened such as Mr. Jackson refused to identify himself, and refused to answer questions.

Know and understand the difference between misdemeanor and felony. A misdemeanor is a lesser offense punishable by less than two years. A felony is a more serious offense and punishable by more than two years. These offenses may also include a fine.

## Revisions

Do not think for an instant that when you finish writing a report that you are actually through. What you have is only a first draft and as you read it over and over you may find that you want to change the way it is worded, or that you may have repeated something or overlooked something. After rereading it over and over you may write several drafts before you have the report the best you can make it. Look for factual errors, inaccuracies, omissions, biases, wordiness, misspellings, repetitive phrases, incorrect word usage, punctuation, and grammar. Word processing applications have features that automatically check the spelling, grammar, and punctuation.

## Easy Reading

- Stick to facts and do not go into unnecessary detail.
- Be very clear on who and what you are referring to.
- Remember that the reader has not gone through the experience of the investigation and in order to understand what happened is totally dependent on your words.

# SAMPLE CONTRACTS

## SAMPLE PRIVATE INVESTIGATOR CONTRACT

This Agreement is entered into as of the _____ day of _____, 20____, between [client's name] hereinafter referred to as "CLIENT" and [private investigator's name] hereinafter referred to as INVESTIGATOR, dab/ (name of agency).

1. **Independent Contractor**. Subject to the terms and conditions of this Agreement, the CLIENT hereby engages the INVESTIGATOR as an independent contractor to perform the services set forth herein, and the INVESTIGATOR hereby accepts such engagement.

2. **Services**. The services to be provided to the CLIENT by the INVESTIGATOR include:

_____

_____

_____

_____

3. **Expenses**. During the term of this Agreement, the INVESTIGATOR shall bill and the CLIENT shall reimburse [him or her] for all reasonable and approved out-of-pocket expenses, which are incurred in connection with the performance of the services as stated in Paragraph 2. Notwithstanding the foregoing, expenses for the time spent by INVESTIGATOR in traveling to and from CLIENT facilities shall not be reimbursable. Expense are not to exceed $_____.

4. **Retainer/Rate**. A retainer in the amount of $_____ is paid at time of signing this Agreement. The _____ (hourly/flat) rate of $_____ will be paid upon completion of investigation. This investigation is not to exceed ___ hours, or $_____ flat fee.

4. **Written Report**. A written results report including, but not limited to, a chronological log of activity, times, and dates of investigation, results of investigation, expenses, copies of records, photos, audio and video tapes, and any other information relevant to investigation will be provided to CLIENT by INVESTIGATOR upon completion of investigation. INVESTIGATOR may keep original audio or videotapes or other original materials that may need to be used in a court proceeding in the event INVESTIGATOR may be required to testify.

5. **Confidentiality**. The INVESTIGATOR acknowledges that during the investigation [he or she] will have access to and become acquainted with personal, private, or confidential information of the CLIENT and/or used by the CLIENT. The INVESTIGATOR agrees that [he or she] will not disclose any of the aforesaid, directly or indirectly, or use any of them in any manner, either during the term of this Agreement or at any time thereafter, except as required in the course of this investigation. All files, records, documents, information, and other investigative items belonging to the CLIENT whether prepared by the INVESTIGATOR or otherwise coming into [his or her] possession, shall remain the exclusive property of the CLIENT. The INVESTIGATOR shall have the right to retain any copies of the foregoing without the CLIENT'S prior written permission. Upon the expiration or earlier termination of this Agreement, or whenever requested by the CLIENT, the INVESTIGATOR shall immediately deliver to the CLIENT all such files, records, documents, information, and other items in [his or her] possession or under [his or her] control. The INVESTIGATOR further agrees that [he or she] will not disclose [his or her] retention as an independent contractor or the terms of this Agreement to any person without the prior written consent of the CLIENT and shall at all times preserve the confidential nature of [his or her] relationship to the CLIENT and of the services hereunder.

7. **Conflicts of Interest**. The INVESTIGATOR represents that [he or she] is free to enter into this Agreement, and that this investigation does not violate the terms of any agreement between the INVESTIGATOR and any third party. Further, the INVESTIGATOR, in rendering [his or her] duties shall use discretion to obtain information. No information will be obtained illegally. During the term of this agreement, the INVESTIGATOR shall devote as much of [his or her] productive time, energy and abilities to the performance of [his or her] duties hereunder as is necessary to perform the required duties in a timely and productive manner. The INVESTIGATOR is expressly free to perform services for other parties while performing services for CLIENT.

8. Hold Harmless.

9. **Termination**. The CLIENT may terminate this Agreement at any time by 10 working days' written notice to the INVESTIGATOR. In addition, if the INVESTIGATOR breaches provisions of this Agreement, the CLIENT at any time may terminate the investigation immediately and without prior written notice to the INVESTIGATOR.

10. **Successors and Assigns**. All of the provisions of this Agreement shall be

binding upon and inure to the benefit of the parties hereto and there respective heirs, if any, successors, and assigns.

11. **Choice of Law**. The laws of the state of [_____] shall govern the validity of this Agreement, the construction of its terms and the interpretation of the rights and duties of the parties hereto.

12. **Arbitration**. Any controversies arising out of the terms of this Agreement or its interpretation shall be settled in [_____] in accordance with the rules of the American Arbitration Association, and the judgment upon award may be entered in any court having jurisdiction thereof.

13. **Headings**. Section headings are not to be considered a part of this Agreement and are not intended to be a full and accurate description of the contents hereof.

14. **Waiver**. Waiver by one party hereto of breach of any provision of this Agreement by the other shall not operate or be construed as a continuing waiver.

15. **Assignment**. The INVESTIGATOR shall not assign any of [his or her] rights under this Agreement, or delegate the performance of any of [his or her] duties hereunder, without the prior written consent of the CLIENT.

16. **Notices**. Any and all notices, demands, or other communications required or desired to be given hereunder by any party shall be in writing and shall be validly given or made to another party if personally served, or if deposited in the United States mail, certified or registered, postage prepaid, return receipt requested. If such notice or demand is served personally, notice shall be deemed constructively made at the time of such personal service. If such notice, demand or other communication is given by mail, such notice shall be conclusively deemed given five days after deposit thereof in the United States mail addressed to the party to whom such notice, demand or other communication is to be given as follows:

17. **Entire Understanding**. This document and any exhibit attached constitute the entire understanding and agreement of the parties, and any and all prior agreements, understandings, and representations are hereby terminated and canceled in their entirety and are of no further force and effect.

18. **Unenforceability of Provisions**. If any provision of this Agreement, or any portion thereof, is held to be invalid and unenforceable, then the remainder of this Agreement shall nevertheless remain in full force and effect.

19. **Entire Understanding**. This document and any exhibit attached constitute the entire understanding and agreement of the parties, and any and all prior agreements, understandings, and representations are hereby terminated and canceled in their entirety and are of no further force and effect.

**IN WITNESS WHEREOF** the undersigned have executed this Agreement as of the day and year first written above. The parties hereto agree that facsimile signatures shall be as effective as if originals.

_____   _____

INVESTIGATOR                                    DATE

[name]_____

[street address] _____

[city, state, zip] _____


_____   _____

CLIENT                                          DATE

[name]_____

[street address] _____

[city, state, zip] _____

~ ~ ~

**SAMPLE AGREEMENT FOR INVESTIGATIVE SERVICES**

I, we, the undersigned, do agree to employ the services of

_____,

a private investigative agency, licensed and insured under the laws of the state of _____ solely for the purpose of attempting to:

_____

_____

_____

_____

It is agreed and understood that I, we, shall be responsible for the compensation to said investigative agency at the hourly rate of $_____ per investigator, plus out of pocket expenses including but not limited to: mileage at the rate of \_\_\_\_ per mile, film and developing or processing, long distance calls, or computer database expenses. The taking of depositions and court ordered testimony shall be considered part of the investigation and payable at the rate of _____ per investigator.

Any amounts or expenses incurred above the retainer fee of $_____ shall be due and payable upon notice. A penalty of ____% will be added to any account balance over 15 days. In the event of default in payment of sums due hereunder and if the agreement is placed in the hands of an attorney at law for collection, I, we, agree to pay all costs of collection including but not limited to a reasonable attorney's fee.

In consideration of the foregoing terms and conditions, I, we, understand that said agency shall under its best efforts, investigate the matter set forth above.

I, we, hereby agree to allow said agency to conduct the investigation at its sole discretion via any lawful means it deems to be appropriate.

I, we, Our, My heirs, beneficiaries, devisees, legatees, administrators and assigns further agree to indemnify and hold harmless said agency and/or its agents and employees from any and all actions, causes for actions, claims, damages, and demands of whatever type arising directly or indirectly from the investigation which I, we, have requested above.

If any portion of this agreement is held to be invalid, then the remainder shall remain in full force and affect.

This contract contains all agreements between investigator(s) and client.

_____      _____
Client                                                                            Date

_____      _____
Investigator                                                                   Date

~ ~ ~

**INDEPENDENT CONTRACTOR or SUB-CONTRACTOR**

**Duties, Term, and Compensation**
**DUTIES**: The Contractor will [describe here the work or service to be performed]. [He or she] will report directly to [name] and to any other party designated by [name] in connection with the performance of the duties under this Agreement and shall fulfill any other duties reasonably requested by the Company and agreed to by the Contractor.

**TERM**: This engagement shall commence upon execution of this Agreement and shall continue in full force and effect through [date] or earlier upon completion of the Contractor's duties under this Agreement. The Agreement may only be extended thereafter by mutual agreement, unless terminated earlier by operation of and in accordance with this Agreement.

**COMPENSATION**: (Choose A or B)

A. As full compensation for the services rendered pursuant to this Agreement, the Company shall pay the Contractor at the hourly rate of [dollar amount] per hour, with total payment not to exceed [dollar amount] without prior written approval by an authorized representative of the Company. Such compensation shall be payable within 30 days of receipt of Contractor's monthly invoice for services rendered supported by reasonable documentation.

B. As full compensation for the services rendered pursuant to this Agreement, the Company shall pay the Contractor the sum of _____ [dollar amount], to be paid _____ [time and conditions of payment.]

~ ~ ~

## EMPLOYEE NON-DISCLOSURE AGREEMENT

FOR GOOD CONSIDERATION, and in consideration of being employed by _____ (Company), the undersigned employee hereby agrees and acknowledges:

1. That during the course of my employ there may be disclosed to me certain trade secrets of the Company; said trade secrets consisting but not necessarily limited to:

> (a) Technical information: Methods, processes, formulae, compositions, systems, techniques, inventions, machines, computer programs and research projects.

> (b) Business information: Customer lists, pricing data, sources of supply, financial data and marketing, production, or merchandising systems or plans.

2. I agree that I shall not during, or at any time after the termination of my employment with the Company, use for others, or myself or disclose or divulge to others including future employees, any trade secrets, confidential information, or any other proprietary data of the Company in violation of this agreement.

3. That upon the termination of my employment from the Company:

> (a) I shall return to the Company all documents and property of the Company, including but not necessarily limited to: draw-

ings, blueprints, reports, manuals, correspondence, customer lists, computer programs, and all other materials and all copies thereof relating in any way to the Company's business, or in any way obtained by me during the course of employ. I further agree that I shall not retain copies, notes or abstracts of the foregoing.

(b) The Company may notify any future or prospective employer or third party of the existence of this agreement, and shall be entitled to full injunctive relief for any breach.

(c) This agreement shall be binding upon me and my personal representatives and successors in interest, and shall inure to the benefit of the Company, its successors and assigns.

Signed this _____ day of _____, 20____.

_____    _____
Company                      Employee

~ ~ ~

## BACKGROUND INVESTIGATIONS

**APPLICATION FOR EMPLOYMENT**
**ALL POTENTIAL EMPLOYEES ARE EVALUATED WITHOUT REGARD TO RACE, COLOR, RELIGION, GENDER, NATIONAL ORIGIN, AGE, MARITAL OR VETERAN STATUS, THE PRESENCE OF A NON-JOB RELATED HANDICAP OR ANY OTHER LEGALLY PROTECTED STATUS.**

Position Sought: _____
How did you learn about the position? _____
_____

Name _____
Date _____
Address _____
City _____ State _____ Zip_____
Home Phone _____
Office Phone _____
Other Phone_____

Email Address _____

Social Security Number _____

Date of birth _____

On what date would you be available for work? _____

Desired Wage/Salary $ _____

Are you a U.S. citizen, or are you otherwise authorized to work in the U.S. without any restriction?  ☐ Yes   ☐ No

Have you ever been arrested? ☐ Yes   ☐ No   If yes, please provide date, location, and explain:

_____

_____

Have you ever been convicted of a felony? ☐ Yes   ☐ No   If yes, please provides date, location, and explains:

_____

_____

Have you been involved in civil lawsuit or bankruptcy? ☐ Yes   ☐ No   If yes please provide dates and location and type:

_____

_____

_____

Have you ever been involuntarily terminated or asked to resign from any position of employment? ☐ Yes   ☐ No   If yes, please describes circumstances:

_____

_____

If selected for employment, are you willing to submit to a pre-employment drug-screening test? ☐ Yes   ☐ No

**EDUCATION**

School Name_____

Location_____

Years Attended_____ Degree Received_____

Major_____

Other training, certifications, or licenses held:

_____

_____

List other information pertinent to the employment you are seeking:

_____

_____

**PRIOR RESIDENCES:** (5 YEAR HISTORY)

_____

_____

_____

_____

**EMPLOYMENT HISTORY:** *(Most Recent First.)*

1. Employer_____

Job Title_____

Dates Employed _____

Prior Position Held within Company (if any): _____

Address _____

City _____ State _____ Zip_____

Phone_____

Job Title _____ Supervisor_____

Starting Salary _____ Ending Salary _____

Duties Performed

_____

_____

Reason for Leaving

_____

2. Employer_____

Job Title_____

Dates Employed _____

Prior Position Held within Company (if any): _____

Address _____

City _____ State _____ Zip_____

Phone_____

Job Title _____ Supervisor_____

Starting Salary _____ Ending Salary _____

Duties Performed

_____

_____

Reason for Leaving

_____


3. Employer _____
Job Title _____
Dates Employed _____
Prior Position Held within Company (if any): _____
Address _____
City _____ State _____ Zip _____
Phone _____
Job Title _____ Supervisor _____
Starting Salary _____ Ending Salary _____
Duties Performed

_____

_____

Reason for Leaving

_____


4. Employer _____
Job Title _____
Dates Employed _____
Prior Position Held within Company (if any): _____
Address _____
City _____ State _____ Zip _____
Phone _____
Job Title _____ Supervisor _____
Starting Salary _____ Ending Salary _____
Duties Performed

_____

_____

Reason for Leaving

_____

**REFERENCES:** (Provide three and include relationship.)

_____

_____

_____

## ACKNOWLEDGMENT AND AUTHORIZATION

I certify that answers given herein are true and complete to the best of my knowledge.

I authorize investigation of all statements contained in this application for employment as may be necessary in arriving at an employment decision.

This application for employment shall be considered active for a period of time not to exceed 45 days. Any applicant wishing to be considered for employment beyond this time period should inquire as to whether or not applications are being accepted at that time.

_____

I hereby understand and acknowledge that, unless otherwise defined by applicable law, any employment relationship with this organization is of an "at will" nature, which means that the Employee may resign at any time and the Employer may discharge Employee at any time with or without cause. It is further understood that this "at will" employment relationship may not be changed by any written document or by conduct unless an authorized executive of this organization specifically acknowledges such change in writing.

In the event of employment, I understand that false or misleading information given in my application or interview(s) may result in discharge. I understand, also, that I am required to abide by all rules and regulations of the employer.

_____     _____
Signature of Applicant                        Date

~ ~ ~

## APPLICANT INFORMATION RELEASE

I hereby authorize any person, educational institution, or company I have listed as a reference on my employment application to disclose in good faith any information they may have regarding my qualifications and fitness for employment. I will hold [Your Business], any former employers, educational institutions, and any other persons giving references free of liability for the exchange of this information and any other reasonable and necessary information incident to the employment process.

_____    _____

Signed                                        Date

~ ~ ~

## BACKGROUND INVESTIGATIONS

A background investigation (BI) is a search for information about a person; the search is not intended to prove or disprove, only to provide relevant information so that an objective judgment can be made. The private investigator dredges up the relevant information; the PI's client makes the objective judgment.

Clients may vary widely and their reasons for hiring a PI may vary widely; for example,

- A defense attorney may need background information about the defendant, key witnesses for both sides, the history of a presiding judge, and jury members
- A plaintiff's attorney may need the same information
- An attorney may want to know the opposing attorney's history of courtroom strategy and tactics
- A mother may need to know the background of a babysitter, nanny or child care facility
- A businessman may want to know if his partner or employee is spending beyond his/her means
- A landlord may need information about a prospective renter
- A celebrity wants background information about prospective employees such as a bodyguard, gardener, nanny, and housemaid
- An investor may want background information on a broker or prospective investment
- A spouse or significant other may want to know if his/her partner is cheating

### The Employer Client

PIs provide employee background investigation services to businesses and others. The client may be the owner, operator, manager, or someone in the human resources department. The areas of interest to the client will vary according to the needs of the business and the preferences of management. For example, a company that operates in a safety-sensitive environment will be interested in a job applicant's accident history and a retail sales organization will be interested in a job applicant's honesty or track record for sales. Whatever the client needs, the search for information follows the same course: the requested information is gathered, presented to the client, and the client makes the call.

An employer can be in the private or public sector. When the employer operates a business, the PI and the employer usually have a direct relationship. When the employer is a government organization, the direct relationship usually is between the PI and a group under private contract to the government for the provision of background investigation services.

Typically, the person whose background is to be searched will fall into one of two categories: employees/job applicants and prospective partners. In the first category are people on the payroll and people who want to be on the payroll. In the second category are people with whom the client may be inclined to do business with. These can be vendors, full partners, joint-venture partners, companies to be acquired or merged with, and prospective buyers.

When a client decides to investigate the background of a current employee it may be because the employee is under consideration for a job change; for example, a promotion into a position of great trust and responsibility. The client wants to be assured of the employee's integrity. When an investigation is made of an employee's background in connection with a crime or incident, the investigation is not simply a BI but a component of a more extensive investigation such as a white-collar crime.

PIs conduct more BIs of prospective employees than current employees. A prospective employee is a job applicant, and the BI is often called pre-employment screening.

In case you might wonder why is an employer willing to pay a PI to obtain information about another person? The money paid to a PI is far less than money that can be lost if the applicant later proves to be other than represented. In essence, a background investigation is a cost-preventive measure.

Applicants that are criminal felons, violence-prone individuals, drug abusers, and safety risks can be filtered out, thus reducing costs associated with theft, injury, accidents, and medical assistance benefits.

Pre-employment screening consists of checking and verifying records, checking and verifying references, and interviewing persons who may know the subject of the investigation but may not be listed as references.

The hardest record to check and verify is the criminal history. Unlike law-enforcement, PIs do not have access to NCIC. Not all criminal histories are available in a single database and many cities and counties may need to be checked individually. This single part of the background investigation could easily be overlooked and result in hiring a person with a criminal history that may prove to be costly to the employer in the future. If a less than thorough background investigation is conducted and the PI does not provide complete information that may determine whether or not a person is to be hired, there is a possibility that the PI could be sued for negligence or other legalities.

In this method, the applicant/employee provides personal information requested by the employer. Written consent is obtained prior to checking. When the reference provided by the applicant/employee is a personal reference, the PI can expect the references to answer glowingly. Logically, an applicant will provide references that can be expected to be supportive.

Checking references by mail or e-mail is not nearly as effective as checking in person or by phone. People tend to be candid in face-to-face and voice-to-voice situations. Facial expressions, pregnant pauses, and voice inflections can reveal a great deal; more can be learned from the manner of response than the content of it. Verbally asking, "Would you rehire this employee?" is potentially more revealing than a form letter that comes back with a simple yes or no response.

The employment application form is the main administrative device for capturing employment and personal references. Quite commonly, dishonest applicants provide some truth in their references. For instance, an applicant might provide the correct name of a former employer and change the location, or provide the correct city and state of the school but change its name. The PI shouldn't use only the references and phone numbers provided by the applicant. Personal and work references can produce recommendations that are excellent but totally false. It helps greatly when the PI inquires with the applicant's past and present co-workers rather than the persons named on the form only.

Public records, private sector, and professional databases are the main sources of records and information. Public records may be found at local, state, and federal government levels including but not limited to law enforcement agencies, criminal and civil courts, licensing bureaus, the military, social security administration, and others. Private sector sources include educational institutions, financial institutions, credit bureaus, utility companies, libraries, and professional/fraternal organizations.

**Local Records**

Police stations, city halls, and county courthouses are rich sources of public records. In most cases the PI needs only ask and a clerk will either hand over a copy of the record or give self-help instruction in where to look and how to retrieve records. It is wise to carry lots of spare change for parking meters and copies of records.

Records that are generally available include:
- Criminal records
- Lawsuits and judgments
- Business licenses
- Divorce and marriage records
- Property tax records, deeds, and mortgages
- Uniform Commercial Code (UCC) liens and secured transactions
- Voter registration files*
- Estate records
- Bankruptcy filings
- Utility records
- Permits and inspection files
- Motor vehicle registration files

*A voter registration record can be particularly helpful. It includes full name, current and former addresses, and other details. Information on a voter registration record may reflect data different that that provided by the applicant, and also help the PI track the applicant's history through other records, such as those mentioned above. Voter registration records may not be available for public inspection in all cities and states. It is best to call and ask before making a trip.

Larger cities have a blue book or city/suburban directory that may be found at a public library. Sometimes these books will include an employer, other people living in the household, and neighbors.

**State Records**
- Corporation filings
- UCC filings (loans)
- Bankruptcy filings
- Workers' Compensation claims
- Professional licensing files
- Driving license files
- Motor vehicle registration files

## AUTHORIZATION TO RELEASE INFORMATION

This release hereby authorizes the First American Bank or agents of the Bank to make inquiries of my background and to examine and/or make copies of any and all records or reports pertaining to my employment, credit and financial status, criminal record, military record, education and training records, driving record, insurance records, business and personal references, and other records or reports necessary to conducting a background investigation related to my application for employment with the First American Bank

_____        _____
Signature                                       Date


_____
Printed name

A good deal of information can be found in computer databases. Some databases are easily accessible to the PI directly; in other cases, the PI works through a vendor. Database searches can provide extensive information at low cost and are useful when the person of interest worked or lived in numerous counties or states. A local search, such as one made at a county courthouse, will not reflect an individual's criminal conviction in another county or state. Success with a database service will depend on the quality and quantity of the information provided by the employer. For each name run through a database, there may be hundreds of persons with the same name. Full and accurate information inputted at the front end can produce good information at the back end.

Not all records are computerized and for this reason the PI has to either contact by phone or physically go to the places where the records of interest are stored. Examples of record-storing places are state and federal offices, county court houses, and archive libraries.

## Medical Records

In order for a doctor, hospital, or other medical professional to release medical information, a medical release authorization form is required. This is actually a release form or letter signed by either the party involved or the next of kin. The medical laws of each state may vary and should be researched before proceeding. It is a good idea to make a copy of the existing law (at a public library) in the event the law allows the release of this information and someone denies you the right to this information. Make several copies of the signed authorization. Each place you visit will need a copy, plus you should retain a copy for your records.

**MEDICAL RELEASE
AUTHORIZATION FORM**

Date: _____

This form expires six months from this date unless indicated otherwise or revoked earlier.

I hereby authorize _____ to obtain copies of my medical history.

I hereby authorize any physician, hospital, or health care facility or professional to release copies of all medical records.

Signed: _____

Date: _____

Notary Seal:

~ ~ ~

**SAMPLE CRIMINAL RECORDS CHECK**

Name of Person:  John Joseph Smith
Aliases/AKA:  Joe Smith, Jon Smith, John Joseph, and Joseph John
Date of Birth:  1/15/35
SSN:  123-45-6789
Last Known Address:  123 Main St., Nashville, TN. 37206
Previous Addresses: 456 Scott Ave., Nashville, TN 37206

Records of the Davidson County Criminal Court Clerk's Office, covering the period of January 2003–November 2005 were checked and the following findings are reported:

\_\_\_ No record was found.

_X_ A record was found and the following information noted.

Name shown on the record:  Joe Smith
Date of birth:  1/15/36
SSN:  123-45-6789
Address:  789 Old Hickory Blvd., Nashville, TN 37115
Docket number:  2002-GS-1505
Date of arrest:  11/11/2002
Offense(s):  Driving under the influence
Disposition:  1 night in jail and $250. fine
Arresting officer:  Jim Jones
Date of report:  11/11/2002
Bonding company:  ABC Bonding
Attorney:  Robert Baker
Other:

A first step in this method is to identify people that are likely to know the applicant and likely to be candid. Such persons can be present and former co-workers, neighbors, and police officers who may be aware of integrity issues not reflected in police or court records. Another good source can be the security manager of a company that previously employed the applicant.

It is helpful to corroborate negative information. If the applicant claims in a resume that he/she headed up a certain work project but that a co-worker says otherwise, the PI needs to corroborate that negative piece of information one way or the other. Note in this example that the issue was put forward by the applicant, that he/she headed up a project. The PI's function is to verify the truthfulness of that claim. If the claim is found by one inquiry to be untruthful, the PI is obligated to check further, either to substantiate or refute.

At the opening moment of an interview, the PI must explain to the interviewee that any questions asked will relate to a job application and that the sole reason for the interview is to verify information provided by the applicant.

# CHAPTER V
# TYPES OF INVESTIGATIONS

A private investigator may be asked to work a case that he or she is not qualified to work. You must know when to say "no" and when to refer a client to another investigator. You may choose to specialize in certain types of investigations. It is good to know as much as possible about the cases you work and it is good to have a specialty like a doctor or lawyer.

You would not want a lawyer who specializes in personal injury to handle a murder case or vice versa. You would not want a doctor who specializes in orthopedics to give you a heart transplant and vice versa. Know your limitations.

The duties of private investigators will depend on the needs of their client. In cases for employers involving fraudulent workers compensation claims, for example, investigators may carry out long-term covert observation of subjects. If an investigator observes a subject performing an activity that contradicts injuries stated in a workers' compensation claim, the investigator would take video or still photographs to document the activity and report it to the client

Private investigators offer a variety of services, including pre-employment verification, individual background investigations, civil liability and personal injury cases, insurance claims, insurance fraud, child custody cases, and premarital screening. Investigating individuals to prove or disprove infidelity is one of the most in demand jobs for a private investigator. Some may offer executive, corporate, and celebrity protection.

Legal investigators will need to have a good understanding of both civil and criminal law, and a working knowledge of legal terms.

- **Civil law** is the body of law that deals with conflicts and differences between individuals.

- **Criminal law** is that branch of law that deals with offenses of a public nature. These laws may be federal or state statutes that usually provide penalties, fines, and/or incarceration to persons for their breach. Crimes are divided into two categories based on the amount of punishment involved: misdemeanors and felonies. Misdemeanors are crimes that are less serious and are punishable for less than one year of incarceration. Felonies are more serious crimes punishable by more than one year, loss of certain civil rights (voting and running for public office), and a fine.

It is good to belong to private investigator associations and network with other professionals. Some investigators may even offer other investigators referral fees for cases. These meetings are a great place to swap information.

Private investigators use many means to obtain and determine facts in a variety of matters. Investigations may require the use of various types of surveillances or searches for information. In order to verify facts, such as an individual's place of employment or income, they may make phone calls or visit a subject's workplace. In other cases, especially those involving missing persons and background checks, investigators often interview people to gather as much information as possible about an individual. In all cases, private investigators assist attorneys, businesses, and the public with a variety of legal, financial, and personal problems.

Investigators may perform physical surveillance, often for long periods of time, in a car or van. They may observe a site, such as the home of a subject, from an inconspicuous location. The surveillance continues using still and video cameras, binoculars, and a cell phone, until the desired evidence is obtained. They also may perform computer database searches, or work with a vendor or information broker. Computer database searches allow investigators to quickly obtain information on individuals' prior arrests, convictions, civil legal judgments; telephone numbers, motor vehicle registrations, credit information, neighbors, associates, and other matters. Knowledge of the privacy laws is necessary before accessing personal information on a professional database.

Private investigators may specialize in one field. Those who focus on intellectual property theft, or copyright infringement for example, may only investigate and document acts of piracy. Their job is to help their clients stop the illegal activity by providing intelligence for prosecution and civil action. Other investigators specialize in developing financial profiles and asset searches, often for civil litigation. Their reports reflect information gathered through interviews, investigation, surveillance, and research, including researching public documents.

Legal investigators specialize in cases involving the courts and are normally employed by law firms or lawyers. They frequently assist in preparing criminal defenses, locating witnesses, serving legal documents, interviewing police and prospective witnesses, and gathering and reviewing evidence.

Legal investigators also may collect information on the parties to the litigation, take photographs, testify in court, and assemble evidence and reports for trials.

Corporate investigators conduct internal and external investigations for corporations other than investigative firms. In internal investigations, they may investigate drug use in the workplace, ensure that expense accounts are not abused, or determine if employees are stealing merchandise or information. External investigations typically prevent criminal schemes originating outside the corporation, such as theft of company assets through fraudulent billing of products by suppliers.

Financial investigators may be hired to develop confidential financial profiles of individuals or companies who are prospective parties to large financial transactions. They often are Certified Public Accountants (CPAs) and work closely with investment bankers and accountants. They search for assets in order to recover damages awarded by a court in fraud or theft cases.

Investigators and detectives who work for retail stores, hotels, casinos, or banks are responsible for loss control and asset protection. In-house detectives, also known as loss prevention agents or security, are responsible for safeguarding the assets of their clients by apprehending anyone attempting to steal merchandise or destroying property. Their job is to prevent theft by shoplifters, vendor representatives, delivery personnel, and employees. In-house detectives also conduct periodic inspections of stock areas, dressing rooms, restrooms, and sometimes assist in opening and closing the property. They may prepare loss prevention and security reports for management and testify in court against persons they apprehend. Hotel detectives protect guests of the establishment from theft of their belongings and preserve order in hotel restaurants and bars. They also may keep undesirable individuals, such as known criminals, off the premises. Armed detectives and security guards are required to have a gun permit and meet certain licensing requirements. These detectives do not have any special arrest powers other than those of a private citizen unless the law states otherwise. Upon the apprehension of a suspect the private detective will contact local law enforcement. Law enforcement may arrest the suspect and the private detective will provide the details of the matter and will become the prosecutor or witness.

Private detectives and investigators often collect information and protect the property and other assets of companies and individuals. There are many types of private investigations. Here is a partial list:

Asset location
- Judgments
- Liens
- Collection
- Subrogation

Background investigations
- Employment
- Pre-marital
- Pre-trial

Civil
- Liability
- Property Disputes

Criminal defense
- Murder
- Rape
- Theft
- Vehicular homicide
- Robbery
- Fraud
- Drugs
- Vice
- Criminal financial investigations

Domestic cases
- Divorce
- Child custody

Environmental cases
- Hazardous chemicals

Insurance claims/fraud
- Worker's compensation
- Disability
- Death claims

Missing persons
- Criminals
- Collection
- Foul play
- Families & friends

Personal injury
- Accident

Process serving

## BACKGROUND INVESTIGATIONS

A lawyer may hire a private investigator to obtain background information pertaining to a personal injury case, a criminal defense case, a divorce case, a child custody case, a lawsuit, or any other type of case. An insurance company may hire a private investigator to obtain background information for a claimant. An individual may hire a private investigator to check out someone for personal reasons. An employer may hire a private investigator to check out a new employee.

Background investigations may involve verification of information that has already been provided, such as for employment purposes. The information requested on an employment application might consist of previous addresses, previous employment, education, previous arrests, and references. If a prospective employee has something in their background they don't want the employer to know about, they simply don't include it on the employment application. For this reason it is important for an investigator to verify the information provided and discover the information that was left out. Some employment applications may not ask the right questions; therefore the information might be incomplete. The more information provided, the easier it is to verify. The investigator will need to pay attention to detail. Because private investigators do not have access to N.C.I.C. (the database used by law-enforcement), conducting a thorough criminal history background investigation may not be possible. A private investigator will have access to some online criminal databases, but these databases may only be for a certain state or jurisdiction. A person who is arrested in a place other than where they reside may not show up unless that exact location is searched. If a criminal history background investigation is being conducted in Dallas, Texas, records may be in seven counties.

Never assume anything. Don't assume that a criminal history is going to be found only in the counties in which the subject resides. Don't assume that educational information is correct without verifying it. Don't assume that information is going to be verified with just a computer and a phone. Even though an application may not ask for liens, judgments, lawsuits, traffic tickets, or warrants, it will not hurt to go that extra mile to find as much information as possible for a client.

A signed release will authorize an investigator to obtain credit or medical information. There are some laws that prevent investigators from getting information without written consent. The Fair Credit Reporting Act, The Privacy Act, the Driver's Protection Act and other laws protect privacy and require written consent for obtaining certain information. Persons who are applying for employment or insurance claims will usually sign a written consent form.

Background investigations may be conducted for a potential spouse or significant other, or for other personal reasons. This type of background investigation will not have a form providing useful information and will probably not have a written consent form to obtain information protected by privacy laws. The information will most likely be verbal. The person who hires an investigator to check out someone for personal reasons may not have much to work with. It will be up to the investigator to find out as much as possible based on the information provided by the client. It is not unusual for someone to want background information simply for his or her own peace of mind.

## ASSET SEARCH

Lawyers, collection agencies, and skip tracers each have a need to track the assets of a debtor for liens or judgments, or other legal purposes.

Assets may include real estate properties; bank accounts, stocks, bonds, and other financial investments; vehicles and other motorized forms of transportation; and personal property. Some of the financial records may be available on a public record and others may require either a written signature, or a subpoena.

An asset search begins with whatever information is provided by the client. From that information a report might be generated from one of the professional databases. The database report will provide the subject's known addresses for five or more years, property owned by the subject, corporate affiliations, bankruptcies, employers, names of relatives, neighbors, and associates. This is a good start. Next is to verify the ownership of the properties with a tax assessor or trustee's office.

Every place the subject has lived might have other records in the county court house. At a county court house, liens, judgments, divorce, and criminal histories can be found. A secretary of state's office should have any UCC filings, bankruptcies, and corporation records.

A divorce or bankruptcy record may be a good source of information because assets must be disclosed.

There are asset search services offered by some of the online professional database brokers. It might be required that you provide a copy of a lien or judgment to prove the purpose of the investigation.

## CRIMINAL FINANCIAL INVESTIGATIONS

There are various types of criminal financial investigations including:

- **Fraud.** Fraud is a generic term involving all the ways one person can falsely represent a fact to another in order to induce that person to surrender something of value.
- **Tax evasion.** Tax evasion occurs when a person deliberately commits fraud in filing or paying taxes.
- **Bribery.** Bribery occurs when money, goods, services, information, or anything else of value is offered with the intent to influence the actions, opinions, or decisions of the recipient. Whether you offer the bribe or accept it, each party can be charged with bribery.
- **Embezzlement.** Embezzlement occurs when a person who is entrusted with money or property appropriates it for his or her own use and benefit.
- **Larceny.** Larceny occurs when one person wrongfully takes another person's money or property with the intent to appropriate, convert, or steal it. If someone steals your car and then sells it, he or she commits larceny.
- **Forgery.** Forgery occurs when a false or worthless instrument such as a check or counterfeit security is passed with the intent to defraud or injure the recipient.
- **Counterfeiting.** Counterfeiting occurs when copies or imitations of an item are passed off for genuine or original items. This can be money, jewelry, clothing, accessories, or anything that is an imitation of the original.
- **Blackmail.** Blackmail is a demand for money or other considerations under threat to do bodily harm, to injure property, to accuse of crime, or to expose secrets, or other embarrassing acts.
- **Extortion.** Extortion occurs when one person illegally obtains property from another by actual or threatened force, fear, or violence, or under cover of official right.
- **Kickback.** A payment or reward to a person who sells an item and is paid back a portion of the purchase price.
- **Racketeering.** Charges of racketeering can cover a wide range of things, but the bottom line is that racketeering is running an illegal business for personal profit.
- **Insider trading.** Insider trading occurs when a person uses "inside," confidential, or advance information to trade in shares of publicly held corporations.

- **Money laundering.** Money laundering is the transfer or investment of money from racketeering, drug transactions, and other illegal sources into legitimate channels so the original source cannot be traced.

A criminal financial investigation might involve hidden assets in offshore tax havens or foreign countries. Tax havens are places with little or no taxes and are not to be confused with tax shelters. A tax haven is a term that generally connotes any foreign country that has either a very low tax or no tax at all on certain categories of income. People who do not want to report their assets to the Internal Revenue might have their money in banks out of the U.S. Often criminals cannot put their illegal money in a regular bank, so they might set up a dummy company and deposit the money in with the dummy company's money. This is referred to as money laundering. Money laundering is the investment or transfer of money from racketeering, drug transactions, and other illegal activity into legitimate channels so that its original source cannot be traced. Money is moved into an account that will not be easy to trace.

## ASSET LOCATION/UNCLAIMED PROPERTY

http://dor.wa.gov/docs/pubs/ucp/Alocater.pdf

This is the guide for all asset locators or searches for owners of unclaimed property.

## UNCLAIMED PROPERTY

Every state has an office that keeps records of unclaimed properties. Usually this office is under the Treasury Department.

Unclaimed property (assets) may be in a bank, the IRS, investment companies, courts, and other places. Assets belonging to a missing or deceased person will be held for seven years. If, in that time no one comes forward to claim the property, the assets are then turned over to the state office of Unclaimed Property. The assets will remain in this office until the owner or next of kin claims it.

The state office of Unclaimed Property keeps a record of all unclaimed properties and this information is usually available for public inspection. A private investigator may be allowed by the state law to charge a small fee to locate the missing people or next of kin. Once the missing person is located, they must prove they are the owner of the property or the next of kin, and they must sign a consent form that will allow the investigator to receive compensation. There is no guarantee that anyone will agree to signing the form after being located. This means that the investigator has done the work for nothing.

http://www.unclaimed.org/
http://www.missingmoney.com/
http://www.nupd.com/

## DOMESTIC CASES

Every time a client has told me they believe their spouse is cheating, it has been true. I have not had a single domestic case in which the suspecting spouse was wrong. I tell people to listen to their instincts and intuitions because they are usually correct. It is true with cheating spouses. Clients with a cheating spouse will usually experience three distinct and recognizable stages: 1) denial; 2) acceptance; 3) anger.

Many spouses go into "denial" because they don't want to believe their suspicions are true. They don't want to break up their family. They don't want to lose their bread and butter. They may blame themselves and feel guilty. Whatever the reason, they don't want to face reality. During this stage they may want a consultation with a private investigator or attorney, but are not ready to proceed with any action.

When a suspicious spouse reaches a stage referred to as "acceptance" and is ready to find out the truth that is when they hire a PI. They need proof to know that their suspicions are right. The truth will set them free. Some live with guilt that they have suspected their spouse of cheating. Whatever their reason for needing to know, I personally think they can handle the truth better than the unknown.

Once the client gets proof, documenting for sure that their spouse is cheating, they finally reach a stage of "anger." When they are angry, they are ready for an attorney.

People develop patterns, especially people who are married. Some of the first signs of a cheating spouse are a change in appearance and behavior. When a new relationship begins, the old pattern usually changes and that is one of the first signs of a cheater.

In order for people to cheat there has to be both opportunity and desire. They will have to find an excuse to meet. Sometimes it is "working late" every Tuesday night and getting home about 11 P.M. Or what about a woman who has to take a bath, shave her legs, fix her face and hair, and wearing those high heels to "run out to the grocery store"? People want to look good for new relationships, and must find an opportunity to be with that person. A pattern usually develops. It is a different pattern if one or both is married. That limits the time they can be together. People who work together have many more opportunities. Work places might be the only place they can be together or can easily slip out for a "nooner" or "quickie."

Some other signs include a new interest in how their bodies look. All of a sudden they join a health club and start working out, or start jogging, or doing something to firm up the old bod.

Then there is the new underwear…especially the ladies. They like to stock up on sexy lingerie. And guys swap the old boxers for some streamline speedos. No old underwear for the new lover.

And what about the new Post Office Box key on the key ring? Having the credit card bills sent to the new address is a sure sign that there are some charges that the spouse should not see. Getting a copy of the credit card statement catches a lot of cheaters.

## Q. What are the signs of a cheating spouse?

Speaking of the key ring, what about a new key to an apartment, condo, or other "love nest"?

At the beginning of an affair the cheating spouse will probably be more attentive to the spouse due to guilt that the cheater may be experiencing.

After the affair has been going on for some time the cheating spouse will begin to find fault with their spouse to justify the affair.

A cheating spouse will have a change in attitude about their family and home and will probably gradually lose attention in the activities of their family and will lose interest in repairs to the home.

Another sign of a cheating spouse is that they will probably want to experiment with new sexual acts.

And then there are the physical signs such as lipstick, cologne, smoke, and underwear stains. The wastebasket or garbage can may contain a crumbled paper with a note or phone number. Receipts may be found in a glove compartment, billfold, purse, or pocket.

Some spouses will write down the mileage on the car and keep up with how many miles the spouse is driving. This will establish a pattern.

Cheating spouses will need to communicate with their "lover." Checking the cell phone calls and keeping a list of incoming and outgoing calls may help to identify the "lover." "Lovers" have to communicate. Getting a copy of the cell calls is not going to be easy. Only the party on the cell account can request copies of the bills, and whom the calls are made to. So if the bill is not in your client's name, why not ask them to purchase a new cell phone as a gift to their spouse?

Most cheating spouses are not hardened criminals and are not pros at not leaving a trail. Finding and following a trail is what catches them.

Of course surveillance will also catch them most of the time. Once a pattern is established that will narrow the time frame of when to watch the cheating spouse. If you follow them enough, you will eventually find them with their new partner. Surveillance of a cheating spouse usually takes between 10–20 hours.

**Q. Are domestic surveillance cases routine?**

Every detective who works domestic cases has "war stories." You never know what might happen on a surveillance case. You might have to sit a long time before anything happens, but when things are happening it is usually not boring and you better be ready to react to the unexpected. On surveillance, when you least expect it, something will happen.

A wealthy cheating spouse may want to transfer some assets or diminish their finances before a divorce is filed. Many a cheater will hide those assets so they won't have to split with the spouse. If there are a lot of assets it is a good idea to freeze them when divorce papers are filed. This will prevent them from being liquidated.

### INSURANCE CLAIMS

Over sixteen billion dollars of fraudulent insurance claims are filed each year. A private investigator may be hired to work several types of insurance claims such as worker's compensation, disability, and death claims. The client may be an insurance company wanting confirmation that a person is indeed injured or disabled. The client may request surveillance and interviews with neighbors or others.

If a death claim is filed and a large sum of money from a life insurance policy is to be paid, the insurance company may want the death investigated to determine if the death was natural, accidental, or suicide. If foul play is involved law-enforcement is either working the case or has closed the case. Your investigation is an extension of what law-enforcement has already done. You will probably need a signed waiver from the next of kin authorizing you to obtain medical records, prescriptions, and other private information. You may be expected to produce records for a ten-year period.

## INSURANCE CLAIMS – SPECULATIVE SITUATIONS

An insurance claim speculative or suspicious situation will generally fall within three general areas:

1) Individual speculation: An individual arranges to receive insurance benefits which exceed his or her loss. This is generally accomplished by arranging to collect benefits from more than one insurance company on the same loss.

2) Group speculation: More than one individual arranges to receive benefits, which exceed the actual loss. There is some sort of organized effort. It is accomplished in the same fashion, i.e., the individuals involved arrange to collect benefits from more than one insurance company on the same loss. Insurance companies are usually more concerned with group efforts than the isolated individual (this is not to imply they are not concerned with individual speculation, merely more concerned with group speculation) because considerable more moneys may be paid in benefits over a relatively short period of time. Also, this type of situation tends to spread and recur periodically.

3) Misrepresentation of circumstances under which claim arises: When an individual, or more than one individual, seeks benefits by misrepresenting the circumstances. This covers such situations as "planned accidents" which never really occurred or, if they did, were prearranged; hospitalization or treatment by a physician either never took place or, if it did, was exaggerated or prolonged intentionally; or those involved acted in some other manner to deceive the insurance company in order to collect benefits.

Special note: This third area is generally more difficult to develop and/or prove. The first two will become self-evident by the mere development of other insurance. Fortunately, in most instances, this third area will involve other insurance in that the person or persons involved will arrange to receive benefits from more than one insurance company when engaging in this third type of activity.

Keep in mind that most claims are in fact legitimate, even if one or more of the following situations exist. Investigator's responsibility should only be to develop facts and let the client draw any conclusions and act upon them. With the above firmly in mind, here are some tips.

1) Claim history: Investigator should be alert to claims involving the same incident (period of disability, hospitalization, etc.) and report claim history to the client.

2) Unwitnessed accidents: Be alert to claimant being able to arrange immediately for medical attention after Unwitnessed accidents, through a friend, relative, or associate who just happened along.

3) Uninvestigated accidents: Be alert to claimants being able to arrange for medical attention immediately after an accident that was not "officially" investigated by authorities.

4) All individuals involved knew one another (no independent "outsider" involved"): Alertness to denials that individuals knew one another, when investigation shows they did (were related in some fashion, had same employer, neighbors at one time, etc.).

5) "Subjective" diagnosis: Injuries were subjective; for example, back injuries, headaches, strains, possible concussion, soft tissue injuries (as opposed to actual fractures).

6) Lengthy period of time involved: Hospitalization, treatment or disability extended beyond normally expected period.

7) Unusual number of claims involving same family or relatives: Be alert to simultaneous hospitalization of various family members – from same accident and for same period of time. These are usually detected by an alert investigator. They will usually signify some sort of an organized effort.

8) Unusual number of claims from various people in a relatively small geographic area: People involved may or may not be related. This may involve the same city, section of the city, one or two streets, or even same address. This may signify an organized effort. This is usually detected by an alert investigator.

9) Unusual number of claims involving same medical facility: Be alert to the use of the same physician or hospital, or other health care facility, especially when it is located out of the way in relationship

to the address of the claimant and/or location of the accident.

10) Those involved are or have been associated with the medical profession or insurance industry: Be alert to the possibility that people involved are more aware than the average person of the availability of other insurance, how claims are handled, etc.

11) Income does not correspond with amount of insurance involved: Be alert to the appearance of financial hardship in affording the amount of insurance involved.

12) If death claim beneficiary is someone other than immediate family member such as friend, other relative, or associate.

13) Medical treatment in a foreign country: The incident itself and/or resulting treatment occurred in a foreign country.

14) Same occupation and/or employer: Be alert to claimants who know one another and are associated with same type of small business.

15) Attitude of claimant: Claimant seems familiar with claims processing. Claimant is generally uncooperative; demands prompt payment; has vague recollection of events; other insurance, etc. Threatens to call insurance commissioner or attorney if claim not handled promptly. Claims to have an attorney but will not divulge name or indicates attorney has told him/her to say nothing.

## Gathering Information

While the investigator may occasionally be provided a tip from a client or, perhaps, obtain it from some local newspaper, it is usually the investigator who will detect such situations by observation, alertness and conscientious asking of questions in order to determine the full facts on individual cases. While the following covers various points of consideration, the investigator my not be able to pursue all during the course of the investigation at hand. Some will require additional effort to pursue completely.

A. A comprehensive report or background investigation from one of the professional databases should provide a list of relatives, neighbors, and associates. It may be necessary to interview all of these people in order to develop leads. This report may also reveal liens, judgments, UCC filings, and bankruptcies.

B. Interviewing the claimant is usually the key element in most investigations. The interview can provide leads that will help the investigator develop all the facts. The key here is the development of other insurance.

1. When interviewing claimants for life and health insurance companies using the first party approach, investigator should always ask about other insurance. In particular, he should ask about other individual coverage, group claims, worker's compensation, disability, etc.

2. If an insurance claim arises from an automobile accident, investigator should obtain a copy of the accident report from the police department or other authoritative agency and if necessary conduct an interview with the officer who made report.

   Investigator should ask about no-fault benefits and liability carrier of other party, especially if other party was at fault. Some states may have a no-fault law, some may require all drivers to be insured.

3. If claim revolves about some other type of liability (a fall on someone else's property, a product liability situation, etc.), should determine details of other pending liability claims.

4. If claimant was on a trip when incident occurred, did claimant have travel insurance? If so, with whom?

5. If claimant was in a rented or leased vehicle, who was liability carrier for the vehicle?

6. If a signed statement is taken, investigator should include a comment about other insurance, either claimant's denial or admission of such other insurance.

C. If disability was the result of an accident, the investigator should attempt to develop full details of the accident. Some special attention points would be:

1. How did claimant get to medical facility for treatment?

2. Who took the claimant to the medical facility?

3. When was the claimant taken for medical treatment? Immediately after the accident?

4. Why was that hospital or facility chosen?

5. What authorities were called or, if not called, why were authorities not called?

6. If others (including all witnesses) were involved in the accident, names and addresses are needed.

7. Were any of the others involved relatives, friends, or associates?

8. Where was damaged vehicle taken? Who repaired it? Where is it now? Who owned it?

D. Confirming details of the accident: If an accident is involved:

1. Consideration to visiting scene should be given. Often a photograph of the accident scene is helpful.

2. Does the claimant's description seem logical? Could the accident have happened exactly as the claimant described. Occasionally, the examination of the scene will preclude the accident happening as the claimant alleges.

3. If vehicle involved, investigator should examine for damages. If not repaired take photos. If repaired, visit the repair shop for confirmation of damage and repairs, as well as identity of insurance company involved.

4. Interview all others involved in the accident for confirmation of claimant's description. If any discrepancy, a signed statement is necessary. Relationship between others and the claimant (relative, friend, etc.) needs to be established. If individual involved was at fault, investigator should get name and address of his or her insurance carrier.

5. If accident was investigated by authorities, obtain a copy of the accident report, any photos, and if possible interview the investigating officer for further details. A check for other traffic accident reports or traffic tickets might establish a pattern.

E. Medical sources may be a prime source of other insurance. A signed medical authorization is required to obtain medical information from physicians, hospitals, and other health care providers. Other insurance coverage can be developed by obtaining medical records from the claimant's physician, hospital, or other health care provider.

If period of treatment or disability was lengthy, why? Did the physician find complications? Did claimant insist on hospitalization, was confinement longer than the physician felt was necessary?

If a physician or a hospital denies treatment, or their information does not correspond with the investigator's, the investigator should attempt to obtain a signed statement to cover the discrepancies.

F. Employer contact: Frequently the employer can be a source for providing other insurance coverage along the following lines:

1. Can provide identity of group insurance and worker's compensation carriers, as well as union coverage in some instances.

2. Some insurance companies require a statement from employer as part of their proofs of loss, especially concerning time lost from work. The employer may have a copy of such a statement or, at least, recall the name of the carrier or carriers involved.

3. If the employer is a small business or claimant is related to the employer, is the business legitimate? Financially sound? Are sources aware that claimant actually worked for that employer?

4. If claimant is self-employed, investigator should cover information through outside sources, not just the claimant.

G. Creditors (known or developed): Many loans include credit disability insurance, which can provide leads to other insurance.

H. Associations: Investigator should be alert to possible membership in various types of associations, which might also provide a type of group coverage. This especially applies to self-employed individuals. Membership should be explored during the claimant interview and through other sources, for example, competitors (if self-employed), employer, checking Yellow Pages for appropriate associations.

I. Follow-up with other insurance companies (developed or provided by claimant): Occasionally the investigator will be asked, or it may appear logical, to contact other carriers. If so, the investigator should obtain particulars of policy and claims, but should not ask for or report medical information without an authorization.

J. Surveillance objective: The purpose of insurance claim surveillance is to observe and document claimant's activities. Client may request photographs or videotapes of claimant.

### Establishing motive on speculative situations

Occasionally a client may ask investigator to develop a motive or it may seem logical to do so. The development of this motive is not always easy; in fact it may be very difficult. The usual motive would, of course, be a monetary gain of some nature. This would be linked to financial difficulties. There are also other motives, for example, a desire for additional monetary gain although already financially well-off, "because insurance companies have it, so why shouldn't I?" plus some other reasons, such as to help finance a political organization, a retirement plan, or other investments, etc.

A client for an insurance claim may be a law firm representing someone who was involved in an automobile accident (or some other type of case), an insurance company, an individual, or an employer.

## Medical Malpractice Investigations

Medical malpractice investigations require that you have a thorough knowledge of the case and understand exactly what you are looking for. Information must be gathered to evaluate the medical validity of the case, and to determine whether the doctor, hospital, health care facility, health care worker, or others will stand up well in a jury trial.

The information obtained from investigating the defendant physician, hospital, technician, health care worker, or others should relate to specific details of the complaint. Any questionable aspects of the complaint must be analyzed against the findings of the investigation. It must be determined that the medical facts and practices derived are recognized and accepted by the medical profession as a whole. If the case is not a criminal case it does not have to be proven beyond a reasonable doubt. A good defense can be damaged by a lack of credibility, questionable procedures, lack of medical support, and lack of medical records. It is important to collect all possible information from every potential source so that the case can be properly analyzed, denied, defended, or settled, based on its merits.

Juries can be sympathetic to a plaintiff regardless of a defendant's credibility, procedures, and documentation. Defending a case may be more difficult than proving a case.

A courtroom can be like a stage and an attorney can be like a director presenting a dramatic, theatrical performance.

The investigator's job is to gather all of the information, compile and submit it for analysis of all the facts.

A good medical malpractice investigation should include:
- Statements from insured physician, hospital, technician, health care facility, or health care workers.

- Statements from all persons whose names are pertinent to the medical records.
- Copies of statements of all physicians, nurses, and other specialists.
- Review the plaintiff's allegations.
- Compare the complaint allegations to the medical information.
- Highlight areas of medical records relating to before, during, and after the incident is alleged.
- Have independent physician examine records.
- Research accepted practices of the medical field as a whole.
- Analyze credibility of all witnesses and participants.
- Determine if there is third party involvement such as an independent anesthetist, independent x-ray service, independent physician, or some other independent involvement.
- Determine if the insured is qualified, has good credentials, and makes a good witness on his or her own behalf.
- Evaluate if there was any negligence involved, if so, by whom, whether independent services and/or the insured.
- Meet with the insured to cover all details once they are collected.

### Medical Malpractice Statement Guide

Name, address, date of birth, Social Security number, telephone number, spouse.

List all education:
- Names of schools, colleges, and special training.
- What specialties studied and degrees earned?
- How many years of schooling?
- Honorary degrees.
- Medical magazine subscriptions.
- Seminars or continuing education courses.
- Internship.
- Medical organization memberships.
- Annual reviews or exams.

Employment history, names, and addresses.

Positions held in the medical profession.

How long employed at each location?

Were normal and acceptable practices carried out in the procedures?

Was there any deviation from normal procedures?

Who advised or assisted in procedure?

Who established these medical procedures?

Any medical history, research, books in support of the procedures?

Review medical records, describe, and explain procedures.

Review complaint allegations, describe, and explain causes.

Was plaintiff advised of risks involved in the procedures?

Did plaintiff sign an affidavit, permission voucher, waiver, or disclosure notice?

Were risks explained to plaintiff properly?

What could cause plaintiff's injuries or illness?

Was there negligence on anyone's part? Explain.

Reviewing plaintiff's medical history prior to the procedures, does anything relate to the present condition?

Was plaintiff cooperative, question anything, accuse anyone, listen to your direction, or contribute to the present condition?

Was the operating room or other facilities adequately furnished and clearly meet evident medical standards?

## WORKER'S COMPENSATION INVESTIGATIONS

The purpose of worker's compensation was to provide support and benefits to an injured worker. Government regulation requires businesses to carry Worker's Compensation. Under this program an injured worker would receive a percentage of his/her income as well as have medical expenses covered. This was intended to protect and subsidize the family until the injured worker could return to work.

The original concept still exists however there have been many changes in the interpretation and procedures by each state. Worker's Compensation is regulated by the state and administered by private insurance companies or self-insured companies. The insurance companies try to do their job while guided by the state. The state is not in the insurance business

Alleged accidents, injuries, and disabilities have put a strain on insurance companies. Independent, experienced, insurance investigative services are needed to gather facts from the insured company, witnesses, personnel records, wage statement, statements from company personnel and claimant (if not represented), and prior medical records.

A good insurance investigator will rely on facts and will be fair to the claimant. Facts will determine if the claim is legitimate or not. Some workers are injured or disabled and deserve to be paid for their accident or injury.

### WORKER'S COMPENSATION STATEMENT GUIDE

1. What are your name, address, and date of birth?
2. What are your phone number and Social Security number?
3. What is your marital status, number of dependent children? If married, does spouse work?
4. In what capacity were you employed? How long employed?
5. Complete job description. Include amount of standing, sitting, lifting, bending, walking, etc.
6. What were your wages? (include overtime)
7. How many days/hours per week did you work?
8. On what date were you injured?
9. What was the location of the accident?
10. How did the accident occur?
11. What part(s) of your body was injured?
12. Was this part of your body ever injured before?
13. Was any other part of your body ever injured before?
14. From whom did you receive medical treatment?
15. Did you receive treatment from any other physicians, hospitals, or medical facilities?
16. Date of your last visit?
17. When did you stop work as a result of the accident?
18. Who did you notify and how did you notify?
19. Were you paid in full for the day of the accident?
20. Have you returned to work? If not, has your physician said when?
21. Name and address of present treating physician or other health care provider.
22. Did the injury occur as a result of defective equipment? If so, explain.
23. Were there any witnesses to the accident?
24. Do you have any other comment regarding this accident?
25. Have the injured worker sign and date the statement.

## MISSING PERSONS

It is hard for a citizen to exist in the U.S. without leaving a paper trail. During their lifetime, the average adult American citizen will leave a paper trail about seven miles long. Exceptions are homeless people, criminals, persons who are deceased and their bodies have not been found, illegal immigrants, and persons who are no longer in this country. Criminals and persons who owe money or who are deliberately hiding know how to exist without leaving a trail. Nothing is in their name and information about them may be incorrect.

The average adult American will probably have a driver's license or some form of identification. A working American will probably have a Social Security number and a bank account. Most Americans have a place to live, utilities, and many will have a vehicle. Many Americans are registered voters. The average American's trail might begin with a phone number listed in a phone book, or with electric, gas, water or other utilities. If the subject owns a car, house, or anything else, there is a trail. Credit cards leave many trails and information from these credit cards and credit bureaus are sold to information brokers. Public records are sold to information brokers. Information brokers create databases and may sell your information to anyone who wants to pay for it. We Americans have a false sense of security thinking privacy laws protect us. There are privacy laws and they are intended to protect us, but there is almost always a way to get the information. Professional investigators have access to many professional databases. Information is available at our fingertips with only a few keystrokes.

Chapter VII will include a list of useful information links on the Internet. Some are free and others charge for the information. These links are subject to change and there is no guarantee that the information in the database is current or correct. The information found may be used as a trail that may or may not lead to finding a person or finding other information. Most of the professional databases have current information.

Some of the best reference sources for investigators are books published by BRB Publications. I highly recommend all of their publications. Their web site has free links to many sources of public information at www.brbpub.com.

## SKIP TRACING

Locating deadbeat parents, persons wanted for collection, persons wanted for process serving, persons wanted for repossession, persons wanted for bond jumping, and others who owe money and skip out without paying can be very challenging, especially if that person has nothing in his or her name. It is difficult to exist without having a trail of some kind even if the missing person changes their name, date of birth, and social security number. People who are deliberately hiding will do anything to keep from being discovered. They may have nothing in their name, but they usually have a trail somewhere. Looking for such a trail might be difficult, challenging, and unpredictable, but not impossible. The more you learn and know about the missing person, the more likely you will find a way to trail them. Maybe they draw unemployment, disability, worker's compensation, welfare, or receive food stamps. Maybe they have been arrested and a bondsman has a record of who signed the bond and who represented the person. Jail records would reveal who visited them while incarcerated. A parole officer may be assigned to check on them. Maybe they needed medicine or medical attention. Try to learn what goes on in that person's life. What do they do with their time? Who do they talk to? Do they have any hobbies or sport activities? Who is their doctor or where do they receive medical attention? Even a person who is deliberately hiding has to eat and have a life. Just because they are hiding doesn't mean they don't go on with their life. In order to have a life there needs to be income from somewhere. The possibilities are unlimited. Talking to a relative, friend, neighbor, employer, or co-worker will usually produce some useful information. Working a case is like working a puzzle. You get a little bit of information, then a little more information, and soon your information will reveal a pattern or trail that will lead to the missing person. A good investigator will go over and over whatever information they have and try to figure out what else that information may lead to. A tenacious investigator will not give up until they find the missing person. Investigators do not like to be defeated. It is a personal challenge for an investigator to solve a case.

Even if someone is deliberately hiding they may still work, have a family, and do things ordinary people do. They may change their identity and go on with life until someone catches up with them.

## ADOPTION SEARCHES

One of the most difficult searches of all is the adoption search. Regardless of whether it is the adoptee searching for their biological family or the biological family is searching for an adoptee, there are many obstacles. In most states the adoption records are protected by laws and identifying information is not readily available. A few states have new laws that allow identifying information to be obtained upon request. Before embarking on an adoption search it is vital to have a name to search for.

There are an estimated 10 million adoptees and biological parents in the United States. Most adoptees have a need to know their identity, their medical information, and their heredity. Most adoptees live with the unknown about themselves, and in many cases the unknown causes a void in their life. This void may cause many problems throughout an adoptee's life. In some cases adoptees are placed with adoptive families that are not compatible. In some cases adoptees feel rejected by their birth mother and may live with anger or depression. An adoptee's search for their identity is not necessarily a search for a relationship with the biological family. Most adoptees have loving and caring adoptive parents who cannot be replaced by the biological family, but some adoptees are not so fortunate.

Adoptees had no choice in the matter of adoption and in some cases feel victimized by laws and the system that regulates adoption. Many states deny adoptees access to their own identity. They do not have any rights to their own birth records, medical records, or other information about themselves. They do not know who they are. Those who are not told they are adopted and find out later in life feel deceived by not knowing the truth. It seems that the truth sets them free, regardless of what it might be.

It takes a very knowledgeable investigator to work on an adoption search. A thorough understanding of the adoption process and the adoption laws for the state in which the adoption took place will increase the opportunity for an investigator to locate identifying information.

Each state may have a different process. There is no set law that all adoptions are handled the same way. The adoption process may differ depending on whether the adoption was handled by an agency or if it was a private adoption or an open adoption.

An adoption agency may be a state or local government, a private non-profit organization, or a religious organization. A private adoption may be arranged by a doctor, lawyer, or other individual. An open adoption may be arranged between the birth mother and adoptive family.

When a baby is born it is usually issued an original birth certificate. If the baby is born in a hospital there is usually a record of the birth and a birth certificate is filed both with the local health department and the state office of vital records. When the baby is adopted a court authorizes a new amended birth certificate to be issued and the original birth certificate to be sealed. This begins the adoptee's paper trail.

One of the first steps for an adoption to take place is for the birth parents to sign a form surrendering or terminating their parental rights. If no birth father is named on the original birth certificate, it may not be required for him to sign the surrender. In some cases a notice will appear in a newspaper stating that the parental rights will be terminated.

Once a birth mother decides to give up her baby for adoption, she may stay in a home for unwed mothers. She may have counseling during the pregnancy and a social worker assigned to her to help her through the process. It is not unusual for a birth mother to go to another state to have a baby. In more recent years birth mothers have more choices. A birth mother may choose which agency may place her baby. The agency may provide the birth mother with unidentified choices of prospective adoptive parents and allow her to choose which family she prefers to adopt her child. The birth mother may choose a family from a particular religion, or with similar physical appearances, or other characteristics.

Some adoptees are placed with a foster family temporarily before they are placed with an adoptive family. Pre-mature babies, or babies with health problems may need special care before they can be adopted.

In order for most legal adoptions to take place the adoptive family will probably have an attorney represent them in a court of jurisdiction. The court that handles adoption should keep a record of all proceedings in a log book or docket appearance book. This book keeps a record of the adopted family's court appearances and the events that take place are recorded in minute books. The docket appearance book will keep a log of the minute books for referral. The court of jurisdiction is usually in the county in which the adoptive parents reside. In rare cases the adoptive family may move before the adoption is completed and the court of jurisdiction may move to another location. The attorney will first file a petition with the court. The court may require a periodic home study by a social worker who will report findings to the court. These findings may be referred to as interlocutory decrees. It may take one year from the time the petition is filed until the final decree of adoption is issued. During this time the adoption is not permanent.

Once the adoption is final the records are sealed and are not available unless the state law permits. In cases of life or death or if there is a serious medical problem a judge may order the records to be opened. Adoption records may be stored in various places. An agency, court, or state office may each have a copy of the records. Court records may be archived after a period of years. Some records may be on microfilm or microfiche. Some records may be destroyed. Some records may be found at a state archives library, or local archives storage facility. Unfortunately adoption records are like looking for a needle in a haystack.

There is one search harder than an adoption search. An abandoned baby with no records and no information is almost impossible to trace. In 1935 a man named Vince Hill was abandoned in a church in New York city. He was left on a church pew. The priest took him to the New York foundling hospital. It was estimated he was about three months old and was malnourished. There was no clue as to his identity. He was eventually placed in a foster home who only took him because they would receive a check to keep him. He was not loved or wanted by this family. At sixteen he ran away. He has spent his entire life trying to find his mother and learning his identity. He has no answers. How many other children were abandoned with similar stories?

There are endless stories of abandonment and adoption. In order to offer some hope to those who live with the unknown in 1994 I began a web site on the internet for these people to post their information in hopes that someone would find them. In 2006 my current web sites are www.get-in-touch.com, www.getintouch.tv, www.nationwidelocate.com, and www.tvreunions.com. There are many adoption organizations and sources of adoption registries on the internet and operated by various states. I recommend that anyone involved in an adoption search place the search on as many registries as possible. Check chapter VII for adoption information sources.

Search and support groups are available in many cities. Often these groups help each other with their searches. It is comforting to be with others who are experiencing the same feelings.

The hardest part of an adoption search is obtaining a name to look for. If it is a common name it may be harder to find, but if it is an uncommon name it may be easier.

It is wise to prepare the client for what you might find. Make sure the client does not have any unrealistic expectations. The person you are searching for may be deceased, ill, or not want any contact. Not all searches will have happy endings. In many adoption searches both parties are looking for each other and are happy to find each other, but not all searches are going to be successful.

Approaching the missing person is another matter and must be handled in a professional, caring, and considerate manner. I do not recommend an adoptee knock on a birth mother's door and say "surprise" nor should a birth mother knock on an adoptee's door and say "surprise." In the most successful adoption reunions both parties are prepared by an intermediary or third party before they meet. Being prepared makes the initial meeting more comfortable for all parties. Some states are now requiring that a certified intermediary be used for adoption searching. Those states will supply a list of the qualified intermediaries.

The adoption triad consists of adoptees, biological families, and adopted families. Each group has a separate set of fears and more likely than not the other groups are unaware of these fears. The adoptee has a need to know their identity but fears rejection by the biological family if they find them. The adopted family fears that the adoptee will leave them for their biological family or love the biological family more than them. The biological mother may live with guilt and regret and have a need for peace of mind that she made the right decision for her child. A birth mother or other member of the biological family fear they will disrupt the child's life or cause a problem with an adoptive family.

## CRIMINAL DEFENSE

### Criminal Defense Investigation (CDI)

By definition a crime is:
- A legal wrong
- Prohibited by criminal law
- Prosecuted by local, state, or federal attorney generals in a formal court proceeding.
- Punishable by a criminal sentence or sanction.

A criminal defense investigation is conducted on behalf of a defendant accused of a criminal offense.

There are two elements of a crime: act and intention. Without act and intention there is not a crime. Act alone is not a crime, intention alone is not a crime, but combined, act and intention make a crime. A crime results from either committing an act that violates the law or omission of a required legal act. An act of commission may be taking the property of another without intention of returning the property. An act of omission is failure to file a tax return.

A criminal investigation by law enforcement will involve collecting facts that lead to the identity and arrest of criminals. The purpose of the criminal court system is to determine if an accused criminal is guilty or innocent and convict those who are found guilty.

The role of the private investigator on a criminal defense investigation is to provide facts that will exonerate the accused person rather than convict the accused person. The private investigator will examine the police report of all facts and attempt to discover new facts.

Death row or death penalty mitigation involves obtaining new information that may prevent a criminal on death row from being put to death. This type of investigation may be court ordered, paid for by the state, and will involve a team consisting of attorneys, private investigators, psychologist, or others. The court may appoint the private investigators who work on these type of cases. Laws may vary from state to state.

The criminal investigation conducted by a private investigator will almost mirror the same investigation by the police. An experienced former law enforcement officer should be able to find weaknesses in the case. Minor technical errors by law enforcement could possibly change the entire outcome of the investigation.

## Criminal Court

Criminal cases are tried in local county, state, and federal criminal courts. Court jurisdiction is decided by where a crime took place and the type of law that was broken. Court systems consists of lower courts, superior courts, and appellate courts. Each jurisdiction has it's own system.

Private investigators who work criminal defense cases need to know and understand the law, rules of evidence, court procedures, and be skilled at giving testimony.

## Private Investigator vs Law Enforcement

Defense: A private investigator conducts criminal defense investigations for attorneys defending persons accused of crimes for the purpose of exonerating the accused.

Prosecutor: Law enforcement conducts a criminal defense investigation so that a prosecutor can prove the accused is guilty of a crime and seek punishment.

Both the private investigator and law enforcement use the same basic investigative techniques. The main difference is that they are playing on separate teams. One team is trying to find the accused person guilty and one team is trying to find the accused person innocent.

It is not uncommon for a private investigator to be a former law enforcement detective. Once a law enforcement detective becomes a private investigator it is like switching teams and animosity builds. Resentment and competition becomes elements of the animosity.

The functions of a criminal defense investigation by a private investigator are to:
- Conduct a separate investigation
- Evaluate the police investigation
- Confer with and inform the client and/or counsel
- Prepare a written report
- Testify

## Defendants

In a criminal investigation the accused person is a defendant. All accused persons of criminal investigations, except in grand jury proceedings, have the right to be present during the criminal proceedings in court. Regardless of a defendant's background he or she is entitled to a lawyer and a fair trial.

The purpose of the private investigator is to provide facts for the attorney to represent the client. A thorough investigation may mean the difference in a person going to prison or being found innocent and free.

## Defense Attorneys

A defense attorney or defender represents an accused person from the time of arrest through the court trial and final appeal. The defense attorney may be court appointed or hired by a defendant or someone representing the defendant. The purpose of a defense attorney is to diligently defend their client. Oftentimes a good defense attorney will use legal technicalities to have a case dismissed, or plea bargain for a reduced sentence. The defender is the "mouthpiece" of the accused and will try to find a way to lessen the client's punishment.

A public defender is an attorney appointed by a court to represent a client. The public defender attorney may work for a private firm or one that is state-funded. Some public defenders work "pro-bono." This means the client does not have to pay. Some public defenders may be under contract for a set fee paid by a court to represent persons of low income. Some public defenders may not have the same level of expertise as an attorney in private practice. Attorneys who work "pro-bono" may not be as motivated as an attorney who is being paid a large fee. Regardless of whether the attorney is paid or not, the learning experience is valuable.

A client's statement of "I am innocent, I did not do it" or "They have the wrong person" is not adequate. Proof of the client's alibi will be required. The investigator's job is to find the proof that will provide the alibi. If the client was out of town, eating in a restaurant, or doing anything that can be documented (such as a parking ticket, a credit card charge, a phone call, etc.), the PI will need to find the evidence or witness to prove the client's innocence.

**Prosecutor**

A prosecutor or attorney general may work for a local county, state, or federal government. The jurisdiction depends on the type of law involved. A local attorney general will prosecute cases on a county level, a state attorney general will prosecute cases involving violations of state law, while a federal attorney general will prosecute cases involving federal laws.

With the court's permission a prosecutor has the authority to plea bargain a case with an attorney representing a defendant. A prosecutor can bring charges against defenders, conduct a trial, plea bargain, and recommend sentencing.

The primary function of the private investigator is to find weaknesses in the law enforcement and prosecutor's case or uncover and provide facts that indicate that the accused is innocent.

# CHAPTER VI

# PRIVACY LAWS

### Fair Credit Reporting Act (FCRA)

The FCRA provides certain protections to job applicants, the effect of which complicates pre-employment screening.

The Federal Trade Commission is mandated by the FCRA to ensure the accuracy and privacy of information in reports made of consumers. A job applicant falls under the definition of consumer.

### Freedom of Information Act (FOIA)

This law was enacted in 1966 to give to any individual or organization access to certain government records. The goal of the FOIA is to make all federal government agency records available to the public, unless those records are protected by one of nine FOIA exemptions.

All federal agencies are required under the Freedom of Information Act (FOIA) to disclose records requested in writing by any person. However, agencies may withhold information pursuant to nine exemptions and three exclusions contained in the statute. The FOIA applies only to federal agencies and does not create a right of access to records held by Congress, the courts, or by state or local government agencies. Accessible records include:
  • Defense Locator Service (military records)
  • Veterans Administration
  • Social Security Administration
  • Federal Bureau of Investigation

### Privacy Act of 1974

The Privacy Act of 1974 protects certain federal government records pertaining to individuals. In general, the Privacy Act prohibits the unauthorized disclosure of the records it protects. It also gives individuals the right to review records about themselves, to find out if these records have been disclosed, and to request corrections or amendments of these records, unless the records are legally exempt.

The purpose of the FOIA and the Privacy Act is to give the public access to existing government records within reasonable limits. Among other records, these include consumer complaints and investigations.

**Drivers Privacy Protection Act**
**18 U.S.C. § 2721 et. seq.**
(Public Law 103-322)

## Section 2721. Prohibition on release and use of certain personal information from State motor vehicle records

(a) In General — Except as provided in subsection (b), a State department of motor vehicles, and any officer, employee, or contractor, thereof, shall not knowingly disclose or otherwise make available to any person or entity personal information about any individual obtained by the department in connection with a motor vehicle record.

(b) Permissible Uses — Personal information referred to in subsection (a) shall be disclosed for use in connection with matters of motor vehicle or driver safety and theft, motor vehicle emissions, motor vehicle product alterations, recalls, or advisories, performance monitoring of motor vehicles and dealers by motor vehicle manufacturers, and removal of non-owner records from the original owner records of motor vehicle manufacturers to carry out the purposes of the *Automobile Information Disclosure Act*, the *Motor Vehicle Information and Cost Saving Act*, the *National Traffic and Motor Vehicle Safety Act of 1966*, the *Anti-Car Theft Act of 1992*, and the *Clean Air Act*, and may be disclosed as follows:

(1) For use by any government agency, including any court or law enforcement agency, in carrying out its functions, or any private person or entity acting on behalf of a Federal, State, or local agency in carrying out its functions.

(2) For use in connection with matters of motor vehicle or driver safety and theft; motor vehicle emissions; motor vehicle product alterations, recalls, or advisories; performance monitoring of motor vehicles, motor vehicle parts and dealers; motor vehicle market research activities, including survey research; and removal of non-owner records from the original owner records of motor vehicle manufacturers.

(3) For use in the normal course of business by a legitimate business or its agents, employees, or contractors, but only —

(A) to verify the accuracy of personal information submitted by the individual to the business or its agents, employees, or contractors; and
(B) if such information as so submitted is not correct or is no longer correct, to obtain the correct information, but only for the purposes of

preventing fraud by, pursuing legal remedies against, or recovering on a debt or security interest against, the individual.

(4) For use in connection with any civil, criminal, administrative, or arbitral proceeding in any Federal, State, or local court or agency or before any self-regulatory body, including the service of process, investigation in anticipation of litigation, and the execution or enforcement of judgments and orders, or pursuant to an order of a Federal, State, or local court.

(5) For use in research activities, and for use in producing statistical reports, so long as the personal information is not published, redisclosed, or used to contact individuals.

(6) For use by any insurer or insurance support organization, or by a self-insured entity, or its agents, employees, or contractors, in connection with claims investigation activities, anti-fraud activities, rating or underwriting.

(7) For use in providing notice to the owners of towed or impounded vehicles.

(8) For use by any licensed private investigative agency or licensed security service for any purpose permitted under this subsection.

(9) For use by an employer or its agents or insurer to obtain or verify information relating to a holder of a commercial driver's license that is required under the *Commercial Motor Vehicle Safety Act of 1986* (49 U.S.C. App. 2710 et seq.).

(10) For use in connection with the operation of private toll transportation facilities.

(11) For any other use in response to requests for individual motor vehicle records if the motor vehicle department has provided in a clear and conspicuous manner on forms for issuance or renewal of operator's permits, titles, registrations, or identification cards, notice that personal information collected by the department may be disclosed to any business or person, and has provided in a clear and conspicuous manner on such forms an opportunity to prohibit such disclosures.

(12) For bulk distribution for surveys, marketing or solicitations if the motor vehicle department has implemented methods and procedures to ensure that —

> (A) individuals are provided an opportunity, in a clear and conspicuous manner, to prohibit such uses; and
>
> (B) the information will be used, rented, or sold solely for bulk distribution for surveys, marketing, and solicitations, and that surveys, marketing, and solicitations will not be directed at those individuals who

have requested in a timely fashion that they not be directed at them.

(13) For use by any requester, if the requester demonstrates it has obtained the written consent of the individual to whom the information pertains.

(14) For any other use specifically authorized under the law of the State that holds the record, if such use is related to the operation of a motor vehicle or public safety.

(c) Resale or Redisclosure — An authorized recipient of personal information (except a recipient under subsection (b)(11) or (12)) may resell or redisclose the information only for a use permitted under subsection (b) (but not for uses under subsection (b)(11) or (12)). An authorized recipient under subsection (b)(11) may resell or redisclose personal information for any purpose. An authorized recipient under subsection (b)(12) may resell or redisclose personal information pursuant to subsection (b)(12). Any authorized recipient (except a recipient under subsection (b)(11)) that resells or rediscloses personal information covered by this title must keep for a period of 5 years records identifying each person or entity that receives information and the permitted purpose for which the information will be used and must make such records available to the motor vehicle department upon request.

(d) Waiver Procedures — A State motor vehicle department may establish and carry out procedures under which the department or its agents, upon receiving a request for personal information that does not fall within one of the exceptions in subsection (b), may mail a copy of the request to the individual about whom the information was requested, informing such individual of the request, together with a statement to the effect that the information will not be released unless the individual waives such individual's right to privacy under this section.

## Section 2722. Additional unlawful acts

(a) Procurement for Unlawful Purpose — It shall be unlawful for any person knowingly to obtain or disclose personal information, from a motor vehicle record, for any use not permitted under section 2721(b) of this title.

(b) False Representation — It shall be unlawful for any person to make false representation to obtain any personal information from an individual's motor vehicle record.

## Section 2723. Penalties

(a) Criminal Fine — A person who knowingly violates this chapter shall be fined under this title.

(b) Violations by State Department of Motor Vehicles — Any State department of motor vehicles that has a policy or practice of substantial noncompliance with this chapter shall be subject to a civil penalty imposed by the Attorney General of not more than $5,000 a day for each day of substantial noncompliance.

### Section 2724. Civil action

(a) Cause of Action — A person who knowingly obtains, discloses or uses personal information, from a motor vehicle record, for a purpose not permitted under this chapter shall be liable to the individual to whom the information pertains, who may bring a civil action in a United States district court.

(b) Remedies — The court may award:

(1) actual damages, but not less than liquidated damages in the amount of $2,500;

(2) punitive damages upon proof of willful or reckless disregard of the law;

(3) reasonable attorneys' fees and other litigation costs reasonably incurred; and

(4) such other preliminary and equitable relief as the court determines to be appropriate.

### Section 2725. Definitions

In this chapter —

(1) "motor vehicle record" means any record that pertains to a motor vehicle operator's permit, motor vehicle title, motor vehicle registration, or identification card issued by a department of motor vehicles;

(2) "person" means an individual, organization or entity, but does not include a State or agency thereof; and

(3) "personal information" means information that identifies an individual, including an individual's photograph, social security number, driver identification number, name, address (but not the 5-digit zip code), telephone number, and medical or disability information, but does not include information on vehicular accidents, driving violations, and driver's status.

### DUE DILIGENCE

The term due diligence refers to the care a reasonable party should take before entering into an agreement with another party. The inquiry serves to confirm all material facts regarding the agreement under consideration. In a big picture context, due diligence is a process for examining the financial underpinnings of a corporation in a pending investment, merger or acquisition, with the goal of understanding risks associated with the deal.

For example, in a sell/purchase deal both parties will want to check out the other party to determine if he/she is acting in good faith. The seller wants assurance that the buyer has the financial ability to meet the sales price, and the buyer wants assurance that the seller's property is worth the price. Due diligence is essentially a way of preventing unnecessary harm or loss to either party.

Due diligence is similar to pre-employment screening. A job applicant wishes to be employed and provides information about his/her qualifications. The employer verifies the qualifications and makes a hiring decision. In due diligence, Party A wishes to connect to Party B and provides information about its qualifications. Party B verifies the qualifications and makes a decision.

Just like pre-employment screening, the other party is asked to fill out forms, provide copies of relevant documents and give consent to being investigated. In due diligence, many documents are requested. For example:

- A management organization chart and biographical information of corporate/executive officers
- Copies of pending or prior lawsuits
- Summaries of disputes with suppliers, competitors or customers.
- Correspondence regarding threatened or pending litigation, assessment or claims
- Decrees, orders or judgments of courts or governmental agencies
- Reports made to regulatory groups such as OSHA
- Summaries of labor disputes
- Correspondence, memoranda or notes concerning pending or threatened labor stoppage
- Consulting agreements, loan agreements and documents relating to outside transactions involving corporate officers, directors, key employees and related parties
- Compensation schedules of corporate officers, directors and key employees showing salary, bonuses and non-cash compensation (such as use of cars, vacations, entertainment, and property, etc.)
- Summary of management incentive or bonus plans
- Confidentiality agreements

The investigative techniques used in a due diligence inquiry are no different than those used when checking records, checking references, and interviewing knowledgeable persons.

Clients that rely on background investigations to make choices among people are likely to believe that past conduct is a very good indicator of future conduct. A job applicant with a high IQ and an excellent aptitude score will look good on paper until a BI turns up a felony record. A prospective business partner with a winning personality may seem perfect until a BI reveals a record of suspicious bookkeeping.

Some PIs bring street smarts to the job. Do not equate street smarts with bending the rules; think of them as little bits of extra knowledge that help cut through red tape and obtain cooperation from otherwise uncooperative people. Street smarts is knowing where to find information, knowing who guards the information, knowing what to ask for, and knowing how to ask. In other words a good street smart PI will have many contacts. It has been said that a detective is only as good as his/her contacts so if you don't have many contacts, try developing them.

# CHAPTER VII

# INFORMATION DATABASES, PUBLIC RECORDS, AND OTHER SOURCES

Listed in this chapter are internet links that are active at the time of this writing. There is no guarantee that the links will remain active in the future or that the information contained in this chapter will remain current. Use the information and links as a reference tool and learn to use a search engine such as Google to find updated and current information that may not be available at the time this book was written.

A good deal of information can be found in computer databases. Some databases are easily accessible to a PI directly; in other cases, the PI works through a vendor. Database searches can provide extensive information at low cost and are useful when the person of interest worked or lived in numerous counties or states. A local search, such as one made at a county courthouse, will not reflect an individual's criminal conviction in another county or state. Success with a database service will depend on the quality and quantity of the information provided by the employer. For each name run through a database, there may be hundreds of persons with the same name. Having full and accurate information to input at the front end of a database search can produce good information results.

There are three main credit bureaus that sell information to private investigators providing there is a permissible purpose under the FCRA: Equifax (www.equifax.com), Experian (www.experian.com), and TransUnion (www.transunion.com). There is a fee for credit information.

Credit reports are subject to the FCRA In order to access a credit report containing account information, a written signature from the subject is required. A client may supply this written authorization from a customer, employee, or prospective employee.

A credit header is limited information from a credit report that does not contain account or financial information and is not subject to the FCRA therefore a written signature from a subject is not required. A credit header should contain the subject's name(s), date of birth, social security number, phone number, current and previous addresses, current and previous employers. This is an excellent source of information for many types of investigations. Credit header information may be obtained directly from the credit bureau or from a vendor that re-sells the information. Information contained in the credit header is dated and updates are added as they occur.

Vendors will usually require a private investigator to select a permissible purpose for obtaining credit and other information. These permissible purposes are required by the FCRA:

1. In response to the order of a court having jurisdiction to issue such and order, or a subpoena issued in connection with proceedings before a federal grand jury.

2. In accordance with the written instructions of the consumer to whom it relates.

3. To a person whom the credit bureau has reason to believe:
   a. Intends to use the information in connection with a credit transaction involving the consumer on whom the information is to be furnished, and involving the extension of credit to, or review or collection of an account of, the consumer; or
   b. Intends to use the information for employment purposes; or
   c. Intends to use the information in connection with the underwriting of insurance involving the consumer; or
   d. Intends to use the information in connection with a determination of the consumer's eligibility for a license or other benefit granted by a governmental instrumentality required by law to consider an applicant's financial responsibility or status; or
   e. Otherwise has a legitimate business need for the information in connection with a business transaction involving the consumer.

The Fair Credit Reporting Act (FCRA) is a federal law that protects consumers. It contains provisions for both criminal and civil prosecutions for abusing the credit reporting system. Any person who knowingly and willfully obtains information on a consumer from a consumer reporting agency under false pretenses shall be fined under title 18, U.S. Code, imprisoned for not more than two years, or both.

Database vendors that sell information to clients such as investigators, law-enforcement, attorneys, insurance companies, and others are self-governed by rules known as the IRSG-Individual Reference Services Group Privacy Principles (www.irsg.org). Clients must agree to abide by the IRSG rules when they subscribe to the database.

The Gramm-Leach-Bliley Act (GLB) was passed by Congress to protect consumer privacy and basically turned the IRSG self-governing rules into law.

## ONLINE INFORMATION SOURCES

This is the information age and the age of high technology. In the past an investigator had to physically go to a library, courthouse, or state office building to obtain information. Now the information is at your fingertips with the use of a computer.

For those who may not be computer literate, don't be intimidated by a computer. Using a computer can save you time and money and is as easy to use as a typewriter. Accessing information simply requires knowledge of how and where to look for it.

When accessing information from a professional database, knowledge of privacy laws is necessary. If you are unfamiliar with privacy laws try searching Goggle for the key words "FCRA," the "Gramm-Leach-Bliley law," the "Patriot Act," and other privacy laws. Some privacy laws may be federal laws and some may be state laws. The privacy laws are intended to protect the public. If you need information that requires a written consent from the person you are investigating, then you must either get a written consent or not obtain the information. If you have to break the law to get information, you are not a good investigator. You must know when to say no and don't cross the line that makes you a criminal.

Professional databases and information brokers sell information.

Google is the leading search engine that will instantly produce results. Searching for key words will lead to online information sources that are both free or fee based. Listed here are but a few of the more popular professional sources of professional information. Don't be afraid to experiment with the Internet and try out various databases. The Internet is a useful research tool.

http://www.irb.com
http://www.merlindata.com
http://www.tracersinfo.com
http://www.chocepoint.com
http://www.knowx.com
http://www.westlaw.com

http://www.lexis.com

http://www.brbpub.com/pubrecsites.asp

http://www.edgar.com

http://www.mapquest.com

http://www.searchsystems.com

http://www.factfind.com

http://www.netr.com

http://www.pacer.psc.uscourts.gov

http://www.anywho.com

http://www.bigfoot.com

http://www.whowhere.com

http://www.whitepages.com

http://www.yahoo.com

http://www.switchboard.com

http://www.dogpile.com

http://www.411.com

http://www.canada411.com

http://www.superpages.com

http://www.411locate.com

http://www.yellowpages.com

http://www.ancestry.com

## Accurint

http://www.accurint.com/

This database is for professional skip tracing. Accurint provides names, aliases, social security numbers, current and previous addresses (going back to up to 30 years), telephone numbers, month and year of birth, current residents or properties, property ownership, names of relatives (up to 3 degrees of separation), neighbors, death information and more. This database is a division of Lexis-Nexis and is fairly inexpensive as compared to other information sources.

## Autotrack XP

http://www.autotrackxp.com/

AutoTrackXP is an excellent source of public information. Find people, corporate records, real property records, deed transfers, professional, firearm, and DEA licenses, motor vehicle records, government, business and residential telephone directories, boat and vehicle registrations, bankruptcies, liens and judgments, and more. Autotrack is a division of Choicepoint, formerly DBT/DataBase Technology. This source is excellent, especially for Florida resident information.

## Aviation/Pilots/Airplanes
http://www.faa.gov/

Find information about current pilots licenses, airplane registration, and other information pertaining to aviation.

## Businesses
http://www.hoovers.com/free/

## Bankruptcy records
http://pacer.psc.uscourts.gov/register.html

## Background information sources
BRB Publications
http://www.brbpub.com/
Public record sources.

## Census
http://www.ancestry.com
http://www.census-online.com/links/
http://www.archives.gov/
http://www.familysearch.org/

Census records are released every ten years and must be forty years old at the time of release. Current census information is not available. One of the best sources of census records is the Mormon Church of Latter Day Saints libraries. Branch libraries are scattered around the country and the headquarters is in Salt Lake City, Utah. Of course the government has census records at the National Archives and it's branches around the country. Many libraries have census records also.

## ChoicePoint
http://www.choicepoint.com

ChoicePoint Online, formerly CDB Infotek and cdb4web, also offers an extensive database of public records. It provides people locating tools, corporate records, real property records, a reverse telephone directory, driver records, boat and vehicle registrations, physician reports including criminal and disciplinary data, bankruptcies, liens and judgments, UCCs, Federal Employer Identification Numbers (FEIN), OSHA investigation records and more. Choicepoint owns DBT (DataBaseTechnology) and AutoTrackXP.

**County Locator**
http://www.netronline.com/frameset.asp?StateID=c_loc
http://resources.rootsweb.com/cgi-bin/townco.cgi

**Criminal Records**
http://www.virtualchase.com/resources/criminal_records.html

**Death Index**
http://ssdi.genealogy.rootsweb.com/
Master Social Security Death Index. Free search.

**DocFinder**
http://www.docboard.org/docfinder.html
Find doctors medical licenses.

**Dun & Bradstreet**
http://www.dnb.com/us/

Better known for its business credit reports, Dun & Bradstreet (D&B) also provides access to public records nationwide. Business credit reports often contain basic information about companies including an address, telephone, SIC classification, major executives, state of incorporation, year it began operations and affiliations. The reports also generally offer a brief business description as well as information about facilities and equipment, sales, ownership, current credit, UCCs, judgments and liens.

**Fair Credit Reporting Act**
http://www.ftc.gov/os/statutes/fcra.htm

**FDA Database**
http://www.sec.gov/edgar/searchedgar/webusers.htm

**Federal Government Information**
http://www.access.gpo.gov/su_docs/gils/

**Free Government Public Record Sites**
http://www.brbpub.com/pubrecsites.asp

## Genealogy
http://www.ancestry.com
http://www.rootsweb.com/
http://www.heritagequestonline.com/
http://www.genealogy.com
http://www.archives.gov/
http://www.familysearch.org/

## Government
Archives Library
http://www.archives.gov/
http://pacer.psc.uscourts.gov/

## Government Information Locator Service (GILS)
http://www.access.gpo.gov/su_docs/gils/agency-pointer.html

## Government Information
http://firstgov.gov

## Government Printing Office
http://www.gpoaccess.gov/databases.html

## Hoover's Business Information
http://www.hoovers.com/free/

Business information on 12 million public and private companies worldwide, including company profiles, in-depth financials, contact names, competitors, etc.

## Health information
http://health.nih.gov/

## IRB
http://www.findanyonenow.com

## KnowX
http://www.knowx.com/

## Lexis-Nexis Research
http://www.lexis.com/

Lexis offers extensive public record coverage. It provides some data not easily found elsewhere online (e.g., jury verdicts and settlements, U.S. federal and state agency sanctions). Lexis also provides access to some public records outside of the U.S.

**Medical/Drug Information**
http://www.nlm.nih.gov/medlineplus/druginformation.html

**Medical Personnel Disciplinary Information**
http://www.citizen.org/hrg/forms/MedBoard_action.cfm

**Merlin Information Services**
http://www.merlindata.com

**Military Information**
http://www.militaryusa.com/

**Pensions**
http://www.freeerisa.com/

**Phone Finder**
http://www.fonefinder.net/
http://www.usinterlink.com

**Political Donors**
http://www.opensecrets.org/2000elect/lookup/AllCands.htm

**Prison Inmate Lookup**
http://www.bop.gov/

**Prisoner Inmate Lookup**
http://www.corrections.com/links/viewlinks.asp?Cat=20

**Public Records Search Systems**
http://www.searchsystems.net/

A great source of free links to states', cities', and other public database records. They provide business information, corporate filings, offenders, inmates, criminal and civil court filings, vital records, property records, unclaimed property, professional licenses, and much more.

**Securities**
http://www.sec.gov/edgar.shtml

EDGAR, the Electronic Data Gathering, Analysis, and Retrieval system, performs automated collection, validation, indexing, acceptance, and forwarding of submissions by companies and others who are required by law to file forms with the U.S. Securities and Exchange Commission (SEC).

**SEC Filings**

http://www.edgar-online.com/

http://www.sec.gov/edgar/searchedgar/webusers.htm

**Sex Offenders**

http://www.nsopr.gov/

http://www.criminalcheck.com/

http://www.sexoffender.com/search.html

http://www.fbi.gov/hq/cid/cac/states.htm

**State & Local Government Links**

http://www.netronline.com/public_records.htm

**Social Security**

http://www.ssa.gov/foia/stateweb.html

**Unclaimed Persons**

http://www.unclaimedpersons.com/

**Unclaimed Property**

http://www.unclaimed.org/

**Westlaw**

http://web2.westlaw.com/

Westlaw offers many of the public records previously mentioned on this page as well as docket sheets, D&B reports, environmental site records, jury verdicts and settlements, obituary pages supplied by Dow Jones, securities filings and trademark registrations.

**ZabaSearch**

http://www.zabasearch.com

Free search for name, address, phone, and sometimes date of birth. Information is not always current but can lead to a trail. This site also has access to paid databases.

## SOCIAL SECURITY NUMBER IDENTIFIER

The first three numbers in a Social Security number identify where the card was originally issued.

| | | | |
|---|---|---|---|
| 001-003 | New Hampshire | 429-432 | Arkansas |
| 004-007 | Maine | 433-439 | Louisiana |
| 008-009 | Vermont | 440-448 | Oklahoma |
| 010-034 | Massachusetts | 449-467 | Texas |
| 035-039 | Rhode Island | 468-477 | Minnesota |
| 040-049 | Connecticut | 478-485 | Iowa |
| 050-134 | New York | 486-500 | Missouri |
| 135-158 | New Jersey | 501-502 | North Dakota |
| 159-211 | Pennsylvania | 503-504 | South Dakota |
| 212-220 | Maryland | 505-508 | Nebraska |
| 221-222 | Delaware | 509-515 | Kansas |
| 223-231 | Virginia | 516-517 | Montana |
| 232-236 | West Virginia | 518-519 | Idaho |
| 237-246 | North Carolina | 520 | Wyoming |
| 247-251 | South Carolina | 521-524 | Colorado |
| 252-260 | Georgia | 525 | New Mexico |
| 261-267 | Florida | 526-527 | Arizona |
| 268-302 | Ohio | 528-529 | Utah |
| 303-317 | Indiana | 530 | Nevada |
| 318-361 | Illinois | 531-539 | Washington |
| 362-386 | Michigan | 540-544 | Oregon |
| 387-399 | Wisconsin | 545-573 | California |
| 400-407 | Kentucky | 574 | Alaska |
| 408-415 | Tennessee | 575-576 | Hawaii |
| 416-424 | Alabama | 577-579 | Washington, DC |
| 425-428 | Mississippi | | |

## PUBLIC RECORDS

Both the government and the private sector require record keeping, to regulate, license, and hire. Paper trails of information begin with a birth certificate and end with a death certificate. Between the birth and death certificate are many other records such as diplomas, a social security number, driver's license, military records, vehicle registration, traffic violations, insurance, utilities, mortgage, financial records, marriage, divorce, licenses, medical records, social and civic organizations, etc.

Public records are maintained by government agencies that are open records without restriction to public inspection. If a record is restricted it is not a public record. Government records may vary by state according to the laws of that state. Some government records may require a written authorization or other qualifications under privacy laws (such as criminal history, driver's records, vehicle records, employment, voter's registration, and worker's compensation records). Some public records are accessible through a database.

Financial records (bank, credit card, credit reports, etc.) and medical records are not public records and may require a written authorization to access. In some locations utility records may be accessed without a written consent (such as gas, electric, or water companies).

Corporate, partnership, UCC filings, limited liability companies, trademarks and copyrights, tax liens, judgments and liens, motor vehicle and drivers records, accident reports, accident reports, criminal records, workers' compensation records, vital records, and sales tax registrations may be accessed online at a local, state, or federal regulatory office. Other agencies include hunting and fishing licenses, occupational licensing, business registration, permits, and archive libraries (local, state, and federal). Other records might include mailing lists, professional associations, alumni records, and scholastic records.

## STATE INTERNET WEB SITES

Alabama – http://alaweb.asc.edu/agency.html
　　　　　http://alaweb.asc.edu/govern.html

Alaska – http://www.state.ak.us

Arizona – http://www.state.az.us

Arkansas – http://www.state.ar.us

California – http://www.state.ca.us

Colorado – http://www.state.co.us

Delaware – http://www.state.de.us

District of Columbia – http://www.capcityonline.com

Florida – http://www.state.fl.us

Georgia – http://www.state.ga.us

Hawaii – http://www.state.hi.us

Idaho – http://www.state.id.us

Illinois – http://www.state.il.us

Indiana – http://www.state.in.us

Iowa – http://www.state.ia.us

Kansas – http://www.state.ks.us

Kentucky – http://www.state.ky.us

Louisiana – http://www.state.la.us

Maine – http://www.state.me.us

Maryland – http://www.mec.state.md.us

Massachusetts – http://www.state.ma.us

Michigan – http://www.migov.state.mi.us

Minnesota – http://www.state.mn.us

Mississippi – http://www.state.ms.us

Missouri – http://www.state.mo.us

Montana – http://www.mt.gov

Nebraska – http://www.state.ne.us

Nevada – http://www.state.nv.us

New Hampshire – http://www.state.nh.us

New Jersey – http://www.state.nj.us

New Mexico – http://www.state.nm.us

New York – http://www.state.ny.us

North Carolina – http://www.state.nc.us

North Dakota – http://www.state.nd.us

Ohio – http://www.state.oh.us

Oklahoma – http://www.state.ok.us

Oregon – http://www.state.or.us

Pennsylvania – http://www.state.pa.us

Rhode Island – http://www.state.ri.us

South Carolina – http://www.state.sc.us

South Dakota – http://www.state.sd.us

Tennessee – http://www.state.tn.us

Texas – http://www.state.tx.us

Utah – http://www.state.ut.us

Vermont – http://www.state.vt.us

Virginia – http://www.state.va.us

Washington – http://www.wa.gov

West Virginia – http://www.state.wv.us

Wisconsin – http://www.state.wi.us

Wyoming – http://www.state.wy.us

## ADOPTION SEARCHING

Of all the missing person cases I have worked on, the adoption search is the most difficult. Laws prevent access to identifying information in many states, however laws are beginning to gradually change because more and more people are speaking up and speaking out, and demanding changes to their anti-quated laws. Many years ago I lobbied the Tennessee legislature for changes to the adoption laws. Several years ago, after many adoption searches, I wrote "The Adoption Searcher's Handbook."

There are many adoption resources and much infighting and power struggles amongst adoption searchers, adoption organizations, and adoption registries.

For many years "The Big Searcher" has been operating his underground searches. The searchers who use "The Big Searcher" extort thousands of dollars from adoptees and biological families who pay only because the laws prevent them from getting the information legally. Several adoption searchers have been caught and served time in prison for obtaining adoption information under false pretenses.

The following information was found on The National Adoption Clearing House web site and is being included in the hope that it might help those who may be involved in adoption searching.

## NATIONAL ADOPTION CLEARING HOUSE

While interest among adopted persons in finding their birth families has always been high, the percentage of adult adopted persons who take action to initiate a search appears to be on the rise. This trend is accompanied by a growing interest on the part of many birth parents in searching for their (now) adult children who were placed for adoption many years earlier. The expanding number of organizations that advocate searching for birth relatives and provide advice and resources for doing so indicate both increased interest in and acceptance of this process. New legislation in some States permits more access to birth information, and new technology has the potential to make the searching process faster. A recent study shows that adopted persons are more likely to seek out information about their birth families now than in the past (Harris Interactive Market Research, 2002). And a study that reviewed estimates abroad and in the United States suggests that 50 percent of all adopted persons search at some point in their lives (Muller & Perry, 2001a).

The purpose of this fact sheet is to provide some guidance on the search process and information access, as well as resources for further help in conducting a successful search. This fact sheet is designed to address the concerns of both adopted persons who are searching for birth parents or other birth relatives, as well as birth parents (both mothers and fathers) who want to locate a child who was adopted. While not a complete "how to" guide to searching, this fact sheet provides information on:
- The decision to search
- Steps in the search process
- Hiring a professional searcher
- International searching
- Reunion issues

In addition, a list of resources is included at the end. The list includes websites on searching, books and articles, and more. The National Adoption Information Clearinghouse (NAIC) website (http://naic.acf.hhs.gov/) is a good starting point for resource information.

## The Decision to Search

Adults who were adopted as infants or young children are the most common group of people searching for adoption information and birth relatives. This group most often searches for birth mothers first (Muller & Perry, 2001b), but may later seek out birth fathers, siblings, or other birth relatives. An event in the life of an adopted person, for instance, the birth of a child or death of an adoptive parent, may trigger the actual search (American Adoption Congress, 2002).

Other groups that search include birth parents searching for children placed for adoption years earlier and a growing number of adoptive parents who search in order to know more about their adoptive children's background or medical history (Freundlich, 2001). In addition, some national organizations that work with children in foster care report increased interest by siblings in finding their siblings who were placed with other families.

The question of why an adopted person or birth parent searches for birth relatives has as many answers as there are searchers. Some of the more common reasons include the following:

- General family information. Searchers may want to know the names of their birth relatives, where they live, and what they are like. Birth parents may want to know whether their birth children have been happy and well treated.

- Family traits and personalities. Many adopted persons and birth parents want to know how their birth relatives look and act and whether they share similar traits.

- Medical history information. Information on genetic diseases and conditions can be crucial for safeguarding an adopted person's own health and the health of their biological children. (The desire or need for family medical history is sometimes the only reason that will compel a judge to open sealed adoption records.)

- Circumstances of the adoption. Often, adopted persons feel a need to know why they were placed for adoption or why the rights of the birth parent were terminated and how that decision was made. Birth parents may want the opportunity to explain the circumstances to their child.

## Steps in the Search Process

Every search is unique in its unfolding, but there are a number of steps and resources common to most searches. This section of the fact sheet addresses the steps in the search process, including:

1. Emotional preparation
2. Assembling known information
3. Researching relevant State laws
4. Registering with reunion registries
5. Obtaining missing documents
6. Filing court petitions

**1. Emotional preparation.** Both adopted persons and birth parents should expect to prepare emotionally for the search process. Such preparation may include reading about other adopted persons' or birth parents' search and reunion experiences and talking to others who are going through or have gone through the same process. Support groups for adopted persons, or for birth parents who are searching, can be extremely helpful, not only in providing emotional support, but also in sharing practical information. (For a State-by-State listing of support groups, see the NAIC's National Adoption Directory at http://naic.acf.hhs.gov/general/nad/)

Gathering emotional support from family and friends also can be helpful. Adopted persons may be reluctant to share their decision to search with their adoptive parents for fear of hurting their feelings. However, in many cases adoptive parents can be an enormous source of support, as well as a source of information. Adoptive parents may take some comfort from knowing that an adopted person's decision to search usually has nothing to do with dissatisfaction with the adoptive parents.

The search process may trigger a number of different emotions at different stages for the searcher. At certain stages, some searchers may feel that they need more emotional or moral support than they are receiving from family, friends, and support groups. In these situations, they may want to talk to a professional counselor. Searchers who seek professional counseling will want to ensure that the counselor is familiar with adoption issues. (See the NAIC's fact sheet on selecting adoption therapists.) In addition, some State laws require a meeting with a counselor before a reunion takes place.

**2. Assembling known information.** Once a decision has been made to search, the first step involves gathering all known and easily obtainable information. For adopted persons, this may mean talking to adoptive parents to find out the name of the adoption agency, attorney, or facilitator involved in the adoption. It also means pulling together all readily available documents, such as the amended birth certificate, hospital records, and any other information, no matter how unimportant it may seem at the time. Birth, death, marriage, divorce, school, church, genealogy, health, military, DMV, and property records related to the birth kin all have potential usefulness for leading to a name and location of a birth parent or birth child. It may be helpful to organize and record all information in a central place for easy reference.

**3. Researching relevant State laws.** Searchers may want to become informed about State laws regarding adoption and records access in the State(s) in which they were born and adopted, keeping in mind that some State laws vary according to the applicable years. Access to information about State laws as well as which States offer reunion registries can be found at the National Adoption Information Clearinghouse (NAIC) website. (Other websites that maintain databases or updates on State laws are included in the Resource List at the end of this fact sheet.)

**4. Registering with reunion registries.** A number of States, as well as private organizations, offer reunion registries that allow adopted persons and birth parents to register the fact that they are searching for each other. Most of these reunion registries are "passive," meaning that both parties (e.g., the adopted person and the birth mother) must independently register in order for a match to be made. When both parties register at the same passive registry and a match is made, registry officials share the mutual information and help to arrange for contact. Passive registries do not actively search for the other party.

The largest passive registry is the <u>International Soundex Reunion Registry</u>. This is open to all adopted adults over 18 years of age, all birth parents, and all adoptive parents of adopted children under 18 years of age.

There are also a number of "active" registries that charge fees to actually go out and search for the birth relative. Some of these are State registries that will initiate a search for a fee. Others are maintained by private search and support groups.

There are few reliable statistics on the success rate of these registries; however, as expected, passive registries tend to show a much lower match rate than active registries. One study of passive State registries found an average success rate of less than 5 percent in 1998, with only two States showing double-digit success rates (Mitchell, Nast, Busharis, & Hasegawa, 1999).

**5. Obtaining missing documents.** At this point, the searcher may want to attempt to acquire some of the missing documents that could help with the search. There are many types of documents that may lead to locating a birth parent or child or provide a breakthrough to this information. The following is a list of potentially helpful documents:

- **Adoption agency records**–If the name of the adoption agency is known, the searcher can request non-identifying information or even records. For instance, in her 1998 book, *Search: A Handbook for Adoptees and Birthparents*, Jayne Askin provides an extensive list of possible questions to be addressed to the agency, including questions about siblings, medical information, and consent to release information. Askin also recommends that the searcher supply a waiver of confidentiality to the agency, so that information about the searcher can be provided to the birth child or birth parent, if that individual also contacts the agency.

• **Hospital records**–Hospital records, when they can be obtained, may provide information on the birth mother, birth father, attending physician, and incidental health information. Adopted persons generally need to know their birth name, as well as the hospital's name and location. If the searcher has difficulty obtaining these records, a request made by a doctor may have a better chance for success.

• **Birth records**–Most adopted persons will not have their original birth certificate but will have, instead, an amended document listing their adoptive parents' names. However, there are a few States that allow adopted adults to have access to their original birth certificate. (See the NAIC information on access to family information by adopted persons.) In other States, the original birth certificate may be available if the adopted person petitions the court.

• **Court adoption file**–The court adoption records consist of a number of documents, including the original, unaltered birth certificate; petition to adopt; finalization papers or final decree; consent to adopt from birth parent(s), relinquishment papers, or orders terminating parental rights; and any agency or attorney papers, including information about birth parents. Many of these documents may also be available elsewhere. For instance, adoptive parents should have copies of the court proceedings finalizing the adoption, although the final court order will not provide the names of the birth parents. If this is not available, an adopted person searching for birth parents may be able to contact the attorney or law firm that handled the adoption to obtain it. A request may also be made to the court. Often, identifying information will be blacked out of the court-supplied document; however, there may be some remaining clues that are helpful. The final adoption papers should provide the name of the attorney, judge, and agency involved in the proceedings. This information may lead to discovering other useful clues.

• **Other court records**–While most or all of the court records may be officially sealed, in some cases a searcher may be able to view the court's Docket Appearance Book, a daily record of who appeared in court and why on a particular day, or even the Minute Book log, with the results of each court appearance (Culligan, 1996). Also, local newspapers from the time of the adoption may carry a notice of the filing of the Petition to Adopt in the classified section. This normally includes the name of the couple adopting, as well as the birth name of the child/infant and the name of the social worker assigned to the case (Culligan, 1996).

- **Other types of records**-Other potentially useful records may include physician records, newspapers (for birth announcements), cemetery and mortuary records, probate records, Social Security information, records of military service, school records (including yearbooks), marriage licenses, divorce or annulment papers, DMV documents, and death certificates.

**6. Filing a court petition.** If none of the above have been successful, adopted persons may petition the court to have the sealed adoption records opened. Whether this is successful may depend on the State, the particular judge, the reason given for the request, and any number of other factors. Petitioning the court does not require an attorney's services, but a petitioner may choose to hire an attorney.

The judge may deny the petition completely or agree to release only non-identifying information or a summary. In some States, the judge may appoint an intermediary, such as the original adoption agency or a professional searcher, to locate the birth parents and determine whether or not they want to release information or be reunited with the adopted person. In other cases, the petitioner may be able to request the appointment of a confidential intermediary, who will conduct a search (for a fee) and determine if the birth parents are willing to be contacted.

Following these steps may lead the searcher to enough identifying information that birth relatives can be located. In cases in which the search seems to be leading nowhere, the searcher may want to review information or begin to research such things as alternative spellings of names or places. In some cases, information may have been falsified, making it difficult or impossible to continue the search without new information.

### Hiring a Professional Searcher

Adopted persons or birth parents searching for birth relatives have the option of hiring a professional searcher. In some cases, it may be useful to hire a professional searcher if specific information needs to be located in another State. For instance, a professional searcher may be able to search courthouse or church records in a faraway locality. This limited professional help may be enough to allow the adopted person or birth parent to continue his or her own search.

Individuals who choose to hire a professional searcher should research the reputation of the searcher or company. There are some searchers who have a certification from Independent Search Consultants, a nonprofit organization that trains in adoption searching. Other searchers may be licensed as private investigators by a particular locality. Individuals should ask whether private investigators have specific adoption search experience before making a decision to hire them. Other professional searchers may be experts in a particular locality or a particular field but may not have a certification. Before hiring anyone, it is crucial to call references and to check with the Better Business Bureau. In addition, support groups can be a ready source of information about professional searchers.

In some cases, a court or agency may refuse to open sealed records or provide full information in response to a petition or request; however, the court or agency may appoint a professional searcher. In such cases, this professional searcher serves as an intermediary whose job is to locate and contact the birth parents (or birth child) and to find out whether they want to have their name and address revealed and whether they want to resume contact. The professional is given access to sealed records, but the petitioner (who generally receives no access to records) pays the fee of the professional searcher. If nothing is found, or if the found person refuses to release information or agree to contact, there is generally no recourse (except that the adopted person or birth parent can continue to search on his or her own).

### International Searching

People who were adopted from outside the United States (through international adoptions) face unique challenges in locating birth parents. Each country has its own laws governing information access. In addition, there is great variation in record-keeping practices across countries and cultures, and in many cases, searchers will find that no information was ever recorded, that records were misplaced, or that cultural practices placed little emphasis on accurate record-keeping. However, in a very few cases, it may actually be easier to gain access to an original birth certificate in a foreign country than in the United States, since some countries do not seal their vital records.

The child-placing agency is the best beginning point for an international search. The U.S. agency should be able to share the name and location of the agency or orphanage abroad and, perhaps, the names of caregivers, attorneys, or others involved in the placement or adoption. The agency, or its counterpart abroad, may be able to provide specific information on names, dates, and places. They also may be able to offer some medical history, biographical information on parents, and circumstances regarding the adoption.

Some other resources for international searchers include the following:

- Adopted persons seeking documents (such as a birth certificate) that the U.S. or foreign child-placing agency is not able to provide may want to apply to government agencies in the birth country. Mailing addresses of offices of vital records in foreign countries can be found on the U.S. State Department website.
- Searchers adopted from another country can contact the U.S. Citizenship and Immigration Services to receive copies of their immigration records.
- An international agency that may offer help is International Social Services, which provides a broad range of social work services, including helping adopted persons find birth families abroad. Their U.S. branch has a website at www.iss-usa.org.
- Support groups for adopted persons from particular countries may be able to offer help and information on searching. Countries that have placed a large number of children with families in the United States, such as Korea, have support groups and organizations with websites and search information. (See the Resource List at the end of this fact sheet.)

In general, searching overseas is more difficult than searching in the United States. In cases in which the search for the birth parent is unsuccessful, some adopted persons may derive some satisfaction from visiting their birth country and experiencing their birth culture. Many agencies and support groups have begun to organize homeland tours for adopted persons and adoptive families. These tours generally provide an introduction to the country and culture. Visiting the birth country for the first time as part of such a group may provide searchers with some emotional security, because the people in the tour group are often looking for answers to similar questions. (The National Adoption Directory lists groups that offer homeland tours.)

## Reunion Issues

Reunions between long-lost birth family members have been the subject of books, articles, and television shows. Two important themes emerge from these accounts:

**1. Participants should be emotionally prepared for the reunion experience.** Adopted persons and birth parents may carry a picture in their mind of the perfect family, but the reunion experience may not live up to that ideal. In preparing for contact and reunion, adopted persons (and birth parents) should prepare for a whole range of realities, including rejection. Although most birth parents are agreeable to further contact, research indicates that a minority, perhaps 9 to 15 percent, reject any contact (Muller & Perry, 2001).

**2. Pacing the contact can be the key to having a successful reunion and relationship.** In a small study of adopted women who experienced reunions with birth kin (Affleck & Steed 2001), it was found that successful reunion experiences were associated with (1) preparation with a support group and (2) a slower pace between initial contact and actual meeting, involving letters and phone calls. This interval between contact and meeting allowed information to be exchanged and gave the "found" relatives some time to become accustomed to the idea. Such an interval can also give the found relatives time to share the news with spouses and 2. children in their family, if they desire.

Some factors that may increase the possibility of a successful longer term relationship include (Muller and Perry, 2001b):
- The establishment of limits regarding each others' lives
- Support from adoptive parents
- Minimal expectations
- Similar lifestyles and temperaments
- Acceptance by other family members

In many cases, a successful reunion with a birth mother may prompt the adopted adult to continue the search process for the birth father. Meeting with birth siblings also may occur, and each reunion experience requires preparation and time to evolve.

**Conclusion**

Each search for a birth relative is guided by a unique set of circumstances. The outcome is uncertain and, even when the birth relative is located, the reunion experience does not always turn out as expected. Nonetheless, many adopted persons and birth parents have conducted successful searches and built successful relationships with their new-found relatives. For those who are just beginning the search, the best preparation may be finding out about the search experiences of others. To that end, a list of resources has been included below. In addition, support groups for adopted persons and birth parents across the country can be found in the online National Adoption Directory on the NAIC website.

## References Cited

Affleck, M. K., & Steed, L. G. (2001). Expectations and experiences of participants in ongoing adoption reunion relationships: A qualitative study. *American Journal of Orthopsychiatry, 71*(1), 38-48.

American Adoption Congress. (2002). Frequently asked questions. Retrieved March 12, 2004, from http://www.americanadoptioncongress.org/search.htm

Askin, J. (1998). *Search: A handbook for adoptees and birthparents, 3rd edition*. Phoenix, AZ: Oryx Press.

Brodzinsky, D. M., Schechter, M. D., & Henig, R. M. (1992). *Being adopted: The lifelong search for self*. NCY: Doubleday.

Freundlich, Madelyn. (2001). *Access to information and search and reunion in Korean American adoptions: A discussion paper*. El Dorado Hills, CA: Korean American Adoptee Adoptive Family Network. Retrieved April 5, 2004, from the Korean American Adoptee Adoptive Family Network at http://www.kaanet.com/whitepaper.pdf

Harris Interactive Market Research. (2002). National Adoption Attitudes Survey. Dave Thomas Foundation for Adoption & The Evan B. Donaldson Adoption Institute. http://www.adoptioninstitute.org/survey/Adoption_Attitudes_Survey.pdf

Mitchell, M., Nast, J., Busharis, B., & Hasegawa, P. (1999). Mutual consent voluntary registries: An exercise in patience and failure. *Adoptive Families 32*(1), 30-33, 63.

Muller, U., & Perry, B. (2001a). Adopted persons' search for and contact with their birth parents I: Who searches and why? *Adoption Quarterly 4*(3), 5-37.

Muller, U., & Perry, B. (2001). Adopted persons' search for and contact with their birth parents II: Adoptee-birth parent contact. *Adoption Quarterly 4*(3), 39-62.

## Additional Resources
## Books and Articles

Bailey, J. J., & Giddens, L. N. (2001). *The adoption reunion survival guide: Preparing yourself for the search, reunion, and beyond.* Oakland, CA: New Harbinger Publications, Inc.

Byrne, M. (2000-2001). Search and reunion etiquette: The guide Miss Manners never wrote. American Adoption Congress (Winter/Spring), 11-13. Retrieved April 14, 2004, from www.americanadoptioncongress.org/articles-archives/search-etiquette.htm

Cox, S. S.-K. (2001). *Considerations for international search.* Retrieved April 21, 2004, from http://www.holtintl.org/reunionsearcharticle.html

Lifton, B. J. (1988). *Lost and found*: The adoption experience. NY: Harper & Row.

McColm, M. (1993). *Adoption reunions: A book for adoptees, birth parents and adoptive families.* Toronto: Second Story Press.

Strauss, J. A. (1994). *Birthright: The guide to search and reunion for adoptees, birthparents, and adoptive parents.* NYC: Penguin Books.

### Websites and Resources for beginning the search:

• The ALMA Society (Adoptees' Liberty Movement Association)

• American Adoption Congress's Search Guidance

• International Soundex Reunion Registry

• Family Search Internet Genealogy Service (sponsored by the Church of the Latter Day Saints)

### Resources for international searches:

• International Social Services

• Korean Adoptee Adoptive Family Network

• U.S. State Department

### Resources on State adoption laws:

• American Adoption Congress

• Bastard Nation

- The Evan B. Donaldson Adoption Institute
- National Center for Adoption Law and Policy
- National Adoption Information Clearinghouse
- The White Oak Foundation

The National Adoption Directory on the NAIC website contains information on State adoption officials, State reunion registries, adoption agencies, and support groups.

Other information on the NAIC website includes resource lists on such topics as organizations that provide adoption research and fact sheets on such topics as international adoption.

A Service of the Children's Bureau,
Administration for Children and Families,
U.S. Department of Health and Human Services

For more information, contact:
National Adoption Information Clearinghouse
Children's Bureau/ACYF
1250 Maryland Avenue, SW
Eighth Floor
Washington, DC 20024
Phone: (703) 352-3488 or (888) 251-0075
Fax: (703) 385-3206
E-mail: naic@caliber.com

## ADOPTION RESOURCES

Listed here is merely a sampling of adoption resources available on the internet. For additional resources go to www.google.com and enter key words such as adoption registries, adoption search and support groups, adoption laws, or adoption.

http://www.get-in-touch.com
http://www.nationwidelocate.com
http://www.getintouch.tv
http://www.tvreunions.com
http://www.americanadoptioncongress.org/articles-archives/vol-reg.htm

http://www.adopting.org/adoptions/national-world-adoption-reunion-
registries.html

http://www.adoption.org/adopt/adoption-registry.php

http://www.isrr.net/

http://registry.adoption.com/

http://www.adopteeconnect.com/

http://www.aci.net/schaefer/page60.html

http://www.plumsite.com/care/

http://www.gensource.com/genealogy/c177.cfm

http://www.niwot.net/adopt/

http://www.findme.org/findme/index.cfm?fuseaction=Main

http://members.tripod.com/~rombergers/linx.html

http://www.cyndislist.com/adoption.htm

http://www.adoption.org/adopt/free-adoption-registries.php

http://www.geocities.com/Wellesley/3686/

http://www.genesearch.com/people/adoptionsearch.html

http://nmar.freeservers.com/ (New Mexico Registry)

http://www.genealogytoday.com/adoption/puzzle/registries.htm

http://www.bastards.org/library/search.htm

http://www.plumsite.com/shea/states.html

http://www.adoptiontriad.org/netregistries.htm

http://www.adoptiontriad.org/netregistries.htm

http://www.vitalrec.com/links3.html

http://www.the-seeker.com/adopt.htm

http://www.fortunecity.com/meltingpot/springhill/801/tornasunder/registries/
am-index.html

http://www.birthfamily.com/register.htm

http://www.epage.com/js/browse/;jsessionid=1A817F3BFE28FC78655E00D
C8F4DBAFC?cat=11203100&b=0&pg=1

http://www.adoptioncrossroads.org/

http://www.adoptioncrossroads.org/

http://www.adoptionregistry.net/about.html

http://www.geocities.com/Heartland/Ridge/2755/

http://www.adoptiontriad.org/registry.htm

http://www.destinyink.com/research/birthline.html

http://thebinkster.com/thebirthmothertree/
http://68.33.85.12:8080/
http://dir.genealogytoday.com/births_n_baptisms.html
http://www.geocities.com/Heartland/Garden/2313/index.htm
http://www.geocities.com/geoadopt/
http://www.kyadoptions.com/
http://www.kindredpursuits.org/
http://www.metroreunionregistry.org/
http://freeweb.wpdcorp.com/relinquished/ccAdoptionSites.asp
http://www.ncpa.org/pd/social/spaug98g.html
http://www.reunite.com/
http://www.ouareau.com/adoptee/start.htm
http://eserver.org/govt/adoption-law.txt
http://www.seeklost.com/
http://dmoz.org/Home/Family/Adoption/Search_and_Reunion/
http://forums.adoption.com/
http://www.faqs.org/faqs/genealogy/adoption/part2/
http://www.adopting.org/ffcwnr.html
http://www.nacac.org/pas_database.html
http://genealogy.about.com/cs/adoption/a/adoption_search.htm
http://dir.groups.yahoo.com/dir/Family___Home/Parenting/Adoption
http://www.genealogyforum.com/gfaol/resource/Adopt0001.htm

## State adoption offices, laws, and registries

**Alabama:** http://ph.state.al.us/Chs/VitalRecords/Adoption/adptee.html

The Department of Health Services

Post Adoption Unit
50 N. Ripley Street
Montgomery, AL  36130
(205) 242-9500

**Alaska:** http://www.hss.state.ak.us/ocs/

Department of Health & Social Services
Division of Family and Youth Services
350 Main Street, Fourth Floor

P. O. Box 110630
Juneau, AK 99811-0630
(907) 465-3170
(907) 465-3397 and (907) 465-3190 fax

Alaska Adoption Exchange: (800) 704-9133

**Arizona:** http://www.supreme.state.az.us/cip/

Arizona Vital Records Section
Arizona Department of Health Services
P.O. Box 3887
Phoenix, AZ 85030
(602) 255-3260

**Arkansas:** http://www.arkansas.gov/dhhs/adoption/mcvar.htm

Department of Human Services
Division of Children & Family Services
PO Box 1437 – slot 808
626 Donaghey Plaza South
Little Rock, AR 72203-1437

**California**: http://www.childsworld.ca.gov/Frequently_1359.htm

California Department of Social Services
744 P Street
Sacramento, CA 95814
(800) KIDS-4-US (800-543-7487)

http://www.leginfo.ca.gov/cgi-bin/waisgate?WAISdocID=87634219715+10+0+0&WAISaction=retrieve

**Colorado:** http://www.genealogybranches.com/adoption.html

Department of Human Services
Office of Youth Services
4255 S. Knox Court
Denver, CO 80236
(303) 762-4466
(303) 762-4401 fax

**Connecticut:** http://www.state.ct.us/dcf/FASU/FASU_Search_law.htm

Department of Children and Families
Office of Public Relations
505 Hudson Street
Hartford, CT 06106
(860) 550-6578

**Delaware:** http://www.dhss.delaware.gov/dhss/dph/ss/vitalstats.html

Youth and Family Center
Children and Youth Services
Adoption Services Manager
1825 Faulkland Road
Wilmington, DE 19805-1195
(302) 633-2655

**District of Columbia:**

Dept. Of Health Services Post Adoption Unit
609 H Street
Washington, DC 20002
(202) 727-5930

State adoption records Information Dept
District Bldg.
14th and E Streets
Washington DC 20004
(202) 628-6000

**Florida:** http://adoptflorida.com/Reunion-Registry.htm

Department of Health and Rehabilitative Services (HRS)
Office of Vital Statistics
P.O. Box 210
1217 Pearl Street
Jacksonville, FL 32231

**Georgia:** http://www.adoptions.dhr.state.ga.us/reunion.htm

State Adoption Unit Division of Family & Children Services
2 Peachtree Street, Ste 13-400
Atlanta, GA 30303-3142
(404) 657-3555

**Hawaii:** http://www.hawaii.gov/jud/excite.htm

Dept of Social Services and Housing
P.O. Box 339
Honolulu, HI 96809

Island of Oahu
Family Court, First Circuit
P.O. Box 3498
Honolulu, HI 96811-3498

**Idaho:** http://healthandwelfare.idaho.gov/DesktopModules/ArticlesSortable/
ArticlesSrtView.aspx?tabID=0&ItemID=381&mid=10463

Department of Health and Welfare
450 West State Street, 5th Floor
Boise, ID 83720-5005
(208) 334-5710
(208) 334-0666 fax
(800) 356-9868

**Illinois:** http://www.idph.state.il.us/vitalrecords/adoptioninfo.htm

Illinois Department of Public Health
Division of Vital Records
605 W. Jefferson Street
Springfield, IL 62702-5097

**Indiana:** http://www.in.gov/isdh/bdcertifs/medical_history.htm

Social Services Division
Dept. Public Welfare
402 W. Washington Street
3rd Floor, W-364
Indianapolis, IN 46204
(317) 232-4448

**Iowa:** http://www.dhs.state.ia.us/dhs2005/dhs_homepage/children_family/
adoption/iam_adopted.html

Department of Human Services
Division of Adult
Iowa Dept of Human Services
Hoover Building 5th Floor

Des Moines, IA 50319
(515) 281-5580
(515) 281-8854 fax

**Kansas:** http://www.kdheks.gov/vital/adoption_before_adoption.html

Department of Social and Rehabilitation Services
915 Harrison Street, 6th Floor
Docking State Office Building
Topeka, KS 66612
(785) 296-3271
(785) 296-4685 fax

**Kentucky:** http://chfs.ky.gov/dcbs/dpp/ADOPTION+SEARCH.htm
http://www.kyadoptions.com/

Department For Social Services
Recruitment, Certification and Permanency Planning Branch
6th Floor East
275 East Main Street
Frankfort, KY 40621
(502) 564-2147
(502) 564-3096 fax

**Louisiana:** http://www.dss.state.la.us/departments/ocs/Adoption_Registry.html

State Reunion Registry Voluntary Registry
Department of Social Services, Youth, & Family Services
Located in the Commerce Building
333 Laurel Street
Baton Rouge, LA 70802
(504) 342-4059

**Maine:** http://www.maine.gov/dhhs/reunionregistry.htm

Dept of Human Services
221 State Street, Station 11
Augusta, ME 04333-0011

**Maryland:** http://www.dhr.state.md.us/adoption/

Maryland State Archives
350 Rowe Boulevard
Annapolis, MD 21401

MD toll free (800) 235-4045
(410) 974-3914
(410) 974-3895 fax

**Massachusetts:** http://members.aol.com/Espaura/MAadopt.html

Massachusetts Department of Social Services
24 Farnsworth Street
Boston, MA 02210
(617) 727-0900

**Michigan:** http://www.michigan.gov/documents/FIA1925_10575_7.pdf

Dept of Social Services
235 S Grand Avenue
P.O. Box 30037
Lansing, MI 48909

**Minnesota:** http://www.health.state.mn.us/divs/chs/osr/adoption.html

Department of Human Services
444 Lafayette Road, 4th Floor
St. Paul, MN 55155-3846
SIS General Information: (651) 772-3750
TDD (800) 627-3529
Fax (651) 772-3794
Help Desk (651) 772-3777

**Mississippi:** http://www.ls.state.ms.us/

Mississippi Department of Human Services Adoption Unit
Division of Family and Children Services
750 North State Street
Jackson, MS 39205
(800) 345-6347

**Missouri:** http://www.dss.mo.gov/cd/adopt/adoir.htm

The State of Missouri
Department of Social Services
221 West High Street
P.O. Box 1527
Jefferson City, MO 65102-1527
(573) 751-4815

**Montana:** http://www.dphhs.mt.gov/

Dept of Family Services
1400 Broadway
Helena, MT  59620
(406) 444-5900
(406) 444-2547 fax

Mailing address:
P.O. Box 8005
Helena, MT  59604-8005

**Nebraska:** http://www.hhs.state.ne.us/adp/adoption_searches.htm

Department of Social Services
P.O. Box 95026
Lincoln, NE  68509

Street Address:
301 Centennial Mall S
5th Floor
Lincoln, NE  68509
(402) 471-9103
(402) 471-9455 fax
(800) 831-4573

**Nevada:** http://dcfs.state.nv.us/

Dept of Human Resources
Nevada State Welfare Division
Social Services
2527 North Carson Street
Carson City, NV  89710
(702) 687-4744
(402) 471-9108
TTY (402) 471-9570

**New Hampshire:** http://www.sos.nh.gov/vitalrecords/Preadoption%20
birth%20records.html

Bureau of Child and Family Services
Dept of Health and Welfare
6 Hazen Drive

Concord, NH 03301

Concord
40 Terrill Park Drive, Unit 1
Concord, NH 03301-7325
(603) 271-6200 or (800) 322-919

**New Jersey:** http://www.state.nj.us/humanservices/adoption/registryframe.html

New Jersey Department of Human Services
Division of Youth and Family Services
P.O. Box 717
Trenton, NJ 08625-0717
(609) 292-8816
(609) 984-6800
(609) 984-5449 fax

**New Mexico:** http://www.state.nm.us/hsd/home.html

Human Services Department
P.O. Box 2348
Santa Fe, NM 87504
(800) 432-6217
(505) 827-7750
TDD: (800) 609-4TDD (800-609-4833)

**New York:** http://www.health.state.ny.us/vital_records/adoption.htm

Vital Records Section
New York State Department of Health
Empire State Plaza
Albany, NY 12237-0023
(518) 474-3077

**North Carolina:** http://www.dhhs.state.nc.us/

Children's Services Branch
Division of Social Services
Department of Human Resources
100 East Six Forks Road
Office of Adoption Services
Raleigh, NC 27609-7750
(919) 733-3801

**North Dakota:** http://www.nd.gov/humanservices/services/childfamily/adoption/disclosure.html

ND Department of Human Services
Children & Family Services
600 East Boulevard Avenue
Bismarck, ND  58505-0250
(701) 328-2310
(701) 328-2359 fax

**Ohio:** http://www.odh.state.oh.us/vitalstatistics/legalinfo/adoption.aspx

Vital Statistics
P.O. Box 15098
Columbus, OH  43215-0098
(614) 466-2531

**Oklahoma:** http://www.okdhs.org/adopt/Adoptions/includes/content/reunion.htm

Child Welfare Services Unit
Attention: Adoption Section
Department of Human Resources
P.O. Box 25352
Oklahoma City, OK  73125
(405) 521-3646

**Oregon:** http://oregon.gov/DHS/ph/chs/preadopt.shtml

Department of Human Resources
Children's Services Division
500 Summer Street, NE
Salem, OR  97310-1017
(503) 945-5651
(503) 581-6198 fax

**Pennsylvania:** http://www.dsf.health.state.pa.us/health/cwp/view.asp?a=168&Q=202177

Department of Public Welfare
Office of Children Youth & Families
P.O. Box 8018
Harrisburg, PA  17105

(717) 787-3672
(717) 787-9706 fax

**Rhode Island:** http://www.courts.state.ri.us/family/adoptreg.htm

Rhode Island Child Support Services
Department of Human Services
Dept for Children & Their Families
77 Dorrance Street
Providence, RI  02903
(401) 277-2847
(401) 277-6674 fax

**South Carolina:** http://www.state.sc.us/dss/adoption/
http://www.southcarolinaadoptions.com/

Division of Social Services
Department of Human Resources
100 East Six Forks Road
Raleigh, NC  27609-7750
(919) 571-4114
(919) 571-4126 fax
(800) 992-9457

State Reunion Registry
Division of Social Services
Department of Human Resources
100 East Six Forks Road
Raleigh, NC  27609-7750
(919) 571-4114
(919) 571-4126 fax
(800) 992-9457

**Tennessee:** http://www.tennessee.gov/youth/adoption/accessto.htm

Department of Human Services
Citizens Plaza Building – 12th Floor
400 Deadrick Street
Nashville, TN  37248-7400
(615) 741-2441
(615) 313-4885 fax
(800) 874-0530

State Reunion Registry
Department of Human Services
Post-Adoption Services
Citizens Plaza Building – 12th Floor
400 Deadrick Street
Nashville, TN  37248-7400
(615) 741-2441
(615) 313-4885 fax
(800) 874-0530

**Texas:** http://www.dshs.state.tx.us/vs/reqproc/adoptionregistry.shtm

Central Adoption Registry
Mail Code Y-943
Texas Department of Protective and Regulatory Services
P.O. Box 149030
Austin, TX  78714-9030
(512) 834-4485

**Utah:** http://health.utah.gov/vitalrecords/Links.htm

Division of Family Services
Bureau of Vital Records
P.O. Box 141012
Salt Lake City, UT  84114-1012
(801) 538-6105

Street address:
Cannon Health Building
288 N 1460 W
Salt Lake City, UT  84114-1012

State Reunion Registry
Bureau of Vital Statistics
Voluntary Adoption Registry
P.O. Box 141012
Salt Lake City, UT  84114-1012
(801) 538-6105

Street address:
Cannon Health Building
288 N 1460 W
Salt Lake City, UT  84114-1012

**Vermont:** http://www.dcf.state.vt.us/fsd/registry.html

Department of Social Welfare
Agency of Human Services
103 South Main Street
Waterbury, VT 05671-1901
(802) 241-2319
(802) 244-1483 fax
(800) 786-3214

State Reunion Registry

Vermont Adoption Registry
Social & Rehabilitation Service
103 Main Street
Waterbury, VT 05676
(802) 241-2122

**Virginia:** http://www.dss.virginia.gov/form/

Department of Social Services
730 East broad Street
Richmond, VA 23219
(804) 692-1201

**Washington:** http://www1.dshs.wa.gov/ca/adopt/res_Records.asp

Division of Children and Family Services
Office Building #2
Olympia, WA 98504
(800) 737-0617

**West Virginia:** http://www.childwelfare.com/West_Virginia_Adoption_listings.htm

Department of Welfare
1900 Washington Street E
Charleston, WV 25305

State Reunion Registry

Mutual Consent Registry
Bureau of Human Resources
Office of Social Services

Capitol Complex
Building 6 Room B-850
Charleston, VA 25305

**Wisconsin:** http://dhfs.wisconsin.gov/children/adoption/adsearch.htm

Division of Health & Social Services
Adoption Records Search Program
P.O. Box 8916
Madison, WI 53708-8916
(608) 266-7163

**Wyoming:** http://adoption.about.com/gi/dynamic/offsite.htm?zi=1/XJ&sdn=
adoption&zu=http%3A%2F%2Flegisweb.state.wy.us%2Fstatutes%2Ftitles%
2Ftitle01%2Fchapter22.htm

Department of Health
2300 Capitol Avenue
117 Hathaway Building
Cheyenne, WY 82002
(307) 777-7657
(307) 777-7439 fax
TTY (307) 777-5648

**Canada Adoption Resources:**
http://www.canadianadopteesregistry.org/
http://www.canadianadopteesregistry.org/disc_registrys.html
http://www.adoptionbychoice.ab.ca/search_registries.cfm
http://www.familyhelper.net/ft/ftsup.html
http://www.adoption.org/adopt/canadian-adoption-searches.php

**United Kingdom Adoption Resources:**
http://www.ukbirth-adoptionregister.com/resources.php

**Search and support groups:**
http://www.google.com (keywords: adoption search and support groups)

**Organizations:**
http://www.almasociety.org/
http://www.americanadoptioncongress.org/
http://www.cubirthparents.org/
http://www.isrr.net/
http://www.nacac.org/

http://www.PNPIC.org/
http://www.starsofdavid.org/
http://www.kaanet.com/
http://www.adoptioncrossroads.org/

**Where to write for Vital Records (birth, death, marriage, divorce):**
http://www.cdc.gov/nchs/howto/w2w/w2welcom.htm

National Adoption Registry Search: http://naic.acf.hhs.gov/general/nad/

Public Records: http://www.publicrecordsinfo.com/adoption_records.htm

# CHAPTER VIII

# SURVEILLANCE

# INTERVIEWING TECHNIQUES

## SURVEILLANCE TIPS

Surveillance cases often involve domestic and insurance related investigations. Regardless of the type of investigation, before beginning surveillance it is important to know as much as possible about the subject of the investigation. You will need to know daily activities and patterns, driving habits, places he or she might go, what the subject looks like, what vehicle the subject drives, where the subject works, where the subject likes to eat or drink, and other information that might be useful on the surveillance. Knowing where the subject is probably going before you start is a great way to work surveillance. Depending on where you are working it might be necessary to have several cars on the surveillance. The more you know about someone, the easier it is to anticipate what he or she might do or where he or she might go. If the subject strays from their usual activity, more than likely this is when something might happen.

Surveillance is learned by trial and error. Your job is to remain invisible to the subject. If the subject learns he or she is being followed you will probably have a hard time getting any evidence. You will need to blend into whatever the environment may be. You do not want to stand out or be noticed. Once you are spotted, you are "burned" and after being "burned" you will probably need to be replaced.

Always be prepared on surveillance. This means have a full tank of gas and plenty of batteries for your cameras. Have what you need at your fingertips so you won't have to search for anything. You might want to take along food and drink in case you are stuck for a long time. Forget about pulling off to go to the bathroom or for food. Once in place you probably need to stay put. If possible it is best to work from a van than a car.

If you have to sit for a long time you want the vehicle to look empty. I found that carrying along a dark sheet was useful for several things. I could make a tent in the back seat and no one could see me. I could drape it across the windows to block the view. I could cover a camera and leave the car empty and let the camera do the work. I used the sheet to cover my equipment. I like to rent cars for surveillance work. I can drive a different one every day. Also the tags won't be traced to me without a subpoena. Once I was in Florida and was watching a residence in broad open daylight. It was a busy neighborhood and sitting in a parked car all day would have been too noticeable so I rented two cars and left one parked with the camera running while I left in the other. I have an AC/DC adapter that I bought at Radio Shack. It plugs into the cigarette lighter and allows an electric cord to be plugged into it. So the camera can run off the car battery. If you have your own van you probably will have a spare marine battery for running camera or computer equipment. I have also rigged up a time-lapse recorder in the trunk of my car and placed a pinhole camera in a Kleenex box or some other object in the car window.

A GPS system can be very useful if you are in unfamiliar territory. Tracking devices may be illegal, so be careful about using them. For many years I used a tracking device, but after one of the Legislators was caught cheating on his wife, a new bill was introduced and a new law was passed making them illegal. There may be a way to get around the law without breaking it. You could possibly "rent" or "sell" your tracking device to your client who is a co-owner of the vehicle. Possibly your client can install the transmitter on his/her own vehicle. Check with an attorney to see whether or not this is legal in your state.

If you are going to be sitting in a residential neighborhood for a long time don't be surprised if a neighbor calls in a suspicious subject to the police. I've had neighbors come out and knock on the window of my car and ask whom I am and what I am doing. I know this day and time a stranger is not welcome. Sometimes I tell a neighbor who I am and ask permission to sit in their driveway. I don't have to tell who I are watching or why. The less said the better, although telling them something non-threatening will probably satisfy them... such as I work a lot of insurance cases. That's true, sometimes I do work insurance cases, but I didn't say that this was one of them. Just be prepared to give a non-threatening, convincing answer if a neighbor approaches you.

One time I was honest about who I was and what I was doing. I asked a neighbor if I could park in their drive. That neighbor said okay, but the next-door neighbor came over to see what I was doing. I told the second neighbor I was working an insurance case to see if his neighbor was actually injured and in a wheel chair, or if he was able to get up and walk. The second neighbor marched right over to the subject's house and knocked on his door to tell him I was there.

Sitting on surveillance is not always easy. It can be very stressful. Unlike what you see on television and in the movies, the perfect parking place is not waiting when you first pull up. And also unlike television and the movies your subject does not appear within five minutes. You probably won't get what you need and solve the case in one hour either. The longer you have to wait, the more chance a neighbor is watching you and will probably cause you to have to move.

The moving surveillance is not like what you see on television and in the movies. It is not a chase, you cannot be on the subject's bumper, or bump the subject's car. You have to remain invisible to the subject. If the subject sees you or notices your vehicle you might as well pull off and get someone else to take your place or get another vehicle.

## ASSIGNMENT FORM

Date: _____ Time: _____

Identification number: _____

Type of assignment: _____

Client: _____

Investigator(s) assigned to case: _____

Vehicles working on case: _____

Location of assignment: _____

Subject: _____

Address: _____

City/State/Zip: _____

Phones:  Home _____ Work _____ Cell_____

Employer: _____

Location of employer: _____

Subject's vehicle: _____

Other vehicles: _____

Daily activity schedule: _____

Photographs/Video Tapes: _____

Comments: _____

_____

_____

**SUMMARY:**

On October 25, 2005 at 4:45 P.M. subject was observed wearing blue jeans and a light blue long sleeved shirt. Subject left his employment at Nissan in Smyrna and got into a red Chevrolet Silverado pickup truck, license ABC123, TN. Subject left Nissan in Smyrna and drove to Nashboro Village condos in Nashville, condo # B101. Subject was observed unlocking and entering the front door of this condo at 5:15 P.M. There was another vehicle parked in front of this condo, a blue Ford Mustang, license DEF456, TN. Subject remained in this condo until 7:30 P.M. Subject and a female companion left the condo and got into the red Chevrolet pickup. They drove to Hickory Hollow Mall and went into O'Charley's Restaurant. The female companion was wearing blue jeans and a white pullover sweater. She appeared to be about 5'5, 120#, with short dark hair. Suspect and companion were observed walking with their arms around each other into the restaurant. Inside the restaurant subject and companion were observed sitting at the bar. Investigators sat close by and observed subject kissing the companion several times. After several drinks, subject and companion left and returned to the condo at Nashboro Village at 8:45 P.M. Subject re-entered the condo with companion. In plain view subject was observed kissing the companion inside the condo. Subject and companion went upstairs. At 9:00 P.M. the upstairs lights were turned off and remained off for thirty minutes. At 9:30 P.M. subject and companion were observed in the living room of the condo. At 9:45 P.M. subject left the condo and drove home.

Surveillance is the act of observing a person, a place, or an activity. The person, place, or activity is referred to as the target or subject of the investigation. The main objective of surveillance is to document facts and events, and obtain information. Surveillances are usually photographed and a chronological log or record of all activities is kept by the investigator(s) working on the case.

There are two types of surveillances, overt and covert.

An overt surveillance allows the subject to know he or she is being observed. For instance, a subject who is aware of the surveillance may lead the investigator to other associates, places, or activities of interest. Overt surveillance can consist of conspicuously following and taking photographs of the target in public places.

A covert surveillance is necessary when it is important to gather information about the movements and actions of the target without the target being aware of the surveillance. The methods of covert surveillance can vary: stationary surveillance (stakeout), foot and mobile surveillance, and photographic and electronic surveillance.

Surveillance can be a valuable method for obtaining factual information for the case. Surveillances may be used for:

– Documenting the activities of a spouse in a divorce or child custody action. In many cases the surveillance will consist of monitoring the movements of a spouse to confirm infidelity or to document other activities that will support the client's case in court.

– Observing the activities of persons suspected of filing false insurance claims such as worker's compensation, disability, and other medical claims. The typical surveillance here is to discover if a claimant is or is not demonstrating the symptoms of the disability for which a claim has been made. For example, an employee may claim that an on-the-job accident has injured his back to the extent he can barely walk. With a camera the investigator may create a visual record of the claimant bowling once a week at the bowling alley.

– Providing early warning of an anticipated crime. In this case the investigator receives from a client or other source certain information indicating that a crime is being planned. For example, the client owns a warehouse. A reliable employee has told the owner that other employees have obtained a key to the warehouse and intend to enter the warehouse after working hours for the purpose of stealing certain valuable property. The investigator is engaged to verify the report of the employee-informant and, if appropriate, coordinate with law enforcement a stakeout form of surveillance at the warehouse.

– Gathering information to plan a protective services operation. An example here is an upcoming business trip to be made by the chief executive officer of a large trucking corporation. Threats by the Worker's Union have been made against the CEO and the corporation. A private sector investigative agency has been engaged to conduct surveillances of the places to be visited, the primary and alternate routes to be taken by the vehicles transporting the CEO, and identifying positions of opportunity from which the CEO can be targeted with weaponry. Information developed by the agency is used to develop a plan designed to protect the CEO during the course of the visit.

– Monitoring a public event to spot trouble brewing. Persons who object to the event for one reason or another sometimes disrupt concerts, football games and other crowded public events deliberately. More often, disruption occurs when attendees get into arguments and fight with one another. The task of the private sector investigator is to move among the crowd or take up an elevated position and look for the early warning signals of a disruption. Early notification to event security personnel is made so that preemptive action can be initiated.

– Identifying criminal activity. A client may engage an investigator to determine if his personal or business property has been targeted by a criminal enterprise or if his business processes have been corrupted by crime or are being used to carry out criminal activity. For example, a company with operations in South America may recognize the possibility that cocaine can be smuggled into the United States aboard aircraft owned by or contracted to the company. Surveillance of aircraft operations and the movements of aircrew members can uncover the indications of drug trafficking.

A moving surveillance can be conducted in any manner that involves mobility: on foot, on a bicycle, or by motor vehicle, train, helicopter, airplane, boat, etc.

Depending on the movement of the target, a mobile surveillance can quickly and unexpectedly become stationary or fixed.

Surveillance by motor vehicle usually will not involve more than three vehicles. Vehicle A is typically the second or third vehicle behind the target vehicle, with Vehicle B closely behind. Vehicle C might travel a parallel road that has short-distance intersections that permit intermittent observation of the target, or Vehicle C might drive ahead of the target vehicle. In this latter technique, the three vehicles could "leap frog" as needed to maintain the surveillance while avoiding detection.

### Moving Surveillance Tips

- Drive in a full circle around the target's office or residence.
- Look for a place to set up.
- Evaluate the fields of view.
- Learn the routes in and out of the area.
- Learn the traffic flow.
- Identify possible problems such as traffic lights, construction, etc.
- While moving, keep one vehicle between your vehicle and the target's vehicle.
- Drive in a different lane, preferably to the right and in the target vehicle's "blind spot."
- Close the distance when approaching traffic lights so that you won't be stopped by a red light.

- Close the distance when approaching off ramps.
- On curves, hang back a little so that you will see the target vehicle for an instant before it is around the curve and out of sight.
- Have pocket change handy for parking meters, a toll road, or other expenses.

A fixed surveillance is also known as a stakeout. This method is used when the persons or activities of interest are stationary. The number and positioning of investigators depends on the number of persons to be observed, the nature of their activities, and the size and layout of the area.

When you operate from separate locations, a means of secure communication, such as a radio and cell phone, is essential both for the success of the operation and the safety of yourself and fellow investigators.

It is not unusual for a fixed surveillance to switch suddenly to a moving surveillance and then back again to the fixed mode. For this reason, the planning of the operation has to allow for alternate forms of transportation, well-understood procedures, and coordination among members of the surveillance team.

When on surveillance the unexpected will occur so be ready to react to the unexpected at all times. When the surveillance is strictly covert, the general rule is to abort the operation if there is a chance that the surveillance has been detected. In less critical operations, the leader of the surveillance team often makes instant decisions.

Instinct is defined as a strong impulse or motivation. Intuition is defined as acute insight. With experience comes a development of strong instincts and intuitions. If something does not feel right, look right, sound right, or seem right, it probably is not right and your natural instincts and intuitions will give you a signal. You will probably develop a keen sense of recognizing danger and will know when it is time to back off or call for help.

## Surveillance Equipment

In addition to having binoculars and a good 35mm camera with zoom and wide angle lenses, the investigator should be equipped with a video camera with features that include image stabilizer, zoom lens, time/date stamp, auto focus, and night vision (or low lux). Accessories consist of videotapes, extra batteries, tripod, and power adapter. A fanny pack with batteries hooked up to a pin hole camera allows the investigator to be hands free while photographing the target. These cameras are very small and can be concealed in a hat, pocket, purse, fanny pack, or just about anywhere. They can be placed in a stuffed animal, a plant, a book, a picture, or anywhere. Pinhole cameras can be fish-eye lens and catch a 180 degree view, or a straight lens in which it has to be pointed directly at the target.

When working with this equipment and a covert approach is needed, the investigator can either find a concealed location (inside a van or behind a curtained window) or the operative can work from an open location such as a customer in a restaurant or shopper in a store. The investigator may have to actually go into the place to see what the target is doing or who the target is with.

It is lawful to videotape or film anything in plain view where there is "no expectation of privacy." A person walking from his front door to the mailbox has no expectation of privacy, but if the person is inside his home, the expectation exists. It may be unlawful to "zoom" to the interior of the home or to climb a tree or pole to take pictures unless the target or subject is in plain view from a public location. You must not trespass on a property that is private or marked "No Trespassing." If you obtain permission to be on private property or if the subject or target is in plain view from a public property it would be okay to take photos of anything in plain view. It is okay to take photographs if there can be no expectation of privacy.

If the client cannot provide a daily routine of your target, a random surveillance might be appropriate. A random surveillance is a spot-checking of a target. A common technique is to watch the target in stages of his or her daily routine and then cut it off. The surveillance is resumed the following day at the cutoff point. The process is repeated until the subject's full daily routine has been established and recorded.

The random surveillance is a good choice when the surveillance has to continue over a long period. The investigator does not have to be the same person every time. There should be no set pattern. An investigator and the investigator's vehicle need to remain unnoticed or invisible to the target.

Among the forms of surveillance, foot surveillance is the most difficult to work and the most likely to be discovered. On foot surveillance, several investigators are required, they must be good at what they do, and they must work in teams so that if surveillance is lost or broken off, a backup team is already in place and ready to take over.

Foot surveillance:
- Requires both human and equipment resources.
- Requires experienced, skilled, and dedicated investigators.
- Presents challenges not associated with less demanding forms of surveillance.
- Is not a good choice when surveillance is to occur over an extended period.
- Is often the choice of last resort.

### Fixed Surveillance

When working from an automobile or van, use one that is common to the area and blends in with the neighborhood. Avoid using vehicles that are noticeable, flashy in style or color, decorated with bumper stickers or magnetic signs, or accessorized with antennas and spotlights. Fog lights that are mounted inconspicuously are desirable. Install a switch that will cut off brake lights and back-up lights. Turn off the interior lights. The windows should be tinted and/or curtained. A van is a good choice.

Parking in secluded areas or moving the vehicle from place to place during a random surveillance can better conceal your presence. The idea is to keep from being noticed by the target or by people living or working nearby. Neighborhood watches are everywhere and residents tend to be protective of their "territory" and will communicate their suspicions to one another. Neighbors may communicate by emailing or telephoning the target and alerting him or her that a suspicious vehicle is in the area or by calling the police and asking that a patrol car be dispatched.

When working in area where police patrolling is likely, it may be advisable to inform the zone car that you are in the area working on a case and ask that the surveillance vehicle not be checked out. When there is little chance that the police will be curious, is best to not inform anyone of the surveillance. The chance of being confronted or having a problem increases due to the number of people who are aware of the surveillance.

### Aerial Surveillance

This form of surveillance may be cost effective because a single hour in the air may produce results that would otherwise require many hours on the ground.

Aerial surveillance may work where other forms of surveillance will fail, for example, when the target of the surveillance is alert and on guard, or paranoid, he or she will go to great lengths to loose anyone they think is following them, or if the subject of the investigation is on private property and has posted "No Trespassing" signs. A tailing vehicle can remain out of sight of the target and receive directions by cell phone or radio from a partner flying overhead. Depending on the laws of the state, surveillance of this type can be greatly assisted with the use of a tracking device that has been covertly attached to the target's vehicle.

Aerial surveillance conducted at night can be assisted with a broken tail light or if a small hole has been drilled in the upper facing of the rear light on the target's vehicle. (It has been reported that such a hole can be created using a one-quarter inch drill bit and a battery-operated drill.) In the dark, light escaping from the hole, shines upward, allowing persons in the aircraft to differentiate the target's vehicle from other vehicles. (It is rumored that law-enforcement uses a screw driver to make a hole or crack in the tail light.) Placing black electrical tape over the taillight works just fine without causing any damage to the vehicle.

### Electronic Surveillance

Electronic surveillance is not wire tapping, bugging, eavesdropping, or any type of illegal information gathering.

Private investigators are sometimes called upon to design and set up surveillance systems using electronic-assisted equipment. Such equipment can include CCTV (closed circuit television); miniature cameras that operate with pinhole and low-level light lenses and fiber optic cabling; video and sound recorders; and sensors based on the principles of detecting motion, heat, sound, vibration, and changes in pressure; interrupting an electric or magnetic circuit; and disturbance of an energy field.

A facet of this service may be to detect electronic surveillance from another source, which could be a party attempting to obtain information about the investigator's client. In the corporate arena where information is a highly valued asset, competitors are tempted to eavesdrop for the purposes of acquiring trade secrets, business plans, client lists, research and development information, and plans for introduction of new products or services. Electronic surveillance for the purpose of detecting the adversary's unlawful and unethical attempts to obtain competitive information is often called TSCM (technical services countermeasures).

Electronic surveillance can be put to numerous uses: crime prevention and detection; intruder detection; and access control. The places of use can vary:

homes, offices, children care centers, manufacturing plants, warehouses, shipping terminals, banks, shopping malls, stores, hotels, entertainment venues, parks, and many, many more.

## Foot Surveillances

This technique, called "1-2" surveillance, is worked with two investigators on foot. Investigator 1 walks directly but discreetly behind the target while Investigator 2 takes up the rear, often from the opposite side of the street. If the target makes a turn, Investigator 1 continues straight ahead while Investigator 2 makes the turn. In so doing, 2 now becomes 1, and 1 moves into place at the far rear. These movements are pre-planned and require no signaling between the two investigators.

A three person investigative team on foot is called "1-2-3" surveillance technique and is appropriate when a closer surveillance on foot is required and several investigators are available to "bird dog" the target. Investigator 1 is behind the target, with Investigator 2 behind 1 on the same side of the street. Investigator 3 walks on the other side of the street. If the target turns left, 1 continues straight ahead, crosses the street, and picks up the trail. At this point, 1 becomes 3; 3 becomes 1, and 2 holds his position as the middle investigator.

However, if the target turns right, 1 continues across the street, 2 takes the 1 position; 3 takes the 2 or middle position, and 1 brings up the rear from the other side of the street in the 3 position

## Targets / Subjects

The targets or subjects of investigation may fall into one of the following categories:

- **Easy:** This individual is totally unaware and has no earthly idea he is being followed. Even if he looked directly at the person tailing him, he would not suspect a thing.
- **Suspicious:** This person will constantly look around, yet he doesn't pay attention to what he is seeing or is incapable of interpreting the details of the immediate surroundings. While he appears to be suspicious, he is actually unaware of the surveillance in progress. He appears to be guilty of something just by his behavior.
- **Amateur:** This person has an idea he is being followed, but does not know how it is being done and what he can do about it.
- **Pro:** This is the seasoned professional veteran. He is street smart; is

able to detect the surveillance; and routinely uses anti-surveillance tactics such as driving around in circles, pulling over, getting back into traffic, and going into a mall, hotel, or some other place with a back exit. He will leave his car and get in someone else's vehicle.

## Surveillance Tips

- A one-man surveillance is not nearly as effective as surveillance by two or more investigators.
- Never look directly into the eyes of the target.
- Don't break off the surveillance unnecessarily by being paranoid yourself, thinking that the target is aware of the surveillance.
- Break off the surveillance on the "third strike." If you think you have been spotted three times on the same surveillance, call it off for that occasion. Listen to your gut instincts and intuitions because they are usually correct. If you think the target knows you are there, he or she probably does.
- Show up for the surveillance prepared to deal with everything you might need for the next eight hours. You might need clothes to change into; health and comfort items; personal medicines; water and food; phone; camera; binocular, note taking supplies; foul weather gear; a full tank of gas; spending money; etc.
- Have a recent photo of the target.
- Scout the area and know the details of the geographical area where the surveillance is to occur such as the location of the target's home or office, routes into and out of the area, traffic flow, and the probability of inadvertent interference by police patrols.
- Inform the police of the surveillance only when it is necessary.

## INTERVIEWING TECHNIQUES

In pre-employment screening, the purpose of an interview is to verify information provided by the job applicant. Opinions and value judgments do not verify, and for that reason do not belong in a BI report. Questions that begin with, "Do you believe…" or "Is there a chance that…" are questions that prompt judgmental responses.

Negative questions also must be avoided; for example, "Do you know if Sandra ever shoplifted?" A question should be such that the answer is expected to be positive. If, however, the interviewee offers a piece of negative information without prompting, the PI has to pursue it. Follow-up questions might be:

"How long have you known Sandra?"

"What is your relationship with her?"

"Did you ever see her shoplift?"

"To the best of your knowledge, what stores did Sandra shoplift from?"

"To the best of your knowledge, how many times did Sandra shoplift?"

"Did she show anything that she shoplifted?"

"Did she ever offer to sell you shoplifted items?"

"Who else would know about this matter?"

The truthfulness of the interviewee becomes an issue when negative information is offered. Does the interviewee have an axe to grind? Does the body language of the interviewee suggest animosity? Through skillful questioning the PI can put down on paper what the interviewee is saying with body gestures, eye movements and voice inflections.

## Prohibited Topics

Questions cannot be asked nor discussions made in any manner concerning certain topics. "In any manner" means any communication mode—verbal and written—and by any person—employer and employer's agents. A private investigator is an agent of an employer and is therefore bound to entirely stay away from the prohibited topics. If the PI violates the prohibition, the employer is held responsible. If a PI wants repeat business with an employer/client, the prohibition will be respected. The prohibited topics are:

- Religion
- Age
- Marital status
- Number of children and number of times married
- Ethnicity
- Disabilities
- Sexual orientation
- Political leanings

While the PI cannot prevent an interviewee from bringing up a prohibited topic on his/her own initiative, the PI must immediately divert conversation away from it.

## Human Factors in Interviewing

### Evaluating the Witness

The personality and attitude of a witness needs to be analyzed and evaluated. The more knowledge of a witness that an investigator has, the easier it is to build a rapport and determine the best technique for interviewing. Finding something in common, same interests, or manner of asking questions may make a witness less uncomfortable and more willing to talk openly. (Personally, I get better results if I am non-threatening).

A background investigation of an important witness may reveal prior arrests, convictions, habits, hobbies, and other interests. The more you know about the witness the easier it will be to break any barriers.

Truthfulness and accuracy of information should be carefully assessed if it is observed that there is a sense of personal relationships among the parties involved (relatives, friends, co-workers, neighbors, acquaintances, etc.), and any connection they have with the offense or incident, place of occurrence, or other particulars involved in the case.

A PI needs to mentally prepare and be ready to react to the unexpected at all times. Encounters with individuals may be hostile or friendly, silent or communicative, knowledge of or lack of knowledge of facts, or truthful or lying. Preparation should also include reviewing the case and being familiar with all facts. Review the information about the person to be interviewed, and have an understanding of what information is needed to bring the case to a conclusion. Make a list of questions that need to be answered. Be prepared to rephrase questions to see if the same answer is given.

If possible, a tape recorder or camcorder should be used in order to make sure the facts are reported correctly. All statements should be written, dated, signed, and witnessed.

### Indifference, Fear, and Privacy

Many people are unwilling to cooperate in an investigation because they do not understand and are unfamiliar with investigative methods. Some are reluctant to become involved because they believe it is none of their business, or they may not think the accused person deserves their help, or they may fear retaliation. The average person prefers not to become involved.

## Perception

Witnesses may not all agree on what happened. Some may see or hear things different from others. Not all witnesses are going to be accurate. They may not intentionally give incorrect statements, but based on their perception they report what they believe to have happened.

It is better to discover a perception problem during the investigation rather than during a trial. It should be noted that a person being interviewed has a physical disability that may impair their senses. It should be noted that a witness has a vision or hearing problem. It is not uncommon for witnesses to have:
- A difference in ability to see, hear, smell, feel, and taste.
- Visual differences in relation to an incident at the time it occurred. Both distance and geographical terrain may become visually impaired.
- A difference in times between occurrence and interview.
- A difference in the number and nature of events.

## Memory Erosion

Memory fades and becomes cloudy and discolored both consciously and unconsciously and is primarily influenced by what the witness is exposed to after the incident.

If a witness is exposed to remarks made by other witnesses or media it may tend to fill in gaps or distort the memory with details of which there is no direct knowledge.

## Prejudice

Expect some witnesses to be biased and prejudiced in some way to some degree. In order to keep information from biased distortion is to ask for specific, detailed answers. Then rephrase and repeat the same questions to see if the answers are the same. If given an opportunity to talk in general someone who is prejudiced, will make partially accurate and misleading statements.

## Self-Interest

Even if a victim or witness is cooperative, they may not always have reliable information. A victim with an insurance claim may inflate the severity of an injury or offense and be overly anxious to please the investigator.

## Stress

A person who is subjected to a traumatic, stressful, exciting, or injurious event after observing an incident is likely to forget details.

# CHAPTER IX

# STATE PI LAWS and LICENSING REQUIREMENTS, & PI ASSOCIATIONS

*Note: Not all laws are included but may be found on the web sites of these states.*

## Alabama

Alabama Department of Revenue
50 North Ripley Street
Montgomery, AL 36132
(334) 242-1170

State requirements:
**40-12-93 Detective Agencies**

Each person engaged in the business of operating a detective agency, or each company or corporation doing business as such in this State, shall pay a license tax of:

License Amount $150.00

Fee $1.00

Total $151.00

Each person so engaged who also solicits or receives notes or accounts for collection shall pay an additional license tax of:

License $150.00

Fee $0.00

Total $150.00

- An agency is not required to purchase a license in each county they operate in, only the counties where an office is maintained.

- An out-of-state agency sending a detective to do investigative work in this state and not maintaining an office, answering service, etc., whereby the general public could contact them to obtain services, would not require a license.

- Private investigators and security guards should contact the local authorities (sheriff or city hall) when doing business in a municipality as most municipalities require a license.

- A company providing guard service only is not required to procure this license.

- Part-time detectives are required to procure this license.

http://www.ador.state.al.us/licenses/sec093.html
http://www.revenue.alabama.gov/ador_results.cfm

Association: http://fyiinvestigators.bizland.com/apia/

## Alaska
State requirements:
Licensing Authority:
City of Fairbanks
City Clerk's Office
800 Cushman Street
Fairbanks, AK  99701-4615
(907) 459-6715
(907) 459-6710 fax
Email clcolp@ci.fairbanks.ak.us

License/Exam Fees:

Application $50

License $25

Renewal application $25

Annual license renewal $25

Surety bond $5,000

New licenses and renewals are issued for 1 year each.

Licensing Requirements:

- Applicant must be a U.S. citizen, of good moral character, and have never been convicted of any felony or crime of moral turpitude.

- Applications must be accompanied by a surety bond, a copy of applicants State of Alaska business license, a copy of applicants driver's license, current driving record and criminal background report.

- The applicant will need to provide a criminal history from each state of residency. The Alaska report must be dated the same date that the application is submitted.

http://www.labor.state.ak.us/

Association: http://www.akinvestigators.com/

## Arizona
Dept. of Public Safety, Licensing
P. O. Box 6328
Phoenix, AZ  85005
(602) 223-2120
(602) 223-2398 fax

State requirements:
http://www.dps.state.az.us/license/privateinvestigator/default.asp
(602) 223-2361

Association: http://www.aalpi.org/

## Arkansas
Arkansas Board of Private Investigators & Private Security Agencies
#1 State Police Plaza Drive
Little Rock, Arkansas  72209
(501) 618-8600

State requirements:
**Arkansas Statute 5-77-301**
**Private Investigators and Alarm Installation/Monitoring**

The Arkansas Private Investigators and Private Security Agencies Act (17-40-101-107 & other associated statutes) designates the Arkansas State Police as an administering agency to regulate private investigators, private security agencies and individuals or businesses offering security or investigative services.

Through the Arkansas Board of Private Investigators and Private Security Agencies, the Arkansas State Police administers a variety of licensing functions that involve the private security and investigation industry.

Should you have questions regarding those individuals or companies regulated by the State Police or if you are seeking assistance in obtaining a license, you may e-mail the PI/Alarm License Administrator or telephone the Regulatory Services office at (501) 618-8600.

http://www.asp.state.ar.us/pl/pl.html

Association: http://www.aappi.org/

## California
Licensing Division
Bureau of Security and Investigative Services
400 R Street
Sacramento, CA 95814
(800) 952-5210

State requirements:
**Private Investigator (Fact Sheet)**

**Private Investigator / Qualified Manager**

**Requirements for Licensure**
A private investigator is an individual who (1) investigates crimes, (2) investigates the identity, business, occupation, character, etc., of a person, (3) investigates the location of lost or stolen property, (4) investigates the cause of fires, losses, accidents, damage or injury, or (5) secures evidence for use in court. Private investigators may protect persons only if such services are incidental to an investigation; they may not protect property. An individual, partnership, or corporation licensed as a private investigator may employ a qualified manager to manage the business on a day-to-day basis. To be eligible to apply for licensure as a private investigator/qualified manager, you must meet the following requirements:

- Be 18 or older.

- Undergo a criminal history background check through the California Department of Justice (DOJ) and the Federal Bureau of Investigation (FBI). Have three years (2,000 hours each year, totaling 6,000 hours) of compensated experience in investigative work; or a law or police science degree plus two years (4,000 hours) of experience; or an AA degree in police science, criminal law, or justice and 2-1/2 years (5,000 hours) of experience. Experience must be certified by your employer and have been received while you were employed as a sworn law enforcement officer, military police officer, insurance adjuster, employee of a licensed PI or repossessor, or arson investigator for a public fire suppression agency. (Work as a process server, public records researcher, custodial attendant for a law enforcement agency, bailiff, agent who collects debts in writing or by telephone after the debtor has been located, or person who repossesses property after it has been located is not considered qualifying experience.)

- Pass a two-hour multiple-choice examination covering laws and regulations, terminology, civil and criminal liability, evidence handling, undercover investigations and surveillance. A copy of the Private Investigator Act will be sent to you; and

- Upon notification that you have passed the examination, you must submit a licensing fee of $175 to the Bureau of Security and Investigative Services, P.O. Box 989002, West Sacramento, CA 95798-9002.

To apply for a Private Investigator license, submit your completed application, two recent passport-quality photographs, a $50 application fee and a Private Investigator Live Scan form signed by the Live Scan Operator. A $32 DOJ fingerprint processing fee and a $24 FBI Fingerprint processing fee must be paid for each applicant at the Live Scan site. Send the application package to the Bureau of Security and Investigative Services, P.O. Box 989002, West Sacramento, CA 95798-9002.

### Firearm Permit

Whether you work as a private investigator or qualified manager, you may not carry a gun on duty without having been issued a firearm permit by the Department of Consumer Affairs. To apply for a firearm permit, you must complete:

- A course in the Power to Arrest. The three-hour training covers responsibilities and ethics in citizen arrest, relationship with police, limitations on Power to Arrest, restrictions on searches and seizures, criminal and civil liabilities, terrorism, code of ethics and personal and employer liability. The training and exam may be administered by any licensee.

- A course in the carrying and use of firearms. The 14-hour (8 hours classroom, 6 hours range) training course covers moral and legal aspects, firearms nomenclature, weapons handling and shooting fundamentals, emergency procedures and range training. The course must be given by a Bureau-certified firearms training instructor at a Bureau-certified training facility. Written and range exams are administered at the end of the course. Costs of training are determined by the training facility. For a list of state-licensed training schools, call (800) 952-5210; and

- Be a citizen of the United States or have permanent legal alien status.

Submit a firearm permit application, an $80 application fee and a Private Investigator License w/Firearm Permit Live Scan form signed by the Live Scan Operator. A $28 Firearm Eligibility application, $32 DOJ fingerprint processing fee and $24 FBI fingerprint processing fee must be paid for each applicant at the Live Scan site. Send the application package to the Bureau of Security and Investigative Services, P.O. Box 989002, West Sacramento, CA 95798-9002.

**Note:** a firearms qualification card expires two years from the date of issuance. An applicant must requalify four times during the life of the permit: twice during the first year after the date of issuance, and twice during the second year. Requalifications must be at least four months apart.

http://www.dca.ca.gov/bsis/bsispi.htm

Association: http://www.cali-pi.org/

## Colorado
State requirements: No license required

Association: http://www.ppiac.org/

## Connecticut
Department of Public Safety
Division of State Police
294 Colony Street
Meriden, CT  06450-2098
(800) 392-2122

State requirements:
**Special Licensing and Firearms**
The Special License and Firearms Unit (SLFU) is responsible for the issuance of state pistol permits, oversight and regulation of firearm sale transactions, and issuance of licenses to professional bail bondsman, private security companies, private investigators, and bail enforcement agents (BEA).

The unit is located at Connecticut State Police Headquarters in Middletown, CT. We also have a satellite office at Troop G in Bridgeport to process pistol permit applications and renewal paperwork.

The unit is also responsible for investigating violations of state law relating to the purchase, sale and transfer of firearms, and violations of statutes relating to the various professional licenses it issues

State of Connecticut
Department of Public Safety
Special Licensing and Firearms
1111 Country Club Road
Middletown, CT  06457
(860) 685-8290

http://www.ct.gov/dps/cwp/view.asp?a=2158&Q=294512&dpsNav_GID=16
58&dpsNav=|

Association: http://users.ntplx.net/~calpi/

**Delaware**
Detective Licensing
Delaware State Police
P. O. Box 430
Dover, DE  19903
(302) 736-5900

State requirements:

The Detective Licensing Section is comprised of two uniform employees and one civilian employee who are responsible for the licensing and regulation of the following industries:

- private security agencies and their employees
- private investigative agencies and their employees
- security systems & protective services agencies and their employees
- non-state constables
- bail enforcement agents

The Detective Licensing Section instructed two Bail Enforcement Agent (BEA) classes in 2003. The Legislation mandates the training in order to become a licensed BEA. All Bail Enforcement Agents are required to receive training in the following fields:

- The Constitution and Bill of Rights
- Laws of Arrest
- Laws of Search & Seizure of Persons Wanted
- Police Jurisdiction
- Use of Deadly Force

- Title 24 Chapter 55
- Promulgated Rules & Regulations

During 2003, the section conducted 288 sight inspections of security guards, which consists of checking for their license, wearing of the proper uniform, etc. There was one (1) security guard/private investigative agency office inspection, looking for any inconsistencies with the Law and the Rules & Regulations. There was a total of 3,351 security guards/private investigators, armored car guards, alarm personnel, constables, and bail enforcement agents IDs issued as new or renewals. These IDs consist of criminal history checks and photo ID cards made. A total of 226 Private Investigative/Private Security and Security Systems & Protective Services Agency Licenses issued as new or renewals. These licenses consist of criminal history checks of all owners/partners/corporate officers/license holders/Delaware managers, all bonds and liabilities required, and licenses made. In addition, sixteen DELJIS violation investigations have been conducted.

Lt. Charles Rynkowski is also responsible for SBI North that consists of three (3) civilian employees. This office opened full-time in September 2001 at Newport and moved to Troop 2 on July 31, 2003. They provide fingerprinting for customers desiring criminal history checks, processing of security personnel for ID cards (Fridays Only), and registering change of address for sex offenders – all for New Castle County. There were a total of 11,407 customers fingerprinted in 2003.

http://www.state.de.us/dsp/detlic.htm

Association:
Delaware Association of Detective Agencies
100 N Maryland Avenue
Wilmington DE  19804
(302) 652-2700

**District of Columbia**
Security Officers Management Branch
Metro Police
Security Unit 2000
14th St. NW
Washington, DC  20009
(202) 671-0500

<u>**Florida**</u>
Florida Department of Agriculture and Consumer Services
Division of Licensing
Bureau of License Issuance
P.O. Box 6687
Tallahassee, FL 32314-6687
(850) 488-5381

State requirements:
**For Individuals**

- "C"– Private Investigator

- "CC"– Private Investigator Intern

- "M" or "MA"– Manager of a Private Investigative Agency

**For Agencies**

- "A"– Private Investigative Agency

- "AA"– Private Investigative Agency Branch Office

A private investigator is any individual or agency who, for consideration, advertises as providing or performs the following activities. Individuals or agencies providing or advertising as providing these services for consideration must be licensed.

- Subcontracting with the government to determine crimes or wrongs done or threatened against the United States

- Determining the identity, habits, conduct, movements, whereabouts, affiliations, associations, transactions, reputation or character of any society, person, or group of persons

- The credibility of witnesses or other persons

- The whereabouts of missing persons, owners of abandoned or escheated property, or heirs to estates

- The location or recovery of lost or stolen property

- The causes or origin of fires, libels, slanders, losses, accidents, damage, or injuries to real or personal property

- Securing evidence to be used before investigating committees or boards of award or arbitration or trial of civil or criminal cases

Applications are available by online request or by contacting any of the regional offices.

Any person applying for a license must:

- Be at least 18 years of age
- <u>Be a citizen of the United States or a legal resident of the United States or have been granted authority to work by the U.S. Citizenship and Immigration Services</u>
- Have no disqualifying criminal history
- Be of good moral character
- Have no disqualifying history of mental illness or alcohol or controlled substance abuse

The applicant must provide the following:

- Name
- Date of birth
- Social security number
- Place of birth
- Residence addresses for the past five years
- Occupations for the past five years
- Statement of all criminal convictions
- Statement whether he or she has been adjudicated incompetent or committed to a mental institution
- Statement regarding any history of alcohol or controlled substance abuse
- Two full-face color photographs
- Full set of prints on the Division's fingerprint card
- Personal inquiry waiver
- Appropriate fees

When the application is received, the Florida Department of Law Enforcement and the Federal Bureau of Investigation perform a criminal history record check to determine if the applicant has a criminal history which will disqualify him or her from licensure.

http://licgweb.doacs.state.fl.us/investigations/index.html

Associations:
Private Investigator's Association of Florida, Inc. (PIAF)

Investigative Information Services, Inc
"The Florida Investigator"
PO Box 620712
Orlando, FL 32862-0712
(407) 282-3735
(407) 282-1301 fax
http://www.piaf.org/

Florida Association of Licensed Investigators (FALI)
P.O. Box 12483
Tallahassee, FL 32317
http://www.fali.com/

South Florida Investigator's Association, Inc. (SFIA)
P.O. Box 891
Ft. Lauderdale FL 33302
(561) 625-8771
http://www.webcircle.com/users/sfia/
heatgain@mindspring.com

Florida Association of Licensed Recovery Agents (FALRA)
(800) 99-FALRA
http://www.falra.org/
kelly@falra.org

## Georgia
State Board of Private Security Agencies
237 Coliseum Drive
Macon, GA 31217-3858
(478) 207-1460

State requirements:
**How do I become licensed as a private investigator in Georgia?**

Licenses in Georgia are issued only to companies. The company must have an individual, either the owner, a partner, or an officer of the corporation or LLC, who is qualified by experience or education to be the holder of the license for the company. If you are interested in opening your own company, please refer to the Company License Information for specific details regarding qualifications and requirements.

**What are the experience and education requirements for qualifying for a private detective company license?**

Briefly, the experience required is two years, either in law enforcement, or as a registered private detective employed by a licensed private detective company. The education required is a four-year degree from an accredited college or university in Criminal Justice, or a related field of study.

**I am not interested in opening my own company; I just want to work as a private investigator for a company. What requirements do I have to meet to be employed as a private investigator?**

If you are interested in becoming employed as an investigator with a licensed company, you may be hired by a company without an experience requirement by the Board, if you are at least 18 years of age, and you meet the minimum requirements established by the Board, as detailed in O.C.G.A. 43-38-7. The company is responsible for your training by a Board-approved instructor; however, you may attend Board-approved training classes on your own prior to being hired by a licensed company. The company is also responsible for submitting an Application for Employee Registration on your behalf within 30 days of your hiring.

**I am a veteran law enforcement officer. Do I have to take the exam to become licensed as a private detective or security company?**

All applicants must take the exam for Private Detective &/or Security. There are no exceptions for experience or licensure in other states.

**Does the Private Detective & Security Agencies Board reciprocate with other states?**

The Board does not reciprocate with any other state for licensure. All applicants for company licensure in Georgia must take the examination for Private Detective &/or Security, whether or not they are licensed in another state. The Board has agreements with certain states for limited license recognition.

**What is a Limited License Recognition Agreement?**

The agreement between Georgia and other states allows a licensed private investigator in another state to enter into Georgia for a period not to exceed 30 days per case per year, in order to complete a case that originated in the state of licensure. A Georgia-licensed investigator would also be able to enter into the other state to perform work for a 30-day period on a case that originated in Georgia.

**With which states does Georgia have the Limited License Recognition Agreement?**

Currently, the Board has Limited License Recognition Agreements with Florida, North Carolina, Louisiana, California, Oklahoma, Virginia, and Tennessee.

**I am presently employed as a private investigator (or security guard) with a licensed company. How do I transfer my license?**

In order to work as a private investigator or armed security guard for another licensed company, the company will need to submit an Application for Employee Registration on your behalf, just as the company did with whom you are presently employed. The complete application must be submitted, including the fingerprint cards. If you will no longer be employed with the present company, you must turn in your registration to the company upon termination of your employment.

**Can I work for more than one company at the same time as a private investigator or security guard?**

You may be employed by more than one company at the same time. Each company must submit an Application for Employee Registration on your behalf.

**What are the fees for getting a license?**

Please refer to the Fee Schedule for a current listing of the various fees.

**When will I know if I am approved to take the Private Detective &/or Security Exam?**

Once the Board approves candidates for examination, the approved candidates will be notified by the Exam Section within two weeks of the scheduled exam date. The notification will specify the date, time, and place of the exam, as well as any instructions for the candidate. Candidates who were not approved for the exam will be notified within two weeks after the Board meeting.

**When is the next Private Detective &/or Security Exam?**

Please refer to the Examination Information page of our website for exam dates and information.

**What study materials are available to prepare for the exam?**

No study materials are provided by the Board, other than the Georgia Law and Board Rules.

**Can a private detective or security guard use the weapon permit issued by the Probate Court while on duty?**

No, the weapon permit issued by the Probate Court is not a valid permit while a private investigator or security guard is on duty. You must have a weapon permit issued by the Board to carry a weapon while on duty.

http://www.ganet.org/cgi/bin/pub/ocode/ocgsearch?docname=OCode/G/43/38/3

## Hawaii
Board of Private Detectives & Guards
DCCA, PVL, Licensing Branch
1010 Richards Street
P.O. Box 3469
Honolulu, HI  96801
(808) 586-3000 or (808) 586-2701

Association:
Investigative & Security Society of Hawaii
1000 Bishop Street No 608
Honolulu HI  96813
(808) 526-2002

## Idaho
Private Detective Licensing Board
Rm 1021
Indiana Government Center North
Indianapolis, IN  46204-2246
(317) 232-2980

State requirements: No license required.

Association: http://www.ipiai.org/

**Illinois**
Illinois Department of Professional Regulation
320 West Washington Street, 3rd Floor
Springfield, IL  62786

State requirements:
**Professions and Occupations**
**(225 ILCS 447/) Private Detective, Private Alarm, Private Security, and Locksmith Act of 2004.**
225 ILCS 447/Art. 15 heading
Article 15. Private Detectives.
(225 ILCS 447/15-5)
(Section scheduled to be repealed on January 1, 2014)
Sec. 15-5. Exemptions; private detective. The provisions of this Act relating to the licensure of private detectives do not apply to any of the following:

(1) An employee of the United States, Illinois, or a political subdivision of either while the employee is engaged in the performance of his or her official duties within the scope of his or her employment. However, any such person who offers his or her services as a private detective or uses a similar title when these services are performed for compensation or other consideration, whether received directly or indirectly, is subject to this Act.

(2) A person, firm, or other entity engaged exclusively in tracing and compiling lineage or ancestry who does not hold himself or herself out to be a private detective.

(3) A person engaged exclusively in obtaining and furnishing information as to the financial rating or creditworthiness of persons or a person who provides reports in connection with (i) consumer credit transactions, (ii) information for employment purposes, or (iii) information for the underwriting of consumer insurance.

(4) Insurance adjusters employed or under contract as adjusters who engage in no other investigative activities other than those directly connected with adjustment of claims against an insurance company or a self-insured entity by which they are employed or with which they have a contract. No insurance adjuster or company may use the term "investigation" or any derivative thereof, in its name or in its advertising.

(Source: P.A. 93-438, eff. 8-5-03.)

(225 ILCS 447/15-10)
(Section scheduled to be repealed January 1, 2014)
Sec. 15-10. Qualifications for licensure as a private detective.

(a) A person is qualified for licensure as a private detective if he or she meets all of the following requirements:

(1) Is at least 21 years of age.

(2) Has not been convicted of any felony in any jurisdiction or at least 10 years have elapsed since the time of full discharge from a sentence imposed for a felony conviction.

(3) Is of good moral character. Good character is a continuing requirement of licensure. Conviction of crimes other than felonies may be used in determining moral character, but shall not constitute an absolute bar to licensure.

(4) Has not been declared by any court of competent jurisdiction to be incompetent by reason of mental or physical defect or disease, unless a court has subsequently declared him or her to be competent.

(5) Is not suffering from dependence on alcohol or from narcotic addiction or dependence.

(225 ILCS 447/15-15)
(Section scheduled to be repealed on January 1, 2014)
Sec. 15-15. Qualifications for licensure as a private detective agency.

(a) Upon receipt of the required fee and proof that the applicant has a full-time Illinois licensed private detective-in-charge, which is a continuing requirement for agency licensure, the Department shall issue a license as a private detective agency to any of the following:

(1) An individual who submits an application and is a licensed private detective under this Act.

(2) A firm that submits an application and all of the members of the firm are licensed private detectives under this Act.

(3) A corporation or limited liability company doing business in Illinois that is authorized by its articles of incorporation or organization to engage in the business of conducting a private detective agency, provided at least one full-time executive employee is licensed as a private detective under this Act and all unlicensed officers and

directors of the corporation or limited liability company are determined by the Department to be persons of good moral character.

(b) No private detective may be the licensee-in-charge for more than one private detective agency. Upon written request by a representative of an agency, within 10 days after the loss of a licensee-in-charge of an agency because of the death of that individual or because of the termination of the employment of that individual, the Department shall issue a temporary certificate of authority allowing the continuing operation of the licensed agency. No temporary certificate of authority shall be valid for more than 90 days. An extension of an additional 90 days may be granted upon written request by the representative of the agency. Not more than 2 extensions may be granted to any agency. No temporary permit shall be issued for a loss of the licensee-in-charge because of disciplinary action by the Department related to his or her conduct on behalf of the agency.

(Source: P.A. 93-438, eff. 8-5-03.)

(225 ILCS 447/15-25)
(Section scheduled to be repealed on January 1, 2014)
Sec. 15-25. Training; private detective and employees.

(a) Registered employees of a private detective agency shall complete, within 30 days of their employment, a minimum of 20 hours of training provided by a qualified instructor. The substance of the training shall be related to the work performed by the registered employee.

(b) It is the responsibility of the employer to certify, on a form provided by the Department, that the employee has successfully completed the training. The form shall be a permanent record of training completed by the employee and shall be placed in the employee's file with the employer for the period the employee remains with the employer. An agency may place a notarized copy of the Department form in lieu of the original into the permanent employee registration card file. The original form shall be given to the employee when his or her employment is terminated. Failure to return the original form to the employee is grounds for disciplinary action. The employee shall not be required to repeat the required training once the employee has been issued the form. An employer may provide or require additional training.

(c) Any certification of completion of the 20-hour basic training issued under the Private Detective, Private Alarm, Private Security, and Locksmith Act of 1993 or any prior Act shall be accepted as proof of training under this Act.

(Source: P.A. 93-438, eff. 8-5-03.)

http://www.idfpr.com/dpr/WHO/dtct.asp

Association:
http://www.idfpr.com/
http://www.the-adi.com/

## Indiana
Private Detective Licensing Board
100 N. Senae Avenue, Rm 1021
Indiana Government Center North
Indianapolis, IN  46204-2246
(317) 232-2980

State requirements:
Applications may be submitting either online or in writing at:
Indiana Professional Licensing Agency
Attn: Private Detectives Licensing Board
402 West Washington Street, Room W072
Indianapolis, IN  46204

Please provide your name, full mailing address, and indicate for which profession you need an application.

http://www.in.gov/pla/
Email: pla11@pla.in.gov

Association: http://www.iapi.net/

## Iowa
Administrative Services Division, Iowa Department of Public Safety
Wallace State Office Bldg..
Des Moines, IA  50319
(515) 281-3211

State requirements:
**80A.3 License required.**
A person shall not operate a private investigation business or private security

business or employ persons in the operation of such a business unless the person is licensed by the commissioner. A license issued under this chapter expires two years from the date issued.
84 Acts, ch 1235, § 3

### 80A.4 License requirements.

1. Applications for a license or license renewal shall be submitted to the commissioner in the form the commissioner prescribes. A license shall not be issued unless the applicant:

    a. Is eighteen years of age or older.

    b. Is not a peace officer.

    c. Has never been convicted of a felony or aggravated misdemeanor.

    d. Is not addicted to the use of alcohol or a controlled substance.

    e. Does not have a history of repeated acts of violence.

    f. Is of good moral character and has not been judged guilty of a crime involving moral turpitude.

    g. Has not been convicted of a crime described in section 708.3, 708.4, 708.5, 708.6, 708.8, or 708.9.

    h. Has not been convicted of illegally using, carrying or possessing a dangerous weapon.

    i. Has not been convicted of fraud.

    j. Complies with other qualifications and requirements the commissioner adopts by rule.

2. If the applicant is a corporation, the requirements of subsection 1 apply to the president and to each officer, commissioner or employee who is actively involved in the licensed business in Iowa. If the applicant is a partnership or association, the requirements of subsection 1 apply to each partner or association member.

3. Each employee of an applicant or licensee shall possess the same qualifications required by subsection 1 of this section for a licensee.
84 Acts, ch 1235, § 4; 85 Acts, ch 56, §1

### 80A.5 Licensee fee.

An applicant for a license shall deposit with each application the fee for the license. If the application is approved the deposited amount shall be applied on the license fee. If the application is disapproved, the deposited amount shall be refunded to the applicant. The fee for a two-year private investigative agency and private security agency license is one hundred dollars.
84 Acts, ch 1235, § 5

### 80A.6 Display of license.
A private investigation agency and private security agency shall conspicuously display the license in the principal place of business of the agency.
84 Acts, ch 1235, § 6

### 80A.7 Identification cards.
The department shall issue to each licensee and to each employee of the licensee an identification card in a form approved by the commissioner. The application for a permanent identification card shall include a temporary identification card valid for fourteen days from the date of receipt of the application by the applicant. It is unlawful for an agency licensed under this chapter to employ a person to act in the private investigation business or private security business unless the person has in the person's immediate possession an identification card issued under this section.

The licensee is responsible for the use of identification cards by the licensee's employees and shall return an employee's card to the department upon termination of the employee's service. Identification cards remain the property of the department. The fee for each card is ten dollars.

A county sheriff may issue temporary identification cards valid for fourteen days to a person employed by an agency licensed as a private security business or private investigation business on a temporary basis in the county. The fee for each card is five dollars. The form of the temporary identification cards shall be approved by the commissioner.
84 Acts, ch 1235, § 7; 85 Acts, ch 56, §2; 89 Acts, ch 112, §1

### 80A.8 Duplicate license.
A duplicate license shall be issued by the commissioner upon the payment of a fee in the amount of five dollars and upon receiving for filing, in the form prescribed, a statement under oath that the original license has been lost or destroyed and that, if the original license is recovered, the original or the duplicate will be returned immediately to the director for cancellation.
84 Acts, ch 1235, § 8

### 80A.9 Badges-uniforms.
A licensee or an employee of a licensee shall not use a badge in connection with the activities of the licensee's business unless the badge has been prescribed or approved by the commissioner. A licensee or an employee of a licensee shall not use an identification card other than the card issued by the department or make a statement with the intent to give the impression that the licensee or employee is a peace officer.

A uniform worn by a licensee or employee of a licensee shall conform with rules adopted by the commissioner.
84 Acts, ch 1235, § 9

### 80A.10 Licensee's bond.
A license shall not be issued unless the applicant files with the department a surety bond in an amount of five thousand dollars in the case of an agency licensed to conduct only a private security business or a private investigation business, or in the amount of ten thousand dollars in the case of an agency licensed to conduct both. The bond shall be issued by a surety company authorized to do business in this state and shall be conditioned on the faithful, lawful, and honest conduct of the applicant and those employed by the applicant in carrying on the business licensed. The bond shall provide that a person injured by a breach of the conditions of the bond may bring an action on the bond to recover legal damages suffered by reason of the breach. However, the aggregate liability of the surety for all damages shall not exceed the amount of the bond. Bonds issued and filed with the department shall remain in force and effect until the surety has terminated future liability by a written thirty days' notice to the department.
84 Acts, ch 1235, § 10; 85 Acts, ch 56, §3

### 80A.10A Licensee's proof of financial responsibility.
A license shall not be issued unless the applicant furnishes proof acceptable to the commissioner of the applicant's ability to respond in damages for liability on account of accidents or wrongdoings occurring subsequent to the effective date of the proof, arising out of the ownership and operation of a private security business or a private investigation business.
85 Acts, ch 56, §5

### 80A.11 Written report.
The licensee shall furnish, upon the client's request, a written report describing all the work performed by the licensee for that client.
84 Acts, ch 1235, § 11

### 80A.12 Refusal, suspension or revocation.
The commissioner may refuse to issue, or may suspend or revoke a license issued, for any of the following reasons:

1. Fraud in applying for or obtaining a license.

2. Violation of any of the provisions of this chapter.

3. If a licensee or employee of a licensee has been adjudged guilty of a crime involving moral turpitude, a felony, or an aggravated misdemeanor.

4. If a licensee willfully divulges to an unauthorized person information obtained by the licensee in the course of the licensed business.

5. Upon the disqualification or insolvency of the surety on the licensee's bond, unless the licensee files a new bond with sufficient surety within fifteen days of the receipt of notice from the commissioner.

6. If the applicant for a license or licensee or employee of a licensee fails to meet or retain any of the other qualifications provided in section 80A.4.

7. If the applicant for a license or licensee knowingly makes a false statement or knowingly conceals a material fact or otherwise commits perjury in an original application or a renewal application.

8. Willful failure or refusal to render to a client services contracted for and for which compensation has been paid or tendered in accordance with the contract. 84 Acts, ch 1235, § 12; 85 Acts, ch 56, § 4; 85 Acts, ch 67, §9

## 80A.13 Campus weapon requirements.
An individual employed by a college or university, or by a private security business holding a contract with a college or university, who performs private security duties on a college or university campus and who carries a weapon while performing these duties shall meet all of the following requirements:

1. File with the sheriff of the county in which the campus is located evidence that the individual has successfully completed an approved firearms training program under section 724.9. This requirement does not apply to armored car personnel.

2. Possess a permit to carry weapons issued by the sheriff of the county in which the campus is located under sections 724.6 through 724.11. This requirement does not apply to armored car personnel.

3. File with the sheriff of the county in which the campus is located a sworn affidavit from the employer outlining the nature of the duties to be performed and justification of the need to go armed.
84 Acts, ch 1235, § 13; 85 Acts, ch 56, §7

## 80A.14 Deposit of fees.
Fees received by the commissioner shall be paid to the treasurer of state and deposited in the operating account of the department to offset the cost of administering this chapter. Any unspent balance as of June 30 of each year shall

revert to the general fund as provided by section 8.33.
84 Acts, ch 1235, § 14

### 80A.15 Rules.
The commissioner may adopt administrative rules pursuant to chapter 17A to carry out this chapter
84 Acts, ch 1235, § 15

### 80A.16 Penalties.
A person who violates any of the provisions of this chapter where no other penalty is provided is guilty of a simple misdemeanor. A person who makes a false statement or representation in an application or statement filed with the commissioner, as required by this chapter, or a person who falsely states or represents that the person has been or is a private investigator or private security agent or advertises as such is guilty of a fraudulent practice. A person who engages in a private investigation or private security business as defined in this chapter, without possessing a current valid license as provided by this chapter, is guilty of a serious misdemeanor.
84 Acts, ch 1235, § 16

### 80A.17 Confidential records.
1. All complaint files, investigation files, other investigation reports, and other investigative information in the possession of the department or its employees or agents which relate to licensee discipline are privileged and confidential except that they are subject to discovery, subpoena, or other means of legal compulsion for their release to a person other than the licensee, and are admissible in evidence in a judicial or administrative proceeding other than a proceeding involving licensee discipline. In addition, investigative information in the possession of the department's employees or agents which relates to licensee discipline may be disclosed to the appropriate licensing authority in another state, the District of Columbia, or a territory or country in which the licensee is licensed or has applied for a license. If the investigative information in the possession of the department indicates a crime has been committed, the information shall be reported to the proper law enforcement agency. A final written decision and finding of fact of the department in a disciplinary proceeding is a public record.

Pursuant to section 17A.19, subsection 6, the department, upon an appeal by the licensee of the decision by the department shall transmit the entire record of the contested case to the reviewing court.

Notwithstanding section 17A.19, subsection 6, if a waiver of privilege has been involuntary and evidence has been received at a disciplinary hearing, the court shall order withheld the identity of the individual whose privilege was waived.

2. Lists of employees of a licensed agency and their personal histories shall be held as confidential. However, the lists of the names of the licensed agencies, their owners, corporate officers and directors shall be held as public records. The commissioner may confirm that a specific individual is an employee of a licensed agency upon request and may make lists of licensed agencies' employees available to law enforcement agencies.
85 Acts, ch 56, §6

## 80A.18 Reciprocity-fee.
A person who holds a valid license to act as a private investigator or as a private security officer issued by a proper authority of another state, based on requirements and qualifications similar to the requirements of this chapter, may be issued a temporary permit to so act in this state, if the person's licensing jurisdiction extends by reciprocity similar privileges to a person licensed to act as a private investigator or private security officer licensed by this state. Any reciprocal agreement approved by the commissioner shall provide that any misconduct in the state issuing the temporary permit will be dealt with in the licensing jurisdiction as though the violation occurred in that jurisdiction. The commissioner shall adopt by rule a fee for the issuance of a temporary permit under this section. The fee shall be based on the cost of administering this section but shall not exceed one hundred dollars per year.
88 Acts, ch 1056, §1

www.state.ia.us/government/dps/iowacode/cd9780a.htm

Association: http://www.iowa-investigators.com/

## Kansas
Kansas Bureau of Investigation
1620 SW Tyler
Topeka, KS 66612
(785) 296-8200

State requirements:
### KBI PI Licensing Verification, Kansas Statutes

Kansas Statute 75-7b01 through 75-7b23 is known as the 'Private Detective Licensing Act'. These are the statutes that govern Private Detective Licensure in Kansas.

If you have questions please send an e-mail to Private.Investigator@ kbi.state.ks.us or call the Private Detective Licensing Unit 785-296-4436.

Visit the Kansas Legislature to view the statutes below.

- Statute 75-7b01 Definitions.

- Statute 75-7b02 Licensure required; law enforcement officers ineligible for license.

- Statute 75-7b03 Exemptions from licensure.

- Statute 75-7b04 Licensure; application; references; qualifications; summary proceedings; grounds for denial of license.

- Statute 75-7b05 License, initial or renewal; fee set by attorney general.

- Statute 75-7b06 License; form; display; pocket card; new officer or partner, licensure.

- Statute 75-7b07 License renewal; license not assignable.

- Statute 75-7b08 Information confidential, exceptions; prohibited acts.

- Statute 75-7b09 Record of employees; address of principal place of business to be filed.

- Statute 75-7b10 Soliciting or advertising for business, contents; advertising or conducting business except at principal or branch office prohibited; closing or changing branch office.

- Statute 75-7b11 Surety bond, liability insurance or deposit with treasurer; requirements.

- Statute 75-7b12 Same; failure to maintain on file; term of bond.

- Statute 75-7b13 Suspension or revocation of license; grounds; hearing; conviction defined, evidence; misuse of a firearm permit badge.

- Statute 75-7b14

- Statute 75-7b15 Records and reports; inspection, enforcement and investigation by attorney general; subpoena; unlawful acts; misdemeanor.

- Statute 75-7b16

- Statute 75-7b17 Firearms permit; expiration of; qualifications; application; discharge of firearm, report; suspension or revocation of permit; liability of licensee; firearm permit badge.

- Statute 75-7b18 Attorney general granted exclusive jurisdiction over licensing and regulation of detectives and agencies; cities prohibited from licensing or regulation; rules and regulations.

- Statute 75-7b19 Falsification of fingerprints or photographs; violation of act; penalties.

- Statute 75-7b20 Licensure; examination; interview; investigation.

- Statute 75-7b21 Trainers, firearm handling and use of force; certification; qualifications; fee; renewal.

- Statute 75-7b22 Fees for regulation of private detectives; maximum limitations established; set by attorney general.

- Statute 75-7b23 Private detective fee fund; receipts and expenditures.

https://www.accesskansas.org/kbi/pi_verify/statutes.html

Association: http://www.k-a-l-i.org/

## Kentucky
State requirements:
http://finance.ky.gov/NR/rdonlyres/0717F804-CB47-4092-A56B-FFC7748744B3/0/lawandregulations.pdf

Association: http://www.kpia.org/legislation.htm

## Louisiana
L.S.B.P.I.E.
2051 Silverside Drive, Suite 190
Baton Rouge, LA  70808

State requirements:
Private Investigators Law
(La. R.S. 37:3500-3525)

3501. Purpose
A. The Legislature of Louisiana declares that it is in the best interest of the citizens of Louisiana to require the licensure of private investigators and businesses.

B. The purpose of this Chapter is to require qualifying criteria in a professional field in which unqualified individuals may injure the public. The requirements of this Chapter shall contribute to the safety, health, and welfare of the people of Louisiana.

### 3502. Short title
This Chapter shall be known and may be cited as the "Private Investigators Law."

### 3503. Definitions
As used in this Chapter, the following terms shall have the meanings ascribed to them unless the context clearly requires otherwise:

(1) "Applicant" means a person who seeks to be examined for licensure or certification by the board.

(2) "Board" means the Louisiana State Board of Private Investigator Examiners within the Department of Public Safety and Corrections.

(3) "Contract private investigator company" means any person engaged in the business of providing, or which undertakes to provide, an investigator on a contractual basis for another person.

(4) "Executive director" means the chief administrative officer of the board.

(5) "Licensee" means any person to whom a license is granted in accordance with the provisions of this Chapter and who may certify the successful completion of the required minimum training for private investigator apprentices.

(6) "Person" means an individual, firm, association, company, partnership, corporation, nonprofit organization, or other legal entity.

(7) "Principal corporate officer" means the president, treasurer, secretary, or comptroller, or any other persons who performs functions for the corporation corresponding to those performed by the foregoing officers.

(8) (a) "Private investigator" or "private detective" means any person who holds out to the general public and engages in the business of furnishing or who accepts employment to furnish information or who agrees to make or makes an investigation for the purpose of obtaining information with reference to the following:

(i) Crimes or wrongs committed.

(ii) Identity, habits, conduct, business, occupations, honesty, integrity, credibility, knowledge, trustworthiness, efficiency, loyalty, activity, movement, whereabouts, affiliations, associations, transactions, acts, reputation, or character of any person.

(iii) The location, disposition, or recovery of stolen property.

(iv) The cause or responsibility for fires, libels, losses, accidents, damages, or injuries to persons or to properties. However, scientific research laboratories, technical experts, and licensed engineers shall not be included in this definition.

(v) Securing evidence to be used before any court, board, officer, or investigative committee.

(b) This definition shall not include any of the following:

(i) Insurer employees or agents and insurance adjusters or claims agents who make appraisals for the monetary value or settlement of damages or monetary value or settlement of personal injuries.

(ii) An officer or employee of the United States, this state, or any political subdivision of either while such officer or employee is engaged in the performance of his official duties within the course and scope of his employment with the United States, this state, or any political subdivision.

(iii) A person engaged exclusively in the business of obtaining and furnishing information as to the financial rating or credit worthiness of persons.

(iv) An attorney at law licensed to practice in this state and his employees.

(v) Undercover agents working with the United States, this state, or any political subdivision while engaged in the performance of their official duties.

(vi) A person primarily engaged in the business of furnishing confidential information for the purposes of a consumer reporting agency, as defined by the Federal Fair Credit Reporting Act, 15 U.S.C. 1681 et seq.

(vii) A person licensed by the Louisiana State Board of Private Security Examiners only when investigating at his place of employment during the performance of his duties pursuant to R.S. 37:3272(18).

(viii) A person or corporation which employs persons who do private investigative work in connection with the affairs of such employer exclusively and who have an employer - employee relationship with such employer. Neither such persons or corporations nor their employees shall be required to register or be licensed under this Chapter.

(ix) A person engaged as a professional employment screening consultant conducting face to face interview with an applicant or candidate for employment.

(x) A certified public accountant licensed to practice in this state and his employees.

(9) "Registrant" means an individual who holds a valid registration card issued by the board.

(10) "Registration card" means the identification card issued by the board to a registrant as evidence that the registrant has met the required minimum qualifications to perform the duties of a private investigator or apprentice.

### 3507.2. Types of licenses

A. The board is authorized to issue the following types of licenses to qualified applicants:

(1) (a) "Private investigation agency license" – issued to any person or entity, as defined in R.S. 37:3503(8), where the individual seeking license or the partner of the partnership seeking license or the principal corporate officer of the corporation seeking license (i) has at least three years experience within the last ten years either working as a private investigator or in an investigative capacity and (ii) satisfies all other requirements for licensing.

(b) The provisions of this Paragraph requiring investigative experience for licensing as a private investigator agency shall not apply to any person or entity licensed as a private investigator agency on August 15, 1999.

(2) "Private investigator license" – issued to any person, as defined in R.S. 37:3503(8), who satisfies the requirements for licensing and is

employed by a licensed private investigator agency.

(3) "Apprentice license" – issued to any person who satisfies the minimum requirements for licensing as an apprentice, as established by rules and regulations promulgated by the board.

B. The individual or the partner of the partnership or the principal corporate officer of the corporation with the requisite experience licensed to operate as a "private investigator agency" may operate as a private investigator and hire others licensed as a "private investigator."

C. The individual licensed as a "private investigator" may only operate as a private investigator if employed by a licensed private investigator agency.

3508. Investigations; time; procedure

A. After receipt of an application for a license, the board shall conduct an investigation to determine whether the facts set forth in the application are true.

B. Within sixty days after receipt of an application, the board shall either issue a license to the applicant or notify him of a denial of the license application.

C. If the board requires additional information from the applicant to complete its investigation or otherwise to satisfy the requirements of this Chapter, or if the applicant has not submitted all required information, the sixty day period for action by the board shall commence when the board has received all such information.

D. The board shall deny the application for a license if it finds that the applicant, or the qualifying agent, or any of the applicant's owners, partners, or principal corporate officers have committed any of the following:

(1) Violated any of the provisions of this Chapter or the rules and regulations promulgated by the board.

(2) Practiced fraud, deceit, or misrepresentation.

(3) Knowingly made a material misstatement in the application for a license.

(4) Failed to meet the qualifications of this Chapter.

(5) Been convicted of a felony.

E. The board may refuse to issue a license for good cause shown.

3509. Examination; content; training class required

A. The board shall determine the scope, form, and content of the examinations for licensure. The examination, which shall be written, shall test the applicant's knowledge of the private investigator business and his ability to apply that knowledge and to assume responsible charge in the practice of private investigator.

B. The examination shall include such subject areas as general federal and state constitutional principles and court decisions related to activities which could result in liability for invasion of privacy or other activities, search and seizures laws in general, state criminal laws and related procedures, and general weapons use and concealed weapons laws. The board shall review and make use of nationally accepted and appropriate examinations to the extent practical.

C. The board shall conduct or contract for the conduct of a forty-hour training class covering the subject areas of the licensing examination and shall require completion of approved training class for a licensed applicant prior to the taking of the examination.

   (1) Private investigator agency:

      (a) Application fee – $25.00.

      (b) Examination fee – $50.00.

      (c) Reexamination fee – $25.00.

      (d) Initial license fee – $200.00.

      (e) Annual renewal license fee – $200.00.

      (f) Replacement fee for a lost, destroyed, or mutilated license – $25.00.

   (2) Private investigator or apprentice investigator:

      (a) Application fee – $25.00.

      (b) Examination fee – $50.00.

      (c) Reexamination fee – $25.00.

      (d) Initial license fee per investigator or apprentice – $50.00.

      (e) Annual renewal license fee – $50.00.

http://www.lsbpie.com/

Association: http://www.lpia.net/

## Maine

State Police Licensing Division
State House Station #164
Augusta, ME  04333
(207) 624-8775

State requirements:

**1. License.** No person may act as a private investigator without first obtaining from the commissioner a license to be a private investigator or investigative assistant. 1981, c. 126, § 2 (new).

**2. Exceptions.** This section does not apply to the following:

A. A person employed by or on behalf of the State, any political subdivision thereof, or any public instrumentality, while in the performance of his official duties; 1981, c. 126, § 2 (new).

B. A charitable or philanthropic organization, duly incorporated under the laws of the State, or any agent thereof, provided that the organization is not operated for profit; 1981, c. 126, § 2 (new).

C. A person employed to inquire into the fitness of an applicant for employment with that person's employer; 1981, c. 126, § 2 (new).

D. A bureau or agency, or agent thereof, whose business is the furnishing of information concerning a person's business, financial or credit standing; 1981, c. 126, § 2 (new).

E. An insurance company, or agent thereof, investigating the personal habits and financial responsibility of applicants for insurance or indemnity bonds; 1981, c. 126, § 2 (new).

F. An attorney acting in a professional capacity; 1981, c. 126, § 2 (new).

H. An insurance adjuster or investigator, or an employee investigating claims for or against his employer; 1981, c. 126, § 2 (new).

I. A person engaged in compiling genealogical information; 1981, c. 126, § 2 (new).

J. A person possessing a valid private investigator's license granted under any prior existing provision of law of this State, provided that, upon expiration of the license, the person shall be governed by this section; or 1981, c. 126, § 2 (new).

K. An employee of a person not licensed under this chapter to do private investigative work, including a proprietary security organization, provided that the employee performs investigative functions solely for the employer and relating to the conduct of the employer's business. [1981, c. 126, § 2 (new).] 1981, c. 126, § 2 (new).

The Revisor's Office cannot provide legal advice or interpretation of Maine law to the public. If you need legal advice, please consult a qualified attorney.

Office of the Revisor of Statutes
7 State House Station
State House Room 108
Augusta, ME 04333-0007

http://janus.state.me.us/legis/statutes/32/title32ch89sec0.html

Association: http://www.mlpia.org/

## Maryland
Maryland State Police, PI Licensing Division
Jessup, MD 20794
(410) 799-0191, ext. 331

State requirements:
http://www.mdsp.org/downloads/Licensing_application.pdf
(800) 525-5555

Associations:
http://www.maryland-investigators.com/
http://www.misahq.com/

## Massachusetts
Massachusetts State Police
Special Licensing Unit
485 Maple Street
Danvers, MA 01923
(978) 538-6128
(978) 538-6021 fax

State requirements:
**Private Investigator License Requirements**

1. An application for a license to engage in the private detective business or a

license to engage in the business of watch, guard or patrol agency shall be filed with the colonel of the state police on forms furnished by him, and statements of fact therein shall be under oath of the applicant.

2. Application shall include a certification by each of three reputable citizens of the commonwealth residing in the community in which the applicant resides or has a place of business, or in which the applicant proposes to conduct his business, that he has personally known the applicant for at least three years, that he has read the application and believes each of the statements made therein to be true, that he is not related to the applicant by blood or marriage, and that the applicant is honest and of good moral character.

3. The applicant, or, if the applicant is a corporation, its resident manager, superintendent or official representative, shall be of good moral character.

4. The applicant shall have been regularly employed for not less than three years as a detective doing investigating work, a former member of an investigative service of the United States, a former police officer, of a rank or grade higher than that of patrolman, of the commonwealth, any political subdivision thereof or an official police department of another state, or a police officer in good standing formerly employed for not less than ten years with the commonwealth, or any political subdivision thereof or with an official police department of another state.

5. No such license shall be granted to any person who has been convicted in any state of the United States of a felony. No person convicted of a violation of section ninety-nine or ninety-nine A of chapter two hundred and seventy-two of the general laws shall be granted a license and any license previously granted to such person shall be revoked.

http://www.mass.gov/

Association: http://www.lpdam.com/

## Michigan
The Department of Consumer & Industry Services
P.O. Box 30018
Lansing, MI  48909
(517) 241-5645

State requirements: http://www.michigan.gov/

Association: http://www.mcpihome.com/

**Minnesota**
Department of Public Safety Private Detective &
Protective Agent Services Board
445 Minnesota Street
St. Paul, MN 55101
(651) 215-1753

State requirements: http://www.revisor.leg.state.mn.us/arule/7506/

Association: http://www.mapi.org/

**Mississippi**
No license required.

Association:
Mississippi Professional Investigators Association, Inc.
P.O. Box 4484
Meridian, MS 39304

**Missouri**
P.O. Box 720
Jefferson City, MO 65102

None required on the state level, but Kansas City, St Louis, Joplin, St Joseph
and Springfield require licensing.

**Montana**
Board of Private Security Patrol Officers and Investigators
301 S. Park, Room 430
P.O. Box 200513
Helena, MT 59620-0513
(406) 841-2387
(406) 841-2309 fax

State requirements:
http://www.discoveringmontana.com/dli/bsd/license/bsd_boards/psp_board/
licenses/psp/pi_license.asp

**Nebraska**
Secretary of State
State Capitol, Suite 2300
Lincoln, NE 68509

(402) 471-2554

State requirements:
http://www.sos.state.ne.us/business/regsearch/Rules/Secretary_of_State/Title-435.pdf

## Nevada
Office of the Attorney General
Private Investigator's Licensing Board
100 N. Carson Street
Carson City, NV  89701-4717
(775) 687-3223

State requirements:
**NAC 648.115 "Private investigator" interpreted. (NRS 648.030)**

1. The Board will interpret the term "private investigator," as defined in NRS 648.012, to exclude a gaming licensee who maintains an employer-employee relationship with:

   (a) A natural person to act as a customer or client of the gaming licensee to evaluate the service provided to actual customers or clients of the gaming licensee by its employees;

   (b) A natural person to act as a customer or client of the gaming licensee to evaluate:

      (1) The operational procedures of the gaming licensee;

      (2) The cleanliness of the property of the gaming licensee; or

      (3) The quality, availability and prices of the goods and services of the gaming licensee; or

   (c) A business entity, licensed pursuant to chapter 648 of NRS, to evaluate the operational procedures and methods of prevention and study used by the gaming licensee relating to the problems of gambling and the consumption of alcoholic beverages by minors.

2. As used in this section, "gaming licensee" means a holder of a nonrestricted gaming license issued pursuant to chapter 463 of NRS.

http://www.leg.state.nv.us/NAC/NAC-648.html

**New Hampshire**
State Police
Division of Licenses and Permits
Hazen Drive
Concord, NH  03305
(603) 271-3575

State requirements:
http://www.nhes.state.nh.us/elmi/licertoccs/privatei.htm
(603) 271-3575

**New Jersey**
State Police
Department of Law & Public Safety
Private Detective Unit
P. O. Box 7068
W. Trenton, NJ  08688-0068
(609) 882-2000, ext 2931

State requirements:
**45:19-9. Definition of terms**

Definitions:
(a) The term "private detective business" shall mean the business of conducting a private detective agency or for the purpose of making for hire or reward any investigation or investigations for the purpose of obtaining information with reference to any of the following matters, notwithstanding the fact that other functions and services may also be performed by the same person, firm, association or corporation for fee, hire or reward, to wit:

> (1) crime or wrong done or threatened or assumed to have been done or threatened against the Government of the United States of America, or any State, Territory or Possession of the United States of America;

> (2) the identity, habits, conduct, movements, whereabouts, affiliations, associations, transactions, reputation or character of any person, association, organization, society or groups of persons, firms or corporations;

> (3) the credibility of witnesses or other persons;

> (4) the whereabouts of missing persons;

> (5) the location or recovery of lost or stolen property;

(6) the causes and origin of, or responsibility for, fires, libels, accidents, damage, injuries or losses to persons, firms, associations or corporations, or to real or personal property;

(7) the affiliation, connection or relation of any person, firm or corporation with any organization, society, association, or with any official member or representative thereof;

(8) with reference to the conduct, honesty, efficiency, loyalty or activities of employees, agents, contractors and subcontractors;

(9) the securing of evidence to be used before any investigating committee, board of award, board of arbitration, or in the trial of any civil or criminal cause; provided, however, that the term shall not include a person, firm, association or corporation engaged exclusively in the business of making investigations and reports as to the financial standing, credit and financial responsibility of persons, firms, associations or corporations nor to electrically controlled burglar or fire alarm system with a central unit, nor to any person, firm, association or corporation engaged in the business of making reports for insurance or credit purposes. Also it shall mean the furnishing for hire or reward of watchmen or guards or private patrolmen or other persons to protect persons or property, either real or personal, or for any other purpose whatsoever. The term shall not include and nothing in this act shall apply to any lawful activity of any board, body, commission or agency of the United States of America or of any State, Territory or Possession of the United States of America, or any county, municipality, school district, or any officer or employee solely, exclusively and regularly employed by any of the foregoing; nor to any attorney or counsellor-at-law in connection with the regular practice of his profession, nor to any person employed by any such attorney or counsellor-at-law when engaged upon his employer's business; nor to any employee, investigator or investigators solely, exclusively and regularly employed by any person, firm, association or corporation which is not engaged in any of the businesses hereinbefore described in items numbered one to nine, both inclusive, of this subSection in so far as their acts may relate solely to the business of the respective employers; nor to any person, firm, association or corporation licensed to do a business of insurance of any nature under the insurance laws of this State, nor to any employee or licensed agent thereof; nor to any person, firm, association or corporation conducting any investigation solely for its own account.

(b) The terms "the business of detective agency," "the business of investigator" and "the business of watch, guard or patrol agency" shall mean any person, firm, association or corporation engaged in the private detective business as defined in subSection (a) of this Section, who employs one or more persons in conducting such business.

(c) The terms "private detective" or "investigator" shall mean and include any person who singly and for his own account and profit conducts a private detective business without the aid or assistance of any employees or associates.

(d) The masculine shall include the feminine and the neuter genders.

(e) The term "superintendent" means the Superintendent of State Police.

(f) The terms "firm" and "association" shall include partnerships, but shall not include corporations.

L.1939, c. 369, p. 887, s. 2. Amended by L.1971, c. 342, s. 1, eff. Dec. 13, 1971.

**45:19-10. License to conduct business, violation of Section as misdemeanor**
No person, firm, association or corporation shall engage in the private detective business or as a private detective or investigator or advertise his or its business to be a private detective business or that of a detective agency or investigator without having first obtained from the superintendent a license to conduct such business, as hereinafter provided. Any person, firm, association or corporation who shall violate any of the provisions of this Section shall be guilty of a misdemeanor.
L.1939, c. 369, p. 889, s. 3.

**45:19-11. Application for license; contents; approvals of reputable citizens; signing and verification; false statements as misdemeanor**
Any person, firm, association or corporation desiring to conduct a private detective business or the business of a private detective or investigator, shall for each Bureau or agency, subagency, office and branch office to be owned, conducted, managed or maintained by such person, firm, association or corporation for the conduct of such business, file in the office of the superintendent a written application duly signed and verified, accompanied, in the case of an application by a person, with the written approval of not less than five reputable citizens who shall be freeholders of the county where such applicant resides or in the county in which it is proposed to conduct such business, and in the case of a firm, the written approval of five reputable citizens for each of the members of the firm who shall be freeholders of the county where each member of the firm resides or the county in which it is proposed to conduct

such business, or in the case of an association or corporation, the written approval by five reputable citizens for each officer and director of the corporation who shall be freeholders of the county where such officers and directors reside, or of the county in which it is proposed to conduct such business. Such approvals shall be signed and acknowledged by the respective citizens before an officer authorized to take acknowledgments of conveyances of real property. The application shall state the following: Name, age, residence, present and previous occupations of the applicant, or in case of a firm, of each member of the firm, or in the case of an association or corporation, of each officer and director thereof; that each of the foregoing persons are citizens of the United States; the name of the municipality and the location therein by street number or other apt description where is to be located the principal place of business and the location of each Bureau, agency, subagency, office or branch office for which a license is desired, and such other facts as may be required by the superintendent as will tend to show the character, competency and integrity of each person or individual signing such application. Any person who shall knowingly state any fact falsely shall be guilty of a misdemeanor.
L.1939, c. 369, p. 890, s. 4.

**45:19-12. Issuance of license; inquiries and investigations; fees; bond; duration of license; renewal; revocation; notification of changes; qualifications**
The superintendent, when satisfied from the examination of any application and such further inquiry and investigations as he shall deem proper as to the good character, competency and integrity of the applicant and the persons named in the application, shall issue and deliver to the applicant a license to conduct such business. Such licensee shall be permitted to own, conduct and maintain one or more Bureaus, agencies, subagencies, offices or branch offices for the conduct of such business at the locations stated in said application, upon the payment by the applicant to the superintendent of a license fee for each location so licensed which in the case of an individual shall be $250.00, and in the case of a firm, association or corporation shall be $300.00. Any license or renewal thereof shall be further conditioned upon the applicant executing and delivering to the superintendent a bond with a surety company authorized to be surety in the State of New Jersey, as surety, and approved as to form, manner of execution and sufficiency by the superintendent of the State Police, running to the State of New Jersey and which shall be for the benefit of any person injured by willful, malicious or wrongful act of the applicant (with a sufficient surety bond), which in the case of an individual shall be $3,000.00, and in the case of a firm, association or corporation $5,000.00, which said bond shall be

conditioned for the faithful and honest conduct of such business by the applicant. The license so granted by the superintendent shall be valid for a period of 2 years, and upon renewal thereof said applicant shall pay to the superintendent in the case of an individual a license fee of $200.00 and in the case of a firm, association or corporation $250.00 for each location for which such a license is renewed. The license shall be revocable by the superintendent after hearing for cause. In case of revocation or surrender of any license, no refund shall be made of any license fee paid under the provisions hereof. The license shall be in a form to be prescribed by the superintendent and shall set forth the full name of the applicant, the location of the principal office or place of business, and the location of each Bureau, agency, subagency, office or branch office for which the license is issued, date on which it is issued, the date on which it will expire, and the name or names of the persons named in the application, and their respective addresses. In the event of any change in the membership of the firm or in the officers or directors of any association or corporation or any change in the address of any office or location of such business the superintendent shall be notified in writing of such change within 5 days thereafter, and failure to give such notification shall be sufficient cause for revocation of such license.

No license shall be issued to a person under the age of 25 years, nor to any person, firm, association or corporation unless such person or at least one member of the firm and one officer or director of the association or corporation has had at least 5 years' experience as an investigator or as a police officer with an organized police department of the State or a county or municipality thereof, or with an investigative agency of the United States of America or any State, county or municipality thereof.

The superintendent and all members of the State Police shall hold as confidential all information obtained as a result of any investigation of any applicant or officer, assistant, or employee of any holder of any license issued under the provisions of this act, and the same shall not be divulged except by an order so to do by a court of record of this State.
L.1939, c. 369, p. 891, s. 5. Amended by L.1948, c. 152, p. 881, s. 1; L.1971, c. 342, s. 2, eff. Dec. 13, 1971.

### 45:19-12.1. Employees of licensee; fees payable by licensee; violation; penalty
a. Subsequent to the effective date of this act, every licensee shall pay to the superintendent an additional fee of $15.00 for each person in its employ engaged in said employment in this State as a private detective or investigator which terms shall include watchmen, guards and private patrolmen. Any

licensee who shall employ any person in the aforementioned categories subsequent to its securing a license or renewal thereof and for whom the fee of $15.00 has not been paid shall pay the fee of $15.00 for each of said persons prior to the commencement of said employment with the licensee. Thereafter any licensee at the time of any renewal if its license hereunder shall pay a renewal fee of $5.00 for each of said employees in the aforementioned categories for whom an initial fee of $15.00 has been paid by said licensee.

b. Any licensee who shall employ any person in the aforementioned categories in subSection a. above without having paid the fees in accordance with said subSection a. shall be a disorderly person.
L.1971, c. 342, s. 3, eff. Dec. 13, 1971.

http://www.njsp.org/about/pdet_act.html

Association: http://www.njlpia.org/

## New Mexico
Bureau of Private Investigators
P.O. Box 25101
Santa Fe, NM  87504
(505) 476-7080

State requirements: http://www.rld.state.nm.us/b&c/pipolygraph/index.htm

## New York
Department of State
Division of Licensing Services
84 Holland Avenue
Albany, NY  12208-3490

State requirements:
### §70. Licenses

1. The Department of State shall have the power to issue separate licenses to private investigators, bail enforcement agents and to watch, guard or patrol agencies. Nothing in this article shall prevent a private investigator licensed hereunder from performing the services of a watch, guard or patrol agency or bail enforcement agents as defined herein; however, a watch, guard or patrol agency or bail enforcement agents may not perform the services of a private investigator as defined herein.

2. No person, firm, company, partnership, limited liability company or corpora-

tion shall engage in the business of private investigator, business of bail enforcement agents or the business of watch, guard or patrol agency, or advertise his, their or its business to be that of private investigator, bail enforcement agents or watch, guard or patrol agency, notwithstanding the name or title used in describing such agency or notwithstanding the fact that other functions and services may also be performed for fee, hire or reward, without having first obtained from the Department of State a license so to do, as hereinafter provided, for each bureau, agency, sub-agency, office and branch office to be owned, conducted, managed or maintained by such person, firm, company, partnership, limited liability company or corporation for the conduct of such business.

3. No person, firm, company, partnership, limited liability company or corporation shall engage in the business of furnishing or supplying for fee, hire or any consideration or reward information as to the personal character or activities of any person, firm, company, or corporation, society or association, or any person or group of persons, or as to the character or kind of the business and occupation of any person, firm, company or corporation, or own or conduct or maintain a bureau or agency for the above mentioned purposes, except exclusively as to the financial rating, standing, and credit responsibility of persons, firms, companies or corporations, or as to the personal habits and financial responsibility of applicants for insurance, indemnity bonds or commercial credit or of claimants under insurance policies, provided the business so exempted does not embrace other activities as described in §71 of this article, or except where such information is furnished or supplied by persons licensed under the provisions of §24-a or subdivision 3-b of §50 of the Workers' Compensation Law or representing employers or groups of employers insured under the Workers' Compensation Law in the State Insurance Fund, without having first obtained from the Department of State, as hereafter provided, a license so to do as private investigator for each such bureau or agency and for each and every sub-agency, office and branch office to be owned, conducted, managed or maintained by such persons, firm, limited liability company, partnership or corporation for the conduct of such business. Nothing contained in this section shall be deemed to include the business of adjusters for insurance companies, nor public adjusters licensed by the superintendent of insurance under the Insurance Law of this state.

4. Any person, firm, company, partnership or corporation who violates any provision of this section shall be guilty of a class B misdemeanor.

## §71. Definitions

1. "Private investigator" shall mean and include the business of private investigator and shall also mean and include, separately or collectively, the making for hire, reward or for any consideration whatsoever, of any investigation, or investigations for the purpose of obtaining information with reference to any of the following matters, notwithstanding the fact that other functions and services may also be performed for fee, hire or reward; crime or wrongs done or threatened against the government of the United States of America or any state or territory of the United States of America; the identity, habits, conduct, movements, whereabouts, affiliations, associations, transactions, reputation or character of any person, group of persons, association, organization, society, other groups of persons, firm or corporation; the credibility of witnesses or other persons; the whereabouts of missing persons; the location or recovery of lost or stolen property; the causes and origin of, or responsibility for fires, or libels, or losses, or accidents, or damage or injuries to real or personal property; or the affiliation, connection or relation of any person, firm or corporation with any union, organization, society or association, or with any official, member or representative thereof; or with reference to any person or persons seeking employment in the place of any person or persons who have quit work by reason of any strike; or with reference to the conduct, honesty, efficiency, loyalty or activities of employees, agents, contractors, and sub-contractors; or the securing of evidence to be used before any authorized investigating committee, board of award, board of arbitration, or in the trial of civil or criminal cases. The foregoing shall not be deemed to include the business of persons licensed by the industrial commissioner under the provisions of §24-a or subdivision 3-b of §50 of the Workers' Compensation Law or representing employers or groups of employers insured under the Workers' Compensation Law in the State Insurance Fund, nor persons engaged in the business of adjusters for insurance companies nor public adjusters licensed by the Superintendent of Insurance under the Insurance Law of this State.

1a. "Bail enforcement agent" shall mean and include only the business of bail enforcement and shall also mean and include, separately or collectively, the engaging in the business of enforcing the terms and conditions of a person's release from custody on bail in a criminal proceeding, including locating, apprehending and returning any such person released from custody on bail who has failed to appear at any stage of a criminal proceeding to answer the charge before the court in which he may be prosecuted. The foregoing shall not be deemed to include the business of persons licensed under the provisions of §24-a or subdivision 3-b of section 50 of the Workers' Compensation Law or representing employers or groups of employers insured under the Workers' Compensation Law in the State Insurance Fund, nor persons engaged in the business of adjusters for insurance companies nor public adjusters licensed by the Superintendent of Insurance under the Insurance Law of this state or the business of private investigator, watch, guard or patrol agency or security guard company.

2. "Watch, guard or patrol agency" shall mean and include the business of watch, guard or patrol agency and shall also mean and include, separately or collectively, the furnishing, for hire or reward, of watchmen or guards or private patrolmen or other persons to protect persons or property or to prevent the theft or the unlawful taking of goods, wares and merchandise, or to prevent the misappropriation or concealment of goods, wares or merchandise, money, bonds, stocks, notes or other valuable documents, papers, and articles of value, or to procure the return thereof or the performing of the service of such guard or other person for any of said purposes. The foregoing shall not be deemed to include the business of persons licensed by the industrial commissioner under the provisions of §24-a or subdivision 3-b of §50 of the Workers' Compensation Law or representing employers or groups of employers insured under the Workers' Compensation Law in the State Insurance Fund, nor persons engaged in the business of adjusters for insurance companies nor public adjusters licensed by the Superintendent of Insurance under the Insurance Law of this State.

3. The term the "business of private investigator," and the term "private investigator" shall mean and include any person, firm, limited liability company, partnership or corporation engaged in the business of private investigator as defined in subdivision one of this section with or without the assistance of any employee or employees. The term "business of watch, guard or patrol agency" and the term "watch, guard or patrol agency" shall mean and include any person, firm, limited liability company, partnership or corporation engaged in the business of watch, guard or patrol agency as defined in subdivision two of this section or the business of a security guard company as defined in subdivision five of §89-f of this Chapter with or without the assistance of any employee or employees. For the purposes of this article, a public entity as defined in subdivision seven of §89-f of this Chapter or a security guard company which utilizes security guards solely for its own proprietary use shall not be deemed a security guard company.

4. The term "business of bail enforcement agent" and the term "bail enforce-

ment agent" shall mean and include any person, firm, company, partnership or corporation engaged in the business of bail enforcement as defined in subdivision 1-a of this section with or without the assistance of any employee or employees.

## §72. Application for licenses

Any person, firm, partnership, limited liability company or corporation intending to conduct the business of private investigator, business of bail enforcement agent or the business of watch, guard or patrol agency, and any person, firm, partnership, limited liability company or corporation intending to conduct the business of furnishing or supplying information as to the personal character of any person or firm, or as to the character or kind of the business and occupation of any person, firm or corporation, society or association or any person or group of persons, or intending to own, conduct, manage or maintain a bureau or agency for the above mentioned purposes, or while engaged in other lawful business activities also intending to engage in any one or more of the activities set forth in §71 of this article except exclusively as to the financial rating, standing, and credit responsibility of persons, firms, companies or corporations or as to personal habits and financial responsibility of applicants for insurance indemnity bonds or commercial credit or of claimants under insurance policies shall, for each such bureau or agency and for each and every sub-agency, office and branch office to be owned, conducted, managed or maintained by such person, firm, partnership, limited liability company or corporation for the conduct of such business, file in the office of the Department of State a written application, on forms provided by the department containing such information and documentation, including fingerprints, as the Secretary of State may require by rule and regulation.

1. If the applicant is a person, the application shall be subscribed by such person, and if the applicant is a firm or partnership the application shall be subscribed by each individual composing or intending to compose such firm or partnership. The application shall state the full name, age, residences within the past three years, present and previous occupations of each person or individual so signing the same, that each person or individual is a citizen of the United States or an alien lawfully admitted for permanent residence in the United States and shall also specify the name of the city, town or village, stating the street and number, if the premises have a street and number, and otherwise such apt description as will reasonably indicate the location thereof, where is to be located the principal place of business and the bureau, agency, sub-agency, office or branch office for which the license is desired, and such further facts

as may be required by the Department of State to show the good character, competency and integrity of each person or individual so signing such application. Each person or individual signing such application shall, together with such application, submit to the Department of State, his photograph, taken within six months prior thereto in duplicate, in passport size and also two sets of fingerprints of his two hands recorded in such manner as may be specified by the Secretary of State or the Secretary of State's authorized representative. Before approving such application it shall be the duty of the Secretary of State or the Secretary of State's authorized representative to forward one copy of such fingerprints to the Division of Criminal Justice Services. Upon receipt of such fingerprints, such division shall forward to the Secretary of State a report with respect to the applicant's previous criminal history, if any, or a statement that the applicant has no previous criminal history according to its files. If additional copies of fingerprints are required the applicant shall furnish them upon request. The Secretary shall reveal the name of the applicant to the chief of police and the district attorney of the applicant's residence and of the proposed place of business and shall request of them a report concerning the applicant's character in the event they shall have information concerning it. The Secretary shall take such other steps as may be necessary to investigate the honesty, good character and integrity of each applicant. Every such applicant for a license as private investigator shall establish to the satisfaction of the Secretary of State (a) if the applicant be a person, or, (b) in the case of a firm, limited liability company, partnership or corporation, at least one member of such firm, partnership, limited liability company or corporation, has been regularly employed, for a period of not less than three years, undertaking such investigations as those described as performed by a private investigator in subdivision one of §71 of this article, as a sheriff, police officer in a city or county police department, or the Division of State Police, investigator in an agency of the state, county, or United States government, or employee of a licensed private investigator, or has had an equivalent position and experience or that such person or member was an employee of a police department who rendered service therein as a police officer for not less than twenty years or was an employee of a fire department who rendered service therein as a fire marshal for not less than 20 years. However, employment as a watchman, guard or private patrolman shall not be considered employment as a "private investigator" for purposes of this section. Every such applicant for a license as watch, guard or patrol agency shall establish to the satisfaction of the Secretary of State (a) if the applicant be a person, or, (b) in the case of a firm, limited liability company, partnership or corporation, at least one member of such firm, partnership, limited liability company or corporation, has been regularly employed, for a period of not less than two years, performing such duties or providing such services as described as those performed or furnished by a watch, guard or patrol agency in subdivision two of §71 of this article, as a sheriff, police officer in a city or county police department, or employee of an agency of the state, county or United States government, or licensed private investigator or watch, guard or patrol agency, or has had an equivalent position and experience; qualifying experience shall have been completed within such period of time and at such time prior to the filing of the application as shall be satisfactory to the Secretary of State. The person or member meeting the experience requirement under subdivision one of this section and the person responsible for the operation and management of each bureau, agency, sub-agency, office or branch office of the applicant shall provide sufficient proof of having taken and passed a written examination prescribed by the Secretary of State to test their understanding of their rights, duties and powers as a private investigator and/or watchman, guard or private patrolman, depending upon the work to be performed under the license. In the case of an application subscribed by a resident of the State of New York such application shall be approved, as to each resident person or individual so signing the same, but not less than five reputable citizens of the community in which such applicant resides or transacts business, or in which it is proposed to own, conduct, manage or maintain the bureau, agency, sub-agency, office or branch office for which the license is desired, each of whom shall subscribe and affirm as true, under the penalties of perjury, that he has personally known the said person or individual for a period of at least five years prior to the filing of such application, that he has read such application and believes each of the statements made therein to be true, that such person is honest, of good character and competent, and not related or connected to the person so certifying by blood or marriage. In the case of an application subscribed by a non-resident of the State of New York such application shall be approved, as to each non-resident person or individual so signing the same by not less than five reputable citizens of the community in which such applicant resides. The certificate of approval shall be signed by such reputable citizens and duly verified and acknowledged by them before an officer authorized to take oaths and acknowledgment of deeds. All provisions of this section, applying to corporations, shall also apply to joint-stock associations, except that each such joint-stock association shall file a duly certified copy of its certificate of organization in the place of the certified copy of its certificate of incorporation herein required.

1a. Every such applicant for a license as bail enforcement agent shall establish to the satisfaction of the secretary of state (a) if the applicant be a person, or (b) in the case of a firm, company, partnership, or corporation, at least one member of such firm, partnership, company or corporation, has been regularly employed, for a period of not less than three years, performing such duties or providing such services as described as those furnished by a bail enforcement agent in § 71 of this article, as a sheriff, police officer in a city or county police department, or the Division of State Police, investigator in an agency of the state, county, or United States government, or employee of a licensed private investigator, or has had an equivalent position and experience or that such person or member was an employee of a police department who rendered service therein as a police officer for not less than 20 years or was an employee of a fire department who rendered service therein as a fire marshal for not less than 20 years.

1-b. The person or member meeting the experience requirement under subdivisions 1 and 1-a of this section and any person or member of such firm, company, partnership or corporation who engages in the apprehension and return of suspects who fail to appear before the court must either satisfactorily complete a basic certification course in training for bail enforcement agents offered by a provider that is approved by the Secretary of State; or such person or member must have served as a police officer, as that term is defined in subdivision 34 of section 1.20 of the Criminal Procedure Law, for a period of not less than three years. The basic course of training shall include at least 25 hours of training approved by the Secretary of State and must include instruction on issues involved with the rights and limitations involving the bailee/ fugitive who signs a contract with the bail enforcement agent. Completion of the course shall be for educational purposes only and not intended to confer the power of arrest of a peace officer or public officer, or agent of any federal, state, or local government, unless the person is so employed by a governmental agency.

2. If the applicant is a corporation, the application shall be subscribed by the president, secretary, treasurer, and all other officers and directors working for such corporation within the State of New York, and shall specify the name of the corporation, the date and place of its incorporation, the location of its principal place of business, and the name of the city, town or village, stating the street and number, if the premises have a street and number, and otherwise such apt description as will reasonably indicate the location thereof, where is to be located the bureau, agency, sub-agency, office or branch office for which the

license is desired, the amount of the corporation's outstanding paid up capital stock and whether paid in cash or property, and, if in property, the nature of the same, and shall be accompanied by a duly certified copy of its certificate of incorporation. Each and every requirement as to character of subdivision one of this section as to a person or individual member of a firm or partnership shall apply to the president, secretary, treasurer and all other officers and directors working for such corporation within the State of New York and each such officer and director, his successor and successors shall prior to entering upon the discharge of his duties subscribe a like statement, approved in like manner, as is by said subdivision one prescribed in the case of a person or individual member of a firm or partnership.

3. Each person subscribing an application pursuant to this section shall affirm that the statements therein are true under the penalties of perjury.

4. The Secretary of State may deny, suspend or revoke the license of a corporation if, at any time, 10 per centum or more of the corporate stock is held by a person who cannot meet the character standard set for an individual licensee.

http://www.dos.state.ny.us/lcns/pifaq.html

Association: http://www.aldonys.org/

## North Carolina
Private Protective Services Board
1631 Midtown Place, Suite 104
Raleigh, NC 27609
(919) 875-3611
(919) 875-3609 fax

State requirements:
**Private Investigator License:**
Three years of experience within the past ten years in private investigative work, or three years within the past ten years in an investigative capacity as a member of a law enforcement agency or other governmental agency. [See G.S. 74C-3(a)(8), 74C-8, 74C-9, 74C-10, 12 NCAC 7D .0401].

**Reciprocity** – The Board currently has reciprocal licensing agreements with several states. These agreements allow currently licensed private investigators from states to come into North Carolina for a specific period of time (30 days maximum, except for Tennessee, which is 15 days) to work a case which originated in their home state. Likewise, licensed North Carolina investigators may enter that state to work a case originating there. Investigations exceeding the time limits must be handled by a private investigator licensed in the particular state. See Reciprocal Agreements.

www.ncdoj.com/law_enforcement/cle_pps_licensing.jsp

Association: http://www.ncapi.org/

**North Dakota**
Private Investigative & Security Board
P.O. Box 7026
Bismarck, ND 58505
(701) 222-3063

State requirements:
**North Dakota Eligibility & Licensing Requirements for Security Providers**

Qualifications to become a security provider:

**93-02-02.1-01. Qualifications for individuals providing private security services.**
To receive and maintain any license or registration from the board to provide private security services, an individual first must:

1. Be at least eighteen years of age.

2. Be a high school graduate or hold the equivalent of a high school diploma.

3. Have not been convicted or adjudged guilty in any jurisdiction of one of the following offenses or its equivalent in another jurisdiction, including juvenile adjudication that the individual has engaged in similar conduct: any felony; any class A or B misdemeanor involving an act of violence or intimidation as defined in North Dakota Century Code chapters 12.1-16 through 12.1-25 and chapter 12.1-31.2 , or involving controlled substances as defined in North Dakota Century Code chapter 19-03.1; any offense involving theft as defined in North Dakota Century Code chapter 12.1-23, including shoplifting, or any other offense which must be reported to the North Dakota Bureau of Criminal Investigation under North Dakota Century Code section 12.1-32-15. This subsection will not prohibit the board from issuing a license or registration to an individual if the

board determines the offense does not have a direct bearing upon the individual's ability to provide private security services to the public and the individual has been sufficiently rehabilitated pursuant to the provisions of North Dakota Century Code section 12.1-33-02.1, or a full pardon has been granted.

4. Be free of mental condition or defect, which would interfere with the individual's ability to provide services in a professional and competent manner.

5. Have not committee an act which the board determines is indicative of bad moral character and which has a direct bearing on the applicant's ability to serve the public, including but not limited to offenses other than those listed in subsection three of this section.

The requirements in this section are in addition to any other qualifications established in this chapter. Each individual who is required to meet the qualifications of this section has a continuing duty to notify the board of any conviction or adjudication of guilt of an offense described in subsection three of this section within fourteen days of the conviction or adjudication. For individuals who are licensed ore registered by the board on the effective date of this section, or who are officers or owners of at least a ten-percent interest in a licensed agency on the effective date of this section, this section applies only to convictions or adjudication of guilt which occur after the effective date of this section.

## 93-02-02.1-02. Licensing of individual providing private security services.

1. An individual providing private security services must obtain a license from the board to provide those services unless the individual is registered as an employee of an agency which is licensed under this chapter and is providing those services within the scope of his or her employment with the agency. This section does not apply to individuals who are exempt from the board's jurisdiction under North Dakota Century Code section 43-30-02.

2. An individual is qualified to be licensed to provide private security services if the individual is currently a commissioned security officer and has passed an examination conducted by or under the supervision of the board within the twelve months preceding the date of the individual's application for the license.

**North Dakota Eligibility & Licensing Requirements for Private Investigators**

Qualifications to become a private investigator:

**93-02-01.1-01. Qualifications for individuals providing private investigative services.**
To receive and maintain any license or registration from the board to provide private investigative services, an individual first must:

1. Be at least eighteen years of age.

2. Be a high school graduate or hold the equivalent of a high school diploma.

3. Have not been convicted or adjudged guilty in any jurisdiction of one of the following offenses or its equivalent in another jurisdiction, including juvenile adjudication that the individual has engaged in similar conduct: any felony, any class A or B misdemeanor involving an act of violence or intimidation as defined in North Dakota Century Code chapters 12.1-16 through 12.1-25 and chapter 12.1-31.2 or involving controlled substances as defined in North Dakota Century Code chapter 19-03.1, any offense involving theft as defined in North Dakota Century Code chapter 12.1-23, including shoplifting; or any other offense which must be reported to the North Dakota Bureau of Criminal Investigation under North Dakota Century Code section 12.1-32-15. This subsection will not prohibit the board from issuing a license or registration to an individual if the board determines the offense does not have a direct bearing upon the individual's ability to provide private investigative services to the public and the individual has been sufficiently rehabilitated pursuant to the provisions of North Dakota Century Code section 12.1-33-02.1, or a full pardon has been granted.

4. Be free of mental condition or defect, which would interfere with the individual's ability to provide services in a professional and competent manner.

5. Have not committed an act which the board determines is indicative of bad moral character and which has a direct bearing on the applicant's ability to serve the public, including but not limited to offenses other than those listed in subsection three of this section.

   The requirements in this section are in addition to any other qualifications established in this chapter. Each individual who is required to meet the qualifications of this section has a continuing duty to notify the board of any conviction or adjudication of guilt of an offense described in subsection three of this section within fourteen days of the conviction or adjudication. For individuals who are licensed or registered by the board on the effective date of this section, or who are officers or owners of at least a ten-percent interest in a licensed agency on the effective date of this section, this section applies only to convictions or adjudication of guilt which occur after the effective date of this section.

### 93-02-01.1-02 Licensing of individual providing private investigative services.

1. An individual providing private investigative services must obtain a license from the board to provide those services unless the individual is registered as an employee of an agency which is licensed under this chapter and is providing those services within the scope of his or her employment with the agency. This section does not apply to individuals who are exempt from the board's jurisdiction under North Dakota Century Code section 43-30-02.

2. An individual is qualified to be licensed to provide private investigative services if the individual has passed an examination conducted by or under the supervision of the board within the twelve moths preceding the date of the individual's application for the license and has provided two thousand hours of private investigative services as a registered employee of a detective agency. The experience requirement in this subsection does not apply to an individual who holds a license on the effective date of this section unless the individual's license lapses and is not renewed within one year pursuant to section 93-02-03-03.

http://www.state.nd.us/pisb/index.html

## Ohio
Ohio Department of Commerce
Division of Licensing
77 South High Street
Columbus, OH 43266-0546
(614) 466-4130

State requirements:
**Sec. 4749.01.** As used in this chapter:

(A) "Private investigator" means any person who engages in the business of private investigation.

(B) "Business of private investigation" means, except when performed by one excluded under division (H) of this section, the conducting, for hire, in person or through a partner or employees, of any investigation relevant to any crime or wrong done or threatened, or to obtain information on the identity, habits, conduct, movements, whereabouts, affiliations, transactions, reputation, credibility, or character of any person, or to locate and recover lost or stolen property, or to determine the cause of or responsibility for any libel or slander, or any fire, accident, or damage to property, or to secure evidence for use in any legislative, administrative, or judicial investigation or proceeding.

(C) "Security guard provider" means any person who engages in the business of security services.

(D) "Business of security services" means either of the following:
>    (1) Furnishing, for hire, watchpersons, guards, private patrol officers, or other persons whose primary duties are to protect persons or property;
>    (2) Furnishing, for hire, guard dogs, or armored motor vehicle security services, in connection with the protection of persons or property.

(E) "Class A license" means a license issued under section 4749.03 of the Revised Code that qualifies the person issued the license to engage in the business of private investigation and the business of security services.

(F) "Class B license" means a license issued under section 4749.03 of the Revised Code that qualifies the person issued the license to engage only in the business of private investigation.

(G) "Class C license" means a license issued under section 4749.03 of the Revised Code that qualifies the person issued the license to engage only in the business of security services.

(H) "Private investigator," "business of private investigation," "security guard provider," and "business of security services" do not include:
>    (1) Public officers and employees whose official duties require them to engage in investigatory activities;
>    (2) Attorneys at law or any expert hired by an attorney at law for consultation or litigation purposes;
>    (3) A consumer reporting agency, as defined in the "Fair Credit

Reporting Act," 84 Stat. 1128, 15 U.S.C.A. 1681a, as amended, provided that the consumer reporting agency is in compliance with the requirements of that act and that the agency's activities are confined to any of the following:

(a) The issuance of consumer credit reports;

(b) The conducting of limited background investigations that pertain only to a client's prospective tenant and that are engaged in with the prior written consent of the prospective tenant;

(c) The business of pre-employment background investigation. As used in division (H)(3)(c) of this section, "business of pre-employment background investigation" means, and is limited to, furnishing for hire, in person or through a partner or employees, the conducting of limited background investigations, in-person interviews, telephone interviews, or written inquiries that pertain only to a client's prospective employee and the employee's employment and that are engaged in with the prior written consent of the prospective employee.

(4) Certified public insurance adjusters that hold a certificate of authority issued pursuant to sections 3951.01 to 3951.09 of the Revised Code, while the adjuster is investigating the cause of or responsibility for a fire, accident, or other damage to property with respect to a claim or claims for loss or damage under a policy of insurance covering real or personal property;

(5) Personnel placement services and persons who act as employees of such entities engaged in investigating matters related to personnel placement activities;

(6) An employee in the regular course of the employee's employment, engaged in investigating matters pertinent to the business of the employee's employer or protecting property in the possession of the employee's employer, provided the employer is deducting all applicable state and federal employment taxes on behalf of the employee and neither the employer nor the employee is employed by, associated with, or acting for or on behalf of any private investigator or security guard provider;

(7) Any better business bureau or similar organization or any of its employees while engaged in the maintenance of the quality of business

activities relating to consumer sales and services;

(8) An accountant who is registered or certified under Chapter 4701. of the Revised Code or any of the accountant's employees while engaged in activities for which the accountant is certified or registered;

(9) Any person who, for hire or otherwise, conducts genealogical research in this state.

As used in division (H)(9) of this section, "genealogical research" means the determination of the origins and descent of families, including the identification of individuals, their family relationships, and the biographical details of their lives. "Genealogical research" does not include furnishing for hire services for locating missing persons or natural or birth parents or children.

(10) Any person residing in this state who conducts research for the purpose of locating the last known owner of unclaimed funds, provided that the person is in compliance with Chapter 169. of the Revised Code and rules adopted thereunder. The exemption set forth in division (H)(10) of this section applies only to the extent that the person is conducting research for the purpose of locating the last known owner of unclaimed funds.

As used in division (H)(10) of this section, "owner" and "unclaimed funds" have the same meanings as in section 169.01 of the Revised Code.

(11) A professional engineer who is registered under Chapter 4733. of the Revised Code or any of his employees.

As used in division (H)(11) of this section and notwithstanding division (I) of this section, "employee" has the same meaning as in section 4101.01 of the Revised Code.

(12) Any person residing in this state who, for hire or otherwise, conducts research for the purpose of locating persons to whom the state of Ohio owes money in the form of warrants, as defined in division (S) of section 131.01 of the Revised Code, that the state voided but subsequently reissues.

(13) An independent insurance adjuster who, as an individual, an independent contractor, an employee of an independent contractor, adjustment bureau association, corporation, insurer, partnership, local recording agent, managing general agent, or self-insurer, engages in the busi-

ness of independent insurance adjustment, or any person who supervises the handling of claims except while acting as an employee of an insurer licensed in this state while handling claims pertaining to specific policies written by that insurer.

As used in division (H)(13) of this section, "independent insurance adjustment" means conducting investigations to determine the cause of or circumstances concerning a fire, accident, bodily injury, or damage to real or personal property; determining the extent of damage of that fire, accident, injury, or property damage; securing evidence for use in a legislative, administrative, or judicial investigation or proceeding, adjusting losses; and adjusting or settling claims, including the investigation, adjustment, denial, establishment of damages, negotiation, settlement, or payment of claims in connection with insurance contractors, self-insured programs, or other similar insurance programs. "Independent adjuster" does not include either of the following:

(a) An attorney who adjusts insurance losses incidental to the practice of law and who does not advertise or represent that the attorney is an independent insurance adjuster;

(b) A licensed agent or general agent of an insurer licensed in this state who processes undisputed or uncontested losses for insurers under policies issued by that agent or general agent.

(14) Except for a commissioned peace officer who engages in the business of private investigation or compensates others who engage in the business of private investigation or the business of security services or both, any commissioned peace officer as defined in division (B) of section 2935.01 of the Revised Code.

(I) "Employee" means every person who may be required or directed by any employer, in consideration of direct or indirect gain or profit, to engage in any employment, or to go, or work, or be at any time in any place of employment, provided that the employer of the employee deducts all applicable state and federal employment taxes on behalf of the employee.

## Sec. 4749.04.
(A) The director of commerce may revoke, suspend, or refuse to renew, when a renewal form has been submitted, the license of any private investigator or security guard provider, or the registration of any employee of a private investigator or security guard provider, for any of the following:

(1) Violation of any of the provisions of division (B) or (C) of section 4749.13 of the Revised Code;

(2) Conviction of a felony or a crime involving moral turpitude;

(3) Violation of any rule of the director governing private investigators, the business of private investigation, security guard providers, or the business of security services;

(4) Testifying falsely under oath, or suborning perjury, in any judicial proceeding;

(5) Failure to satisfy the requirements specified in division (D) of section 4749.03 of the Revised Code.

Any person whose license or registration is revoked, suspended, or not renewed when a renewal form is submitted may appeal in accordance with Chapter 119. of the Revised Code.

(B) In lieu of suspending, revoking, or refusing to renew the class A, B, or C license, or of suspending, revoking, or refusing to renew the registration of an employee of a class A, B, or C licensee, the director of commerce may impose a civil penalty of not more than one hundred dollars for each calendar day of a violation of any of the provisions of this section or of division (B) or (C) of section 4749.13 of the Revised Code or of a violation of any rule of the director governing private investigators, the business of private investigation, security guard providers, or the business of security services.

### Sec. 4749.06.

(A) Each class A, B, or C licensee shall register the licensee's investigator or security guard employees, with the department of commerce, which shall maintain a record of each licensee and registered employee and make it available, upon request, to any law enforcement agency. The class A, B, or C licensee shall file an application to register a new employee no sooner than three days nor later than seven calendar days after the date on which the employee is hired.

(B)(1) Each employee's registration application shall be accompanied by one complete set of the employee's fingerprints, one recent photograph of the employee, the employee's physical description, and an eighteen-dollar registration fee.

(2) If the director requests the bureau of criminal identification and investigation to conduct an investigation of a licensee's employee and if the bureau

assesses the director a fee for the investigation, the director, in addition to any other fee assessed pursuant to this chapter, may assess the licensee a fee that is equal to the fee assessed by the bureau. If, after investigation, the bureau finds that the employee has not been convicted of a felony within the last twenty years, the director shall issue to the employee an identification card bearing the license number and signature of the licensee, which in the case of a corporation shall be the signature of its president or its qualifying agent, and containing the employee's name, address, age, physical description, and right thumb print or other identifying mark as the director prescribes, a recent photograph of the employee, and the employee's signature. The director may issue a duplicate of a lost, spoliator, or destroyed identification card issued under this section, upon payment of a fee fixed by the director, not exceeding five dollars.

(C) Except as provided in division (E) of this section, no class A, B, or C licensee shall permit an employee, other than an individual who qualified a corporation for licensure, to engage in the business of private investigation, the business of security services, or both businesses until the employee receives an identification card from the department, except that pending the issuance of an identification card, a class A, B, or C licensee may offer for hire security guard or investigator employees provided the licensee obtains a waiver from the person who receives, for hire, security guard or investigative services, acknowledging that the person is aware the employees have not completed their registration and agreeing to their employment.

(D) If a class A, B, or C licensee, or a registered employee of a class A, B, or C licensee, intends to carry a firearm, as defined in section 2923.11 of the Revised Code, in the course of engaging in the business or employment, the licensee or registered employee shall satisfactorily complete a firearms basic training program that includes twenty hours of handgun training and five hours of training in the use of other firearms, if any other firearm is to be used, or equivalency training, if authorized, or shall be a former peace officer who previously had successfully completed a firearms training course, shall receive a certificate of satisfactory completion of that program or written evidence of approval of the equivalency training, shall file an application for registration, shall receive a firearm-bearer notation on the licensee's or registered employee's identification card, and shall annually equality on a firearms range, all as described in division (A) of section 4749.10 of the Revised Code. A private investigator, security guard provider, or employee is authorized to carry a firearm only in accordance with that division.

(E) This section does not apply to commissioned peace officers, as defined in division (B) of section 2935.01 of the Revised Code, working for, either as an employee or independent contractor, a class A, B, or C licensee. For purposes of this chapter, a commissioned peace officer is an employee exempt from registration.

**SECTION 2.** That existing sections 4749.01, 4749.04, and 4749.06 of the Revised Code are hereby repealed.

**SECTION 3.** Section 4749.01 of the Revised Code is presented in this act as a composite of the section as amended by both Am. Sub. S.B. 162 and Am. H.B. 229 of the 121st General Assembly. The General Assembly, applying the principle stated in division (B) of section 1.52 of the Revised Code that amendments are to be harmonized if reasonably capable of simultaneous operation, finds that the composite is the resulting version of the section in effect prior to the effective date of the section as presented in this act.

http://www.homelandsecurity.ohio.gov/pisg.htm

**Oklahoma**
Council on Law Enforcement Education & Training
Private Security Division
P. O. Box 11476-Cimarron Station
Oklahoma City, OK 73136-0476
(405) 425-2775

State requirements:
**390:35-5-2. Security guard, armed security guard, and private investigator licenses**
(a) Applicants for security guard, private investigator, or armed security guard licenses must meet and satisfy the requirements set forth in 59 O.S., Section 1750.5.
(b) Applicants for Armed Security Guard or firearms authorized licenses must further:
    (1) Successfully pass a psychological evaluation by a licensed psychologist; provided that the applicant shall bear the cost of such evaluation.
    (2) Successfully complete the firearms phase of private security training;
    (3) Be twenty-one (21) years of age, and
    (4) Applicants for an armed security guard license must submit an affidavit that they are gainfully employed as an armed security guard and that a firearm is required within the scope of their employment.

(c) An Armed Security Guard License grants no authority to carry a firearm when not acting directly in the course and scope of employment.

(d) No licensee shall brandish, point, exhibit, or otherwise display a firearm at any time, except as authorized by law, and the rules of this Chapter.

(e) Private Investigators must complete four (4) hours of continuing education training from an approved source, each year to maintain their license. This training will be reported to CLEET at the time of license renewal. Firearms requalification courses will not count towards mandate training. Approved sources are:

> (1) College credit hours, fifteen hours of mandate training will be granted for each successfully completed college hour. Proof of attendance needed is a certified copy of the grade report;
>
> (2) Established Entities (Recognized county, state, and federal associations, vo-techs), one hour of training will be granted for each hour attended. Proof of attendance needed is a copy of a certificate or sign-in roster from the sponsor; or
>
> (3) CLEET Accredited Schools, Seminars, and Conferences, one hour of mandate training credit will be granted for each hour of instruction (minimum four (4) hour course). For approval to conduct mandate training, sponsors must:
>
>> (A) Submit a written request for program accreditation to CLEET;
>>
>> (B) Provide course outline, and course objectives;
>>
>> (C) Provide Resume for Instructors; and
>>
>> (D) After training, submit a roster of attendees completing the training to CLEET.

(f) Any person seeking an Oklahoma Security Guard or Private Investigators license, who has been licensed by a state whose training and standards have been deemed comparable to and approved by the Oklahoma Council on Law Enforcement Education and Training may obtain a license by reciprocity, under the following conditions:

> (1) The applicant must meet the minimum license requirement standards set forth by Oklahoma Law
> including fingerprint requirements. Such fingerprints requirement may be waived by CLEET where a verified records check has been made within a reasonable period of time in the context of existing law requiring fingerprint checks.
>
> (2) The applicant must have an active license in the original licensing state, and not be subject to any administrative action regarding the active status in the licensing state.

(3) The applicant receiving a license by reciprocity in Oklahoma shall at all times while working as a security guard or private investigator in Oklahoma be subject to all laws regarding security guards and private investigators including all applicable fees for such license.

(4) Reciprocity may be granted only from the state in which the applicant was originally licensed and not from any intervening state by reciprocity to the original licensing state.

(5) The applicant must sign a statement of irrevocable consent that service of process, in any complaint or disciplinary action filed against the applicant, arising out of the applicant's private investigative activities in the reciprocating state, may be made by the delivery of such process on the administrator of the private investigation regulatory agency in his/her/its state of residence.

(6) An armored car employee who is primarily employed by an armored car company in another state, and is properly licensed by that state to carry a weapon while acting in the services of that company in the home state, and meets the minimum home state requirements, would be exempt from other requirements of 59 O. S. Section 1750.1 et seq. during such time as the armored vehicle from that state is actively engaged in interstate commerce within Oklahoma pursuant to 15 U.S.C. Section 5901, the Armored Car Industry Reciprocity Act of 1993."

http://www.cleet.state.ok.us/Private_Security.htm

Association: http://www.opia.com/

## Oregon
Oregon Board of Investigators
445 State Office Bldg.
800 NE Oregon Street #33
Portland, OR 97232
(503) 731-4359
(503) 731-4366 fax

State requirements: http://landru.leg.state.or.us/ors/703.html

Association: http://www.oali.org/

## Pennsylvania
Office of the clerk of the court of common pleas of the county wherein the principal office or such business is located

State requirements: http://www.pali.org/papdact.htm

Association: http://www.pali.org/

## Puerto Rico
Policia De Puerto Rico
GPO Box 70166
San Juan, PR  00936
(787) 793-1234

## Rhode Island
State of Rhode Island
Providence Plantations
345 Harris Avenue
Providence, RI 29221
(401) 277-2000

State requirements:

**§ 5-5-3 License qualifications.** – In order to be eligible for a license, an applicant must:

(1) Be a citizen of the United States or a resident alien;

(2) Not have been convicted in any jurisdiction of a felony;

(3) Not have had any previous private investigator license or registration revoked or application for that license or registration denied by the appropriate authority of any local licensing authority;

(4) Not have been declared by any court of competent jurisdiction incompetent by reason of mental defect or disease unless the court has subsequently determined that his or her competency has been restored;

(5) Not suffer from habitual drunkenness or from narcotics addiction or dependence;

(6) Be of good moral character;

(7) Have experience that has been gained through:

(i) At least five (5) years experience as an investigator or as a police officer with a state, county or municipal police department or with an investigative agency of the United States of America or of any state, county or municipality; or

(ii) A degree in criminal justice from an accredited college or university; or

(iii) Employment by a private detective as an investigator for at least five (5) years; or

(iv) Substantively equivalent training or experience.

http://www.rilin.state.ri.us/Statutes/TITLE5/5-5/INDEX.HTM

Association:
State of Rhode Island
Providence Plantations
345 Harris Avenue
Providence, RI  29221
(402) 277-2000

## South Carolina
State Law Enforcement Division
Regulatory Services
P. O. Box 21398
Columbia, SC  29221-1398
(803) 737-9000
(803) 896-7041 fax

State requirements:
### Private Investigations
Any person who obtains or furnishes information defined in Section 40-18-20(A), South Carolina Code of Laws for a fee, or employs others to do so, is required to secure a license and/or registration as a private investigator in South Carolina. The only exceptions to this requirement are listed in South Carolina Code Section 40-18-140. Information clarifying requirements as they relate to various types of information businesses are discussed in the "Frequently Asked Questions" section of this web site.

### Private Investigation Businesses
**SECTION 40-18-20.** Definitions.
As used in this chapter, unless the context otherwise requires, the term:
(A) "Private investigation business" means engaging in business or accepting employment to obtain or furnish information with reference to the:
    (1) identity, habits, conduct, business, occupation, honesty, integrity, credibility, knowledge, trustworthiness, efficiency, loyalty, activity,

movement, whereabouts, affiliations, associations, transactions, acts, reputation, or character of a person;

(2) location, disposition, or recovery of lost or stolen property;

(3) cause or responsibility for fires, libels, losses, accidents, damage, or injury to persons or property; or

(4) securing of evidence to be used in a criminal or civil proceeding, or before a board, an administrative agency, an officer, or investigating committee.

**SECTION 40-18-30.** Powers and duties of South Carolina Law Enforcement Division (SLED).

(B) The Chief of SLED has the following powers and duties as they relate to the practice of private investigation businesses:

(1) to determine the eligibility of applicants for licenses and registration under this chapter;

(2) to investigate alleged violations of this chapter and regulations promulgated by SLED;

(3) to promulgate regulations necessary to carry out this chapter; and

(4) to require training necessary to provide for competent delivery of services to the public;

(C) SLED must keep a record of all information received from other states and the United States Department of Justice pertaining to criminal identification systems. SLED must cooperate with other jurisdictions in criminal identification.

(D) Fingerprint cards submitted to SLED pursuant to Sections 40-18-50, 40-18-60, 40-18-70, and 40-18-100 must be submitted by SLED to the Federal Bureau of Investigation to facilitate a national criminal records check of the applicant.

**SECTION 40-18-40.** Licenses to operate private investigation business; transferability; surrender on termination of business or change of ownership.

Licenses to operate private investigation businesses are the property of SLED and are not transferable. Licenses must be surrendered immediately to SLED upon the termination of a business or upon a change of ownership, possession, or control of a corporation or business entity. The transfer of twenty-five percent or more of corporate stock is considered a change in ownership.

**SECTION 40-18-70.** Private Investigation License; applications; bond; renewal; display of license; qualifications of licensee; contract; reports to clients; arrest of licensee; inspections of business records; prior licensees.

(A) A person who desires to operate a private investigation business in this State must apply for a Private Investigation License from SLED and pay an annual license fee which must be set by SLED regulation.

(1) If the applicant is an association or corporation, the chief executive officer of the association or corporation must be the applicant or must designate in writing the corporate officer or principal who is the applicant.

(2) If the applicant is a partnership, all partners must complete an application form.

(3) The application for license must be made, under oath, on a form approved by SLED. The application must state the applicant's full name, age, date and place of birth, current residence address, residence addresses for the past ten years, employment for the past ten years, including names and addresses of employers, the applicant's current occupation with the name and address of the current employer, the date and place of any arrests, any convictions for violations of federal or state laws, excluding traffic violations, and any additional information as SLED requires. Each applicant must submit with the application one complete set of the applicant's fingerprints on forms specified and furnished by SLED and one color photograph of the applicant's full face, without head covering, taken within six months of the application.

(B) The applicant must post a ten thousand dollar bond with SLED in a form approved by the Attorney General in favor of the State. The bond must be issued by a surety insurer licensed to transact surety insurance in this State. The surety on the bond may cancel the bond upon giving thirty days' notice to SLED and is relieved of liability for a breach of condition after the effective date of cancellation.

(C) Upon receiving the application, bond, and license fee and upon satisfaction after investigation of the competency and integrity and qualifications of the applicant, SLED must grant a license to the applicant to conduct the private investigation business stated in the application. Licensure is for one year and application for renewal must be on a form approved by SLED. The initial and annual renewal license fee for conducting a private investigation business must be set by regulation.

(D) Issuance of a license authorizes the licensee to engage in the private investigation business and to operate branch offices. Immediately upon receipt of the license certificate issued by SLED pursuant to this chapter, the licensee must post and at all times display the license in a conspicuous place at his primary place of business. A copy or duplicate of the license certificate must be conspicuously posted at each branch office. The licensee must immediately notify SLED of the address of each branch office opened or closed.

(E) SLED may issue a license to a person who:

(1) is at least twenty-one years of age;

(2) has a high school diploma or equivalent;

(3) is a citizen of the United States;

(4) has not been convicted of a felony or a crime involving moral turpitude;

(5) is of good moral character;

(6) does not unlawfully use drugs;

(7) does not use alcohol to such a degree as to affect adversely his ability to perform competently the duties of a private investigator, has not been adjudicated an incapacitated person without being restored to legal competency, and who has no physical or mental impairment which would prevent him from competently performing the duties of a private investigator;

(8) has not been discharged from the military service with other than an honorable discharge;

(9) has at least three years' experience:

  (a) as a private investigator employed by a licensed private investigation agency;

  (b) as an investigator for a law firm, a government agency, a private corporation, a nonprofit organization, or in a capacity that SLED determines has provided the requisite investigative experience; or

  (c) as a sworn officer with a federal, state, county, or municipal law enforcement agency.

(F) A private investigator licensed under this chapter must, prior to commencement of services or investigation ordered by a client, secure a contract signed by the client and the private investigator, on a form approved by SLED, describing in detail the services to be provided, fees to be charged, and an understanding by both parties concerning delivery of the written report. A client may waive the right to a written contract by signing a form approved by SLED.

(G) A private investigator licensed under the provisions of this chapter must provide to each client, in compliance with the contract describing the investigation or other services, and within a reasonable time of the conclusion of contracted work, a written report accurately detailing hours worked, activities accounting for time charged, and results of an investigation. This requirement is satisfied if the private investigator maintains in his files a waiver of written report signed by a client.

(H) A private investigator licensed under the provisions of this chapter must maintain for a period of three years copies of all written service contracts and investigation reports.

(I) Evidence of criminal activity discovered by a licensed or registered private investigator must be immediately reported to the Chief of SLED.

(J) A licensee who is arrested must report the custodial arrest to SLED within seventy-two hours of the arrest.

(K) Licensees must make business records available during normal business hours for inspection by the Chief of SLED or his designee.

(L) A person initially licensed as a private investigator before the effective date of this section, and who has maintained his license, is not required to meet the requirements contained in subsections (E)(1), (4), and (8).

**SECTION 40-18-80.** Private investigator registration certificates; application; qualifications of applicants; exemptions.

(B) Within thirty days of the employment of a person who will perform the functions of a private investigator, a private investigator licensee, or the person to be employed as an investigator must make application to SLED for registration of the person to be employed as a private investigator. After thirty days, a licensee may not authorize a person to perform the duties of a private investigator unless that person holds a valid private investigator registration certificate or has applied for one. The licensee may apply and pay the fee for the private investigator registration certificate or may require the person to be employed as an investigator to apply and pay the fee. For purposes of the penalties provisions of this chapter, the licensee and the person to be employed as an investigator are both responsible for ensuring that the person performing duties of an investigator is registered or has made application to be registered.

http://www.sled.state.sc.us/default.htm

Association: http://www.scalinv.com/

**South Dakota**
No PI license, but business license through Department of Revenue required.
Main Department of Revenue Office number: (800) 829-9188

State requirements:
http://legis.state.sd.us/IssueMemos/IssueMemos/im95-08.pdf

**Tennessee**
Department of Commerce & Insurance
Private Protective Services Division
500 James Robertson Parkway
Nashville, TN 37243-1158

(615) 741-6382

State requirements: http://tennessee.gov/commerce/boards/sil/pi/fees.html

Association:
http://www.tpia.com/
http://www.tai.com

## Texas
Texas Commission on Private Security
4930 S. Congress, Suite C-305
Austin, TX 78745
P. O. Box 13509
Austin, TX 78711
(512) 463-5545
(512) 452-2307 fax

State requirements:
**Private Investigator**
Licensing and Duties of Investigations Companies and Security Services
Contractors

**Sec. 1702.101.** Investigations Company License required. Unless the person holds a license as an investigations company, a person may not:
(1) act as an investigations company;
(2) offer to perform the services of an investigations company; or
(3) engage in business activity for which a license is required under this chapter.

**Sec. 1702.104.** Investigations Company. A person acts as an investigations company for the purposes of this chapter if the person:

(1) engages in the business of obtaining or furnishing, or accepts employment to obtain or furnish, information related to:
>  (A) crime or wrongs done or threatened against a state or the United States;
>  (B) the identity, habits, business, occupation, knowledge, efficiency, loyalty, movement, location, affiliations, associations, transactions, acts, reputation, or character of a person;
>  (C) the location, disposition, or recovery of lost or stolen property; or
>  (D) the cause or responsibility for a fire, libel, loss, accident, damage, or injury to a person or to property;
(2) engages in the business of securing, or accepts employment to secure,

evidence for use before a court, board, officer, or investigating committee;
(3) engages in the business of securing, or accepts employment to secure, the electronic tracking of the location of an individual or motor vehicle other than for criminal justice purposes by or on behalf of a governmental entity; or
(4) engages in the business of protecting, or accepts employment to protect, an individual from bodily harm through the use of a personal protection officer.

**Sec. 1702.114.** Additional Qualifications for Investigations Company License
(a) An applicant for a license to engage in the business of an investigations company or the applicant's manager must have, before the date of the application, three consecutive years' experience in the investigative field as an employee, manager, or owner of an investigations company or satisfy other requirements set by the Private Security Bureau.

(b) The applicant's experience must be:
  (1) reviewed by the Private Security Bureau; and
  (2) determined to be adequate to qualify the applicant to engage in the business of an investigations company.

**Sec. 1702.130.** Use of Certain Titles, Uniforms, Insignia, or Identifications Prohibited.
(a) A license holder, or an officer, director, partner, manager, or employee of a license holder, may not:
  (1) use a title, an insignia, or an identification card, wear a uniform, or make a statement with the intent to give an impression that the person is connected with the federal government, a state government, or a political subdivision of a state government; or
  (2) use a title, an insignia, or an identification card or wear a uniform containing the designation "police."

(b) Subsection (a) does not prohibit a commissioned security officer employed by a political subdivision of this state from using a title, insignia, or identification card, wearing a uniform, or making a statement indicating the employment of that individual by the political subdivision.

**Sec. 1702.131.** Advertising. An advertisement by a license holder soliciting or advertising business must contain the license holder's company name and address as stated in Private Security Bureau records.

**Sec. 1702.132.** Reports to Employer or Client.
(a) A written report submitted to a license holder's employer or client may only be submitted by the license holder or manager or a person authorized by a license holder or manager. The person submitting the report shall exercise dili-

gence in determining whether the information in the report is correct.

(b) A license holder or an officer, director, partner, manager, or employee of a license holder may not knowingly make a false report to the employer or client for whom information is obtained.

**Sec. 1702.133.** Confidentiality, Information Relating to Criminal Offense.
(a) A license holder or an officer, director, partner, or manager of a license holder may not disclose to another information obtained by the person for an employer or client except:

    (1) at the direction of the employer or client; or
    (2) as required by state law or court order.

(b) A license holder or an officer, director, partner, or manager of a license holder shall disclose to a law enforcement officer or a district attorney, or that individual's representative, information the person obtains that relates to a criminal offense.

http://www.txdps.state.tx.us/psb/pi.aspx

Association: http://www.tali.org/

## Utah
Department of Public Safety & Law Enforcement Services
Bureau of Regulatory Licensing
4501 South 2700 West
Salt Lake City, UT 84119
(801) 965-4461

State requirements:
**53-9-108. Qualifications for licensure.**
(1) (a) An applicant for an agency license under this chapter shall be at least 21 years of age, a citizen or legal resident of the United States, and of good moral character.
    (b) An applicant may not have been:
        (i) convicted of a felony;
        (ii) convicted of an act involving illegally using, carrying, or possessing a dangerous weapon;
        (iii) convicted of an act of personal violence or force on any person or convicted of threatening to commit an act of personal violence or force against another person;
        (iv) convicted of an act constituting dishonesty or fraud;

(v) convicted of an act involving moral turpitude;

(vi) placed on probation or parole;

(vii) named in an outstanding arrest warrant; or

(viii) convicted of illegally obtaining or disclosing private, controlled, or protected records as provided in Section **63-2-801**.

(c) In assessing good moral character under Subsection (1)(b), the board shall consider mitigating circumstances presented by an applicant regarding information under Subsections (1)(b)(vi) and (viii).

(d) If previously or currently licensed in another state or jurisdiction, the applicant shall be in good standing within that state or jurisdiction.

(e) An applicant shall have completed a minimum of two years, or 2,000 hours, of investigative experience that consists of actual work performed as a private investigator for a private agency, the federal government, or a state, county, or municipal government.

(f) (i) An applicant for an agency license shall substantiate investigative work experience claimed as years of qualifying experience and provide the exact details as to the character and nature of the experience on a form prescribed by the department and certified by the applicant's employers.

    (ii) If the applicant is unable to supply written certification from an employer in whole or in part, the applicant may offer written certification from persons other than an employer covering the same subject matter for consideration by the board.

    (iii) The applicant shall prove completion of the required experience to the satisfaction of the board and the board may independently verify the certification offered on behalf of the applicant.

(2) (a) (i) An applicant for a registrant license shall meet all qualification standards of this section, except Subsection (1)(d).

    (ii) An applicant shall have a minimum of one year, or 1,000 hours, of investigative experience that consists of actual work performed as a private investigator for a private agency, the federal government, a state, county, or municipal government.

(b) A licensed registrant shall only work as an employee of, or an independent contractor with, licensed agencies as provided in Subsection **53-9-102**(19), and may not:

    (i) advertise his services or conduct investigations for the general public; or

    (ii) employ other private investigators or hire them as independent contractors.

(3) (a) An applicant for an apprentice license, lacking the experience required for a registrant license, shall meet all of the qualification standards in Subsection (1), except Subsection (1)(d) and complete an apprentice application.

(b) (i) An apprentice shall work under the direct supervision and guidance of a licensed agency, full-time for one year, or 1,000 hours, prior to eligibility for a registrant license.

(ii) A licensed apprentice shall only work under the direction of a licensed agency as provided in Subsection **53-9-102**(5), and may not:

(A) advertise his services or conduct investigations for the general public;

(B) employ other private investigators; or

(C) obtain information from the Utah State Tax Commission Motor Vehicle Division or Driver License Division within the Department of Public Safety, except the apprentice may utilize such information for a legitimate business need under the direct supervision of a licensed agency.

(4) (a) An applicant for an agency, registrant, or apprentice license may be eligible for a license without meeting all or part of the investigative work experience required by this section if the applicant:

(i) has a criminal justice degree from an accredited college or university;

(ii) is certified by Peace Officer Standards and Training; or

(iii) can substantiate other similar law enforcement or investigative training in the areas set forth in Subsection **53-9-102**(17).

(b) The board shall determine whether or not training may replace the work experience requirement and to what extent.

http://www.le.state.ut.us/~code/TITLE53/53_08.htm

Association: http://www.piau.com/p_home.asp

## Vermont
Board of Private Investigative and Armed Security Services
Office of Professional Regulation
109 State Street
Montpelier, VT 05609-1101
(802) 828-2837

State requirements:
**§ 3173. Private detective and private detective agency licenses**

(a) No person shall engage in the business of a private detective or operate a private detective agency in this state without first obtaining a license to do so from the board. The board shall not issue a license to a private detective or private detective agency without first obtaining and approving the following:

(1) An application filed in proper form.

(2) An application fee as established pursuant to section 3178a of this title.

(3) Evidence that the applicant has attained the age of majority.

(4) Evidence that the applicant has successfully passed the examination required by section 3175 of this title.

(b) The board may inquire of the Vermont criminal information center for any information on criminal records of the applicant, and the center shall provide such information to the board. The board, through the Vermont criminal information center, may also inquire of the appropriate state criminal record repositories in all states in which it has reason to believe an applicant has resided or been employed, and it may also inquire of the Federal Bureau of Investigation, for any information on criminal records of the applicant. When fingerprinting is required, the applicant shall bear the costs associated with the return and resubmission of illegible fingerprint cards. The board may also make such additional inquiries it deems necessary into the character, integrity and reputation of the applicant.

(c) The board shall require that the person has had appropriate experience in investigative work, for a period of not less than two years, as determined by the board. Such experience may include, but not be limited to, having been regularly employed as a private detective licensed in another state or as an investigator for a private detective licensed in this or another state, or has been a sworn member of a federal, state or municipal law enforcement agency.

(d) An application for a license may be denied upon failure of the applicant to provide information required, upon a finding that the applicant does not meet a high standard as to character, integrity and reputation or for unprofessional conduct defined in section 3181 of this title. (Added 1981, No. 98, § 1; amended 1989, No. 250 (Adj. Sess.), § 67; 1995, No. 144 (Adj. Sess.), § 8; 1999, No. 133 (Adj. Sess.), § 26.)

http://www.leg.state.vt.us/statutes/sections.cfm?Title=26&Chapter=059

Association:
Vermont Association of Licensed Detectives & Security Services
RR#1 Box 1112
Hardwick, VT 05843

## Virginia
Department of Criminal Justice Services
Private Security Section
P.O. Box 10110
Richmond, VA 23240-9998
(804) 786-4700

State requirements:
Course Time: 60 Hours

1. Orientation: applicable sections of the Code of Virginia; Administrative Code 6VAC 20-171; standards of professional conduct; and ethics – 6 hours

2. Law: basic law; legal procedures and due process; civil law; criminal law; evidence; and legal privacy requirements – 16 hours plus one practical exercise

3. General Investigative Skills, Tools and Techniques: surveillance; research; and interviewing – 16 hours plus one practical exercise

4. Documentation: Report preparations; photography; audio recording; general communication; and courtroom testimony – 8 hours plus one practical exercise

5. Types of investigations: accident; insurance; background; domestic; undercover; fraud and financial; missing persons and property; and criminal – 14 hours plus one practical exercise

www.dcjs.virginia.gov/pss/howto/registrations/privateInvestigator.cfm

Association: http://www.pisa.gen.va.us/

## Washington
Department of Licensing, Public Protection Unit
405 Black Lake Boulevard
P.O. Box 9649
Olympia, WA 98507-9649

State requirements: http://www.dol.wa.gov/ppu/pifront.htm

Associations:
http://www.pnai.com/html/index.htm
http://www.wali.org/

## West Virginia
Secretary of State

Licensing Division
Private Investigator Licensing
Charleston, WV  25301

State requirements: www.wvsos.com/licensing/piguard/basiceligibility.htm

Association:
Private Investigators & Private Security
Professionals of West Virginia
Email: cookpi@citynet.net

**Wisconsin**
Department of Regulation & Licensing
P.O. Box 8935
Madison, WI  53708
(608) 266-0829

State requirements: http://drl.wi.gov/index.htm

Association: http://www.pawli.com/

**Wyoming**
Regulated by local jurisdictions.

**1. Do I have to have a license to be a private investigator in Wyoming?**
No, but some municipalities may regulate private investigators and security
alarm companies via city ordinance. You should check with the municipalities
where you will conduct business.

**2. Do I have to have a license to operate a security firm in Wyoming?**
No, but you may need to register with the Secretary of State if your company
conducts business in Wyoming, the Wyoming Department of Revenue if you
are subject to the state revenue laws and some municipalities may regulate
private security firms.

> *Be advised that all internet information is subject to change (daily).
> There is no guarantee that these web site links or this information will
> remain active. If a link does not work go to Google.com and enter the
> state, private investigator/detective license or association. (Example:
> Tennessee private investigator license)*

## NATIONAL AND INTERNATIONAL ASSOCIATIONS

National Council of Investigation & Security Services:
http://www.nciss.org/

N.A.L.I. National Association of Legal Investigators:
http://www.nalionline.org/

World Association of Detectives:
http://www.world-detectives.com/home.htm
http://www.wad.net/

# CHAPTER X

# WAR STORIES

War stories are stories based on real cases. In order to protect the privacy of the individuals involved, no names or places are identified. In almost all of these stories the unexpected happened when I least expected it. Any resemblance to anyone, guilty or innocent, is purely coincidental.

## CHEATING SPOUSE

Spouses who listen to their instincts and intuitions are usually correct. It is almost predictable that a spouse who thinks their spouse is cheating will first experience denial. They don't want to believe it is happening to them so they just pretend it is not happening. Eventually they will reach the next stage, acceptance. When a spouse reaches acceptance they have to deal with the situation one way or another. This is when they will probably hire a private investigator or consult with an attorney for advice. Finally a spouse will reach a stage of anger. When a spouse gets angry they are ready for divorce.

It seems that as many men as women are cheating spouses. Regardless of which one is the client, most of them just want to know the truth, that their suspicions are correct. State divorce laws dictate whether it is a no-fault divorce or not. If the divorce occurs in a no-fault state, then it does not matter, one way or another, what either spouse has done. All that is involved is how to divide the marital assets, who gets custody of the kids, and what kind of settlement will be arranged. In states that do not have no-fault laws, the results of an investigation may be used as leverage in cases where there are children or a large settlement is involved.

One married man made his wife suspicious after he retired from a successful self-employed occupation and took a part time job working as a janitor at the airport at night. He began giving a ride to work to a young female co-worker. They worked the night shift as janitors at the airport. The airport was closed at night, so there was no way to watch them. Security was tight. They had access to every door in the building. The husband would come home talking about his co-worker fixing a pot of coffee for them up in the Admiral's Club (a private section of the airport for members only). The husband talked about his female co-worker so often that the wife had no doubts of what was going on. It was later learned by the wife that this same married man often gave money to another of the younger female co-workers who had quite a reputation for having sex with all the men.

The wife enjoyed her flying privileges so much that she never confronted her husband about cheating. She just traveled and stayed gone all the time and gave him more and more opportunity to cheat.

Some spouses reach a point where they give up and just don't care. Maybe they are dependent or don't want to lose their "bread and butter," so they compromise. Some let the husband cheat while the wife spends his hard earned money. It becomes a "trade-off."

Another time the husband told the wife (who just had a baby) that he had to get up and go to work an hour early because of extra work that needed to be done. After the husband left for work the wife remembered something to tell him so, after giving him plenty of time to arrive at work, she placed a call. The phone rang and rang, but no answer. The wife kept calling, thinking that either her husband had been involved in an accident or that he had lied and was meeting another woman. Finally on the last call she let it ring a good thirty minutes until finally her husband answered. He was huffing and puffing and said he had just run downstairs to get something. Asked how long he had been downstairs, he said only a few minutes. He did not know the phone had been ringing for thirty minutes. The wife immediately knew he had lied, and never trusted him again after that. She decided not to leave but stay and make his life miserable after that.

## THE OLD FOOL

It has been said that there is "No fool like an old fool." In another case the husband was about 75 years old and had been married for about 50 years. His wife had no knowledge of him having a girlfriend until he was in a car accident and broke his hip. The girlfriend showed up at the hospital and offered to sit with him. The wife did not know who she was and questioned why this woman would offer to sit with her husband. The woman told the wife she did volunteer work for her church. The wife became suspicious that this woman was actually her husband's girlfriend. When the husband returned from the hospital the wife put a recorder on their phone and every time she left he would call the girlfriend. Instead of filing for a divorce, the wife wanted to stay married. She decided she needed to do something to break him and his girlfriend up. After the husband was able to drive again, the wife contacted me to talk about hiring me to follow him and catch him with the girlfriend. This was going to be too expensive. She already knows they are seeing each other. All she wants to do is stop the affair. Instead of following him, the wife asked me if I would make a call to their house while they were gone and leave a message on their answering machine. She wanted me to pretend to be the girlfriend. The wife planned what she wanted me to say. She wanted me to say that I have been seeing some other men and that she had tested positive for AIDS. I have been asked to do a lot of crazy things, but this one was one of the craziest. I went to a pay phone and left a message on the recorder. I pretended to be crying and was very apologetic for causing any problem, but that I had something very important to tell the husband. I left the message about seeing the other men and that I was tested positive for AIDS and was worried about him. I am a person who does not like to use a pretext for anything. I have never done anything like this before and had no experience. But apparently I was very convincing. When the couple returned home the wife knew that I was going to leave this message, but when she actually heard it she said it sounded real and she began to cry and locked herself in the bathroom. She said her husband was banging on the door and apologizing and promising he would never see that woman again. Later the wife left and the husband called the girlfriend and told her he never wanted to see her again. Of course the wife had a recorder on the phone line and was sure this was the end of the affair. The wife called me later and thanked me for "saving her marriage."

And then there was the time that the wife learned the husband was seeing prostitutes and told him she was going to divorce him and take everything he had. He said "before you get your hands on a dime I will spend every penny. When the money runs out I will kill myself. You will not get anything."

The husband had someone forge the wife's name to a second mortgage on his or her home. He was an executive vice president of a large corporation and had a lot of stock in the company. One day he took over $100,000.00 from his company and left work without telling anyone where he was going. The wife was so upset, thinking he would kill himself, that she asked me to locate him and try to prevent him from suicide. There was not much I could do without a trail.

One day his secretary received a call. A topless dancer in Texas had been given a large check by the missing executive and she was calling to verify that the check was good. Apparently he had told her where he worked and to call if she wanted to check him out. The secretary notified his wife.

The wife called me to ask me to go to the topless bar in Texas and talk with the dancer who called about the check. Now I had a trail to follow. I called the dancer and told her the story about the missing executive and that everyone was worried that he might kill himself. I told her I was coming there and wanted to talk to her. She was expecting me and was very cooperative.

Apparently the missing executive had been a regular visitor to the topless bar and was a big tipper. Several of the dancers knew him. I learned that he was attracted to one of the dancers and he was probably with her, but she was not there.

With permission from the manager I was allowed to be inside the club without an escort. The manager requested I sit over to the side, so as not to distract from the dancers. Now I am the oldest woman in there and the only one fully dressed. I was sitting all alone and way out of the way. On two separate occasions two men wandered over to my table to ask me what I was doing there. I asked for their business card, then gave them mine and said, "Your wife said to tell you to have a good time."

Several days went by and there was no sign of the missing executive or the dancer he was probably with. Finally one of the dancers heard that the girl he was attracted to was currently dancing in a club in Georgia. A call to her parents resulted in the motel where she was staying and they verified that he was with her there.

I contacted the wife to tell her where her husband was then returned to Nashville. His brother drove to the motel in Georgia and picked up the missing executive. He was later admitted to a sexual addiction clinic.

After the divorce the wife was left penniless and in debt. The executive later went to work for another company and eventually married the topless dancer who was as young as his daughter.

I could fill this book with endless "war stories." From these examples you see that the main reason anyone hires a private investigator to catch a cheating spouse is to find the truth. People can deal with the truth. It is the unknown and suspicions that people cannot deal with. The truth sets them free.

From years and years of dealing with domestic cases I learned that divorce can be devastating to many people. Not only the two people who were married, but the children and other relatives, and everyone they know may be affected. Divorce causes many people a lot of pain. It is probably one of the most traumatic experiences a person will ever experience. Recovering from divorce may take years. For some it may take a lifetime.

## THE KINGPIN

An attorney contacted me to come to his office and meet his client. He explained that the woman thought her husband was having an affair with his bookkeeper. I went to the office and signed a contract to check on the cheating husband.

I followed the husband and his bookkeeper as they made their daily rounds. I watched them go from place to place but did not know exactly what was going on. For all I knew he was collecting rent. It was later that I learned the husband was involved in money laundering and illegal activities.

A tracking device was placed on the husband's car. At that time it was legal to do so. As the batteries on the device became weak I had to actually get under his car to retrieve the transmitter and change them. I had to wait for a good opportunity to do this. I could not do it at his business or home, so it had to be a public place. I followed him to a country club where he went to play golf. This was the perfect opportunity. I was able to get the transmitter and change the batteries without being detected. It turned out that he was playing golf with some local politicians, including the police chief. Later it was suggested that the golf course was a meeting place for politicians to receive their payoffs.

One day as I waited for the husband I realized that he did not leave as expected. I waited and waited and finally I saw him run out of the house and get into his car and take off at a high rate of speed. He was unaware that anyone was watching him. I trailed him to work then received a call from his daughter. Then the unexpected happened. While I was waiting for him to leave his house, he had just attempted to kill the wife, my client. He had choked her and left her in the floor of their home. After that the wife told me he kept over $100,000. cash in a floor safe in their home. She had taken this money and that's when he beat her up. Little by little I learned more and more about the husband and his activities.

The wife went to an undisclosed location so the husband could not find her. She told me that she expected her husband and some of his other friends to take a private plane out of the country to launder some money. She asked me to follow him to the airport and make sure he got on the plane so that she would feel safe to go back to their home and get her things out. The woman was in fear of her life. I watched the husband in the airport. He was carrying a lot of cash on him. I sat in the waiting area as each person boarded the private plane. The husband told the others he was expecting his wife and pretended to be waiting for her. As he paced around the waiting area and it was time for the plane to take off he turned to me and said "We have an extra seat, do you want to go?" I shook my head no.

The wife packed up and moved out while the husband was out of the country. Even though she feared for her life, knew her husband was having an affair, and knew about the illegal activities the husband was able to persuade her not to file for divorce and offered to build her the home of her dreams as a peace offering.

Last I heard there was no divorce and she has a beautiful new mansion. They are members of the country club and thought of as fine upstanding pillars of the community.

## POLITICAL CORRUPTION

I was contacted and asked to work on what appeared to be a background investigation. It did not seem to be a big deal. My client was an out of state attorney who was referred to me by a former FBI agent friend of mine. My friend had recently been elected to a new job and was unable to work the case for the attorney. The attorney wanted a female with a southern accent to blend into a small southern town without being detected. My mission was not that easy. I was to go to this small town and not talk to anyone. No one was supposed to see me or know I was there. Yet my mission was to obtain certain information for the client. The client asked me to find out if a certain small town lawyer was representing some politicians.

I called my ex-FBI friend to thank him for the referral and he cautioned me to be careful and not work on this case alone. He told me I could get killed. I didn't think it sounded that important or dangerous. He told me to meet him and he would brief me on what was going on. It turned out that it was much more than I expected. The people I was asked to investigate were thought to be involved in a federal bid-rigging.

My client gave me the names of three well known politicians. I was to sit and watch the attorney's office, follow the attorney, get the garbage, or do whatever was required to determine if these three politicians were connected to this attorney. I thought I could do this without being noticed. As I sat in a parked rental car across from the attorney's office watching for any activity I became aware that I probably looked suspicious to the locals. So I decided to get out of the car and walk around the local courthouse and square. I could not talk to anyone or ask questions. I was not to call attention to myself. I decided to go in the courthouse and look at some court docket books to get a feel for the attorney. I looked for lawsuits, judgments, and leins. The office workers tried to talk to me, to find out who I was and what I was doing. I didn't mean for anyone to notice me, so I thought I had better leave. As I started to walk back to the car I thought this was going to take longer than I expected and I might be there for days, maybe weeks. I thought I would wait for the attorney's office to close then go to the back and check for garbage. It is not uncommon for law enforcement and other investigators to get information from garbage. Before I got to the car I had a strong impulse to stick my head in the attorney's office and see what it looked like. On the spur of the moment I opened the door and saw a young female receptionist. My first reaction was to leave, but now that she had seen me I thought I would draw too much attention by leaving without saying anything, so I said "Do you have something called a Martingale Hubbell book? I knew that was not the correct name but she didn't know what I was talking about anyway. She asked what it was. I said "It is a book that has listings of attorneys, and I was looking for an attorney who represented song writers." This was not a well thought out plan….it was a spur of the moment impulse. Then the unexpected happened, the attorney heard me and came out of his office to tell me there was a book back in the library conference room. The attorney did not ask who I was, or what I was doing. I was escorted to the library and was given a Martindale-Hubbell directory to look at. As I sat down and began flipping pages I glanced around the room. I was sitting at a six foot long conference table with papers stacked everywhere.

I could not have planned this to happen, but the attorney told the receptionist that he was going to lunch and would be back in an hour. I wished I was able to get to my rental car and follow the attorney to see who he was going to meet, but since I got into the office and didn't raise any suspicions, I thought I would sit tight and make the most of the opportunity. As luck would have it the receptionist got on the phone with a personal call. She forgot I was there and was not paying me any attention. I peeked at the papers in plain view on the conference table and they were all about the case my client was working on. I found a pen and began taking notes…..I did not have any paper so I wrote all over my body. I noticed a brand new Rolodex next to the phone. I flipped through it to see if the three politicians were by any chance in it and guess what? All three were in there…their unlisted private numbers, cell phones, faxes, etc. In fact, those were the only three people in the new Rolodex.

I left before the attorney returned and called my client to give him the unbelievable news. He was thrilled that I was able to accomplish this without arousing suspicions. With the information I obtained, my client was able to win a civil lawsuit that involved these politicians. No criminal charges were filed, but there was plenty of criminal activity involved. I'm saving the rest of this story for another book.

## DISABLED

A woman who worked as a LPN in a hospital claimed that while alone on the elevator a ceiling panel fell and injured her neck and shoulder. The alleged injury was going to prevent her from turning and lifting patients and she filed a lawsuit for $5,000,000.00 against the hospital. She said she had to wear a tinge machine to help with the pain. She also claimed she could not drive a car. She lived in a very rural area and it was practically impossible to sit on surveillance. After several attempts to watch the woman I decided to talk to her neighbor and learned that the neighbor did not like the woman next door. I asked for permission to park in her drive. From the next door neighbor's house I was able to watch the allegedly injured woman. I learned that her truck driver husband was drawing disability for a back injury. I photographed the disabled husband in the yard digging a garden, climbing a ladder to work on the roof, and lifting a concrete birdbath to mow the yard with a push mower. While video taping the husband the woman ran to the car (not wearing her tinge machine) and started to back it out of the drive. The husband jumped on the hood and she backed up and slammed on the brakes and threw him off. It was quite a show. Needless to say the woman's attorney decided to settle out of court because he did not want the video shown. State laws allowed her to receive "pain and suffering."

## AERIAL SURVEILLANCE

A cheating spouse went up a private drive on top of a hill. There were three houses using the same private drive. Not wanting to trespass or alarm the watch dogs, I decided to take my camera and go up in a helicopter. While the pilot circled the hillside I was able to shoot photos of the wife's car parked at one of the houses to determine who it was she was visiting.

This was actually a case of "pay-back." My client, the husband, had already been caught cheating with his girlfriend in Cancun by his wife's private investigator and he just wanted to catch the wife doing the same thing.

My client was so intent on catching his estranged wife and paying her back that he put a recording device in his wife's house and was recording her phone calls. He did not tell me he was doing this until the night when he got caught. He called me and asked me to come to his house immediately. Upon my arrival he asked me to open my trunk and put all the recording equipment in my car and tried to set me up as if I was the one doing the recording. I had no knowledge of it until that moment. Needless to say my client was in deep trouble. The wife's private investigator turned out to be a person I knew very well. That PI had installed a video camera to capture the person who placed the recording equipment at the wife's house. The husband was video taped changing the tapes in the recording equipment which he had placed under the wife's house. He could access it from outside her house, so when he had visitation with the children he could swap the tapes.

## THE MAN WITH THE MARBLE EYES

A birth father hired me to locate his twenty-one year old adopted son whom he never saw. The birth father and mother had dated for many years. Both were in separate colleges when she became pregnant. The father wanted to marry her and raise their child, but the mother did not want to get married and chose to give the child up for adoption. The father's name was not given and he had no parental rights.

After college both the father and mother married other people and both had other children and went on with their lives, however the father lived with an obsession to find his son. He agonized over whether the son was loved and had good adopted parents and even had counseling to help him deal with this situation. He felt guilty and responsible and unfortunately had no say-so about the adoption. He purposely waited until the son was twenty one before he tried to find him. He did not want to interrupt his life or cause a problem. He did not want to upset the adopted family. He only wanted peace of mind to know his son was all right.

The father contacted the birth mother, was married with a teen age son, to tell her he was going to search for their adopted son and wanted to know if she would like to meet him if he is located. Her husband had recently had heart surgery. She had never told them about the adopted son, so it was not a good time for her to break the news to her family and she did not want to be included in the search for her son.

The father began calling me regularly for updates on whether or not I had found the son and what was happening. The search took several months. I think he became addictive to my encouragement and every time we talked I reassured him that everything was going to be okay.

When I finally found the son he was working in a music store, so I was able to go in and shop around and strike up a conversation with him. I told him I was a private investigator and was working on a case in the small town where he lived. The son became intrigued and was very friendly and easy to talk to. When the right moment and opportunity presented itself I was able to bring up adoption. I told him I specialized in finding missing persons and had written a book on adoption searching. At that time he seemed completely unaware that I might be looking for him. He told me his girlfriend was adopted and he wanted her to meet me. He said his girlfriend was looking for her birth parents. I asked him if by any chance was he adopted to and he said yes. Then I asked if he had searched for his birth parents and he said no because he believed his biological parents were probably less than desirable people. He went on to tell me that he had been told his father was in the Navy and that he assumed his mother was a prostitute. He envisioned a drunken, drug addicted father living under a bridge. When the son told me why he did not want to find his biological family I knew that was the unexpected moment that seems to always occur when I work a case. I seized the moment and immediately reacted. This was a perfect opportunity to plant a seed for him to think about so I said "But what if your biological parents were people you are not ashamed of, people you would be proud of?" I could tell by his reaction that this had not occurred to him and that the seed was planted immediately. All I had to do was wait for the seed to take root and stir his curiosity.

A week passed before I returned to the music store. The minute I walked in the son said "Can we go outside and talk?" I had a feeling that he had given this some thought and was ready to ask some questions. Sure enough when we got outside he said "Do you think you can help me find my biological parents?" This is exactly what I hoped would happen. I could not have planned for this to go any better than it was going. I said "Well after we talked last week I did some checking and I think I know who his father is, and I assure you he is a very nice person that you would be proud of, not someone you would be ashamed of." Again when I least expected it, the unexpected happened….he said "Can you arrange for me to meet my father?" I said I would try. He said he wanted me to be with him when he met them and I told him I would be glad to be with him. I asked him when to arrange the meeting and he again surprised me with the unexpected…."How about tonight?" I said I would try to make arrangements and get back with him.

It was Saturday afternoon. I left and drove a few blocks away and called the father. He was home alone, watching a basketball game on tv. I asked if he had plans for that night and he said "no." I asked if he would like to have some company and he said "are you coming to see me?" I said "Yes, and I am bringing someone else." He said "Your husband?" I said, "No." There was a silent pause and he said "Is it who I think it is?" I said, "Yes, your son would like to meet you." The father was stunned. It was an overwhelming, unexpected surprise and he just began crying and sobbing. He was so happy and wanted to hear exactly what happened and how this was possible. I told him the whole story and he was so excited. I was so happy for him.

I called the son and told him that the father was going to be home and was expecting us. The son asked me to pick him up as soon as he got off work. I drove him to his father's mansion. His father had never been in the Navy. He was a very well educated business man from an affluent family and the son was in disbelief. As we arrived at the father's house the son just seemed to freeze. We walked up to the door and as the door opened the father seemed to freeze. I introduced them and immediately took a photograph of them meeting for the first time. The father had eyes that were like cracked marbles…and the son had those same cracked marble eyes. They were unmistakably the same eyes.

The father offered us something to drink. I told him to get out his family album so the son could get a feel for how the father had grown up. At first they did not know what to say to each other, but slowly they began asking questions and began learning about each other. After about three hours both of them were talking like old friends. It was about midnight when we left.

A week went by and the son had not contacted the father who was waiting for a call. The father was becoming depressed because he feared the son did not like him. Finally the son called and wanted to bring his girlfriend to meet the father. It was a gradual thing but the father and son took their time and got to be friends. Then the son wanted his adopted family to meet the father. All was going well. A year went by and the father had quit calling to keep me updated on how things were going. As far as I knew everything was fine. One day the father called and told me the son was getting married and that both he and the adopted father were going to be the best men at the wedding. This was one of the most successful adoption reunions I have ever experienced.

After a few years had passed I received a call from the father. He was at the hospital about to go into surgery. He said "I need to hear you tell me once again that everything is going to be okay." I said "Everything is going to be okay, call me when you wake up." And sure enough, everything was okay.

What a small world it is. After all these years I recently moved to a new house and guess who also lived on the same street? The father.

## PARENTAL ABDUCTIONS

The mother had not seen her daughter since she was six years old. The parents were divorced and the mother was remarried with other children. The child's father had visitation right and one day he took his daughter for a visit but did not return her. Instead he came back and set fire to the mother's house with the intent of burning up her and her family.

After that the father was on the run from the law with his daughter at his side. He told the daughter her mother did not love her or want her anymore and that she was going to live with him.

The daughter was twenty one when I was contacted by the mother to find her.

Even though the father had changed their names, the daughter had been issued a social security number when she was a baby and the mother gave me that information. When I ran the number I found the daughter and contacted her. She feared her father and was actually hiding from him and living with her boyfriend's family. At first she thought her father had hired me to locate her. She was quite shocked to learn that her mother had been looking for her all those years. She confided in me that her father had been very abusive and was in jail on an unrelated charge.

Instead of telling the mother I found her daughter, I arranged for her to appear on a local television show in hopes that someone in the viewing audience might know something. She came on the show with photos of her daughter at age six sitting on Santa's lap. She brought along her daughter's favorite stuffed animal. The mother could not talk about her daughter without crying, so needless to say it was a tearful plea for her daughter. Then after a few minutes the host of the show told her that her daughter had been located and was in fact at the studio. The mother turned pale and appeared totally surprised and shocked when the daughter appeared. They embraced and it was a wonderful reunion.

About a year later the daughter was planning to marry her boyfriend and wanted me to come to the wedding. The daughter treated me like I was her mother. She became very close to me.

Another year passed and the daughter was pregnant and ready to have a baby. About five o'clock in the morning my phone rang and it was the mother calling. My first reaction was that she was inconsiderate calling me at that time of the morning to tell me she was a grandmother. Instead the unexpected happened...the daughter had just died, three days after giving birth. Her spleen had ruptured and was undetected. What a terrible shock to everyone. The daughter had been so happy to be reunited with her mother and learn the truth that her mother really loved her. Then to marry and have her first baby....her life was going so great. I was so sorry to hear this news. To this day I still get choked up when I think about it. This was one of the saddest endings to a case that I had ever experienced.

## BACK FROM THE DEAD

In another parental abduction case the mother was looking for her forty-six year old daughter who had been missing since her father took her for a visit when she was six years old. The father told the daughter that her mother died and was cremated and for forty years this daughter grieved for her mother.

I located this daughter and contacted her and of course the unexpected happened. Instead of being happy she seemed angry and said "My mother is dead. What kind of cruel joke are you trying to pull on me?" I had no way of knowing that the father had lied to her and told her the mother was dead. I tried to assure her that her mother was alive and had been looking for her for forty years. The girl was in disbelief and wanted to call her father immediately. She called her father and he confessed that he had lied to her most of her life. She called me back and told me that now she believed me. She further explained that she had been in counseling most of her life and now she was going to need more. It was a very unusual situation, one that I had not experienced before.

I acted as an intermediary between the mother and daughter before they actually had any contact. Both needed to be prepared before they were finally reunited on television.

## FALSELY ACCUSED

A few years ago I planned to write a book based on a true case I had worked. I thought I needed a literary agent to represent me and asked another writer if he knew of one. The other writer said the literary agent had given him a business card, but that he did not know him personally. I called the literary agent to make an appointment to talk to him. He told me he already knew who I was and would like to meet me in a nice restaurant in downtown Nashville and talk about my new book.

> *Note: This should have been a red flag...why meet in a restaurant and not his office?*

I met the literary agent for lunch. He brought along some materials to show me who he was and told me that he represented another client whose book was being made into a movie. He said that he was talking to DreamWorks and others. He dropped a lot of names and sounded legitimate.

> *Note: This should have been a red flag...why did he have to prove to me who he was?*

He asked if I could possible turn my project into a screen play. I told him I did not know how to write a screen play, but would consider learning. I was totally surprised when he presented me with a contract and even more surprised that I signed it without reading it.

> *Note: This was another red flag...I should not have signed it without reading it...and he should have had an extra copy for me.*

I asked for a copy and he said he would send it to me. By the time I received a copy and read it, it was too late. He had included in the contract that he would receive 10% of everything I made.

Now I know when you feel a gut instinct that something does not look right, sound right, or feel right, that it probably is not right. Even though I did feel a "red flag" that this was too good to be true, I wanted to have an agent so bad that I did not listen to my instincts. Instead I chose denial that there was a problem. Before lunch was over I was convinced that this agent could get me a book deal and possibly a movie deal. I was totally blindsided.

About a week after signing the agent's contract he began calling and telling me bizarre stories. One story was that someone had broken into his automobile and stolen his gun. (I wondered why he felt the need to carry a gun.) Then he thought someone was trying to kill him. He contacted the sheriff's office to have them bring out drug sniffing dogs because he believed drugs were planted at his home. He asked me to run vehicle tags and do background investigations for him. One of his former clients was causing him a problem and he wanted to know if he was dangerous and if he had a prior criminal history. There was no end to all the favors he asked for my professional investigative services. I realized he was using me to get information for him. After months of nothing happening with my book deal, I was contacted for a possible movie deal. This was not something the agent had anything to do with until I told him about it and included him in the negotiating. During the negotiating the agent began acting strange. I was unable to contact him by phone. He was not in his office. I did not know what was going on, but whatever it was, I did not want him to represent me anymore. Finally I wrote a letter and terminated him. He responded with a threat of "I'll get you for this." I didn't know what he would do to "get me" but it was not a good feeling.

The movie deal never materialized and I never received a penny. Apparently the agent thought I fired him and cut him out of the deal and that I had received some money from it. I feel sure that what happened next was because he felt like I owed him some money from the movie deal.

After he threatened me he began harassing me. It was the most bizarre behavior I had ever seen. He began mailing me Bible verses. Then one day he mailed me an audio tape that had nothing but heavy breathing on it. It was getting stranger and stranger. Finally I reported it to the local authorities and they contacted him and told him to leave me alone.

Then there was a long period of silence and nothing else happened until one day when I received a phone call from a reporter. The reporter asked me about the lawsuit that the agent had just filed against me. I was caught completely off guard. I had no idea what the reporter was talking about. I asked him to fax me a copy and he did. That was the first I knew about all the false accusations this agent had made up to "get me."

After the local authorities told the agent to quit harassing me and leave me alone, he began filing false police reports monthly in another county, each with a different false accusation.

In his mind he thought I worked for a man he considered his enemy. The police reports named me and the other man as suspects for each false accusation. On one of the reports the officer had noted that the agent did not want him to contact me. Also on the reports he could not state the date or time of the alleged incidents. I assume this was because I traveled so much he was not sure if I was in town or not when his alleged incidents occurred. He made it clear that he did not want the police to investigate or interview me or the other man he thought I worked for. He had no proof the incidents ever occurred because the incidents never happened.

One of the false accusations was that someone broke into his office and tampered with his computer and stole some files. Breaking and entering is a criminal matter, yet there was no criminal investigation and no arrests were made. A criminal matter belongs in a criminal court, not a civil court. Apparently this man was only interested in obtaining money from me.

Of course I hired an attorney to represent me and was not worried because I believe the truth would prevail. I had not done anything to this man and I was not worried that he could prove anything. I knew he could not prove any of the accusations against me, they never happened.

The first day in court I told the judge that I believe the agent had a mental problem. The judge decided that before we began the case that the agent should be examined by a psychiatrist, to determine if he had a mental problem or not. The judge ordered me to pay for the examination by the doctor of my choice. The judge also ordered that the results of the mental examination to be sealed. The judge told the agent that if he could not prove I had done the things he accused me of that he would have to reimburse my legal fees. This gave me a sense of satisfaction because I knew I had not done anything and that he could not prove anything and that he would have to reimburse my expenses.

He was extremely paranoid and in his mind he believed there was a conspiracy against him and that I was doing all the things he accused me of. The judge had four cameras in the courtroom and extra security was standing by. My attorney told me not to come to court for fear the agent may harm me. The agent began harassing my attorney and the judge. He never got around to showing any proof that any of the false accusations had ever occurred. He decided to dismiss the case because he believed the judge was part of the "conspiracy" against him.

Sadly, to my disappointment, the judge did not order him to reimburse me a penny. I felt like the justice system had completely let me down. I felt totally victimized and that my legal expenses should have been reimbursed. I was completely innocent and this is not the way an innocent person should be treated.

After dismissing this lawsuit, the agent threatened to take me to another court. As the statue of limitation was almost up, I decided to file a lawsuit against him. He began harassing my attorney and his staff and they began to fear him. Although I felt totally victimized by this man, I listened to my attorney's advice when he told me that I should dismiss the case. My attorney convinced me that this agent had nothing of value and it would be pointless to win the case against him because I would probably not collect any damages. Reluctantly I agreed to dismiss the case.

Again, when I least expected it – the unexpected happened. *It happened to me, and it can happen to you!*

~ ~ ~

I sincerely hope that this book has helped you in your pursuit of a new career. Use this book as a guide, but most importantly, use your common sense and practice the Golden Rule.

Always remember, you don't have to lie, cheat, or steal to get information or to solve a case! A good investigator knows when and how not to cross the line that makes their investigation and hard work illegal.

Best wishes for much success and happiness.

–Norma

---

For Consultations, Speaking Engagements,
and Seminar Training Programs

email nt007@bellsouth.net

or write
Norma Tillman
P.O. Box 158543
Nashville, TN  37215-8543

Printed in the United States
65345LVS00006B/118

9 780963 442413